Build your own

Sports Car

ON A BUDGET

This book is dedicated to the memory of
my Mother, Maureen Gibbs 1935–2006

Published in February 2007
Reprinted July 2008 and October 2010

A catalogue record for this book is available
from the British Library

ISBN 978 1 84425 391 3

Library of Congress control no. 2006933581

Published by Haynes Publishing,
Sparkford, Yeovil, Somerset BA22 7JJ, UK

Tel: 01963 442030 Fax: 01963 440001
Int. tel: +44 1963 442030
Int. fax: +44 1963 440001
E-mail: sales@haynes.co.uk
Website: www.haynes.co.uk

Haynes North America, Inc.,
861 Lawrence Drive, Newbury Park,
California 91320, USA

Design and layout by Richard Parsons

**Whilst every effort is taken to ensure the accuracy
of the information given in this book, no liability
can be accepted by the author or publishers for
any loss, damage or injury caused by errors in, or
omissions from the information given. If you have
any doubts about your ability to safely build your
own car then it is recommended that advice is
sought from a professional engineer.**

Printed and bound in the USA

www.haynes.co.uk/forums/index.php

E-mail: roadster@haynes.co.uk

Build your own

Sports Car

ON A BUDGET

Chris Gibbs

HAYNES

HAYNES

SHOEI

HAYNES MANUALS

See Haynes See How

ACKNOWLEDGEMENTS

First of all I'd like to thank Martin Keenan of MK Engineering. Martin helped build the prototype car, and without his input into the design of the suspension the car's handling wouldn't be nearly as good as it is. Martin is, quite simply, a genius when it comes to welding and engineering. I'm grateful to have had the use of his fantastic facilities, and my thanks also go to Tammy, for the tea and sandwiches, and to Clarice, for the cakes (and the welding!).

Special thanks to Dave Flavell, for all his hard work in translating my design into the 2D CAD drawings appearing throughout this book.

Thanks, too, to Steve Rendle for his encouragement and support throughout the building of the car and the writing of the book, and also to all the other helpful people at Haynes. And to the experts who give us the benefit of their knowledge and experience in Chapter 14.

Finally, I want to thank my long-suffering wife Julie and my girls Emma and Amy. Their love and support has sustained me; they even kept me calm when my computer tried to wipe out the first ten chapters! I couldn't have written this book without you.

Chris Gibbs
February 2007

CONTENTS

INTRODUCTION 6

CHAPTER 1 SKILLS REQUIRED 14

CHAPTER 2 TOOLS AND EQUIPMENT 18

CHAPTER 3 PARTS AND MATERIALS 26

CHAPTER 4 MAKING THE CHASSIS 34

CHAPTER 5 MAKING THE FRONT
& REAR SUSPENSION 56

CHAPTER 6 FITTING THE ENGINE,
GEARBOX & BACK AXLE 78

CHAPTER 7 MAKING A FUEL TANK 86

CHAPTER 8 MAKE AND FIT
BODY PANELS 90

CHAPTER 9 BRAKING SYSTEM 108

CHAPTER 10 ELECTRICS 112

CHAPTER 11 INTERIOR 114

CHAPTER 12 LEGAL ISSUES 120

CHAPTER 13 WHAT'S NEXT? 128

CHAPTER 14 THE EXPERTS 134

APPENDIX 1 TUBE DETAILS 160

APPENDIX 2 FURTHER INFORMATION 190

INTRODUCTION

▼ The prototype
Haynes Roadster – a
'special' for the 21st
century. *(John Colley)*

Not many people can say that their life was
changed by a visit to their local newsagents.
Mine was!

One day in late 1996 I was flicking through
the car magazines when a picture caught my
eye. It was of a little green and yellow two-seater
sports car of the type that I really wanted. I
bought the magazine and headed home to read
the article. It told of a new book claiming that
this handsome car could
be built for as little as
£250. The book, of
course, was *Build
Your Own Sports*

Car by Ron Champion. I was amazed that such
a car could be built for so little money, but that
wasn't the main attraction for me. Instead, I saw
it as the ultimate car-building challenge – a car
from the ground up.

Cars have always been my passion. I learnt to
drive on a farm at the age of ten, on a tractor,
scattering livestock in all directions! My first car
was a Hillman Imp, which I bought for the grand
sum of £20 (I was robbed). It was sky blue and
always overheating, as they all did!

Since then I've had a vast selection of mostly
impractical cars and motorcycles. Ones that
spring to mind are the Chevrolet Camaro I
purchased when I was 18, and sold two
weeks later because I'd spent almost £500
on fuel; a Ford Popular hot-rod that parted

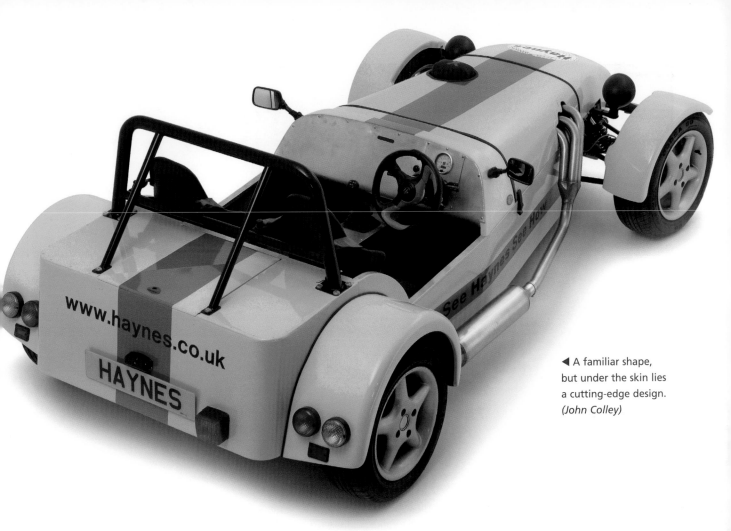

◀ A familiar shape, but under the skin lies a cutting-edge design. (John Colley)

company with its V8 engine on the M1 motorway; and the Mazda MX-5 two-seater that I purchased just before my first daughter was born.

I've also had a succession of kit cars that either remained in bits, or regularly broke down on the highways and byways around my home. The local RAC man and I were on first-name terms!

My first restoration was a very rusty, yellow, Dolomite Sprint, which probably wasn't the best choice as a 'starter classic'. I had to take the engine out to change the starter motor! Many other restorations followed and I decided that some sort of proper training would be a good idea, so I enrolled on a two-year full time restoration course at the Leeds College of Technology. The course included panel beating (in the traditional sense, i.e. actually making and repairing panels) as well as mechanics, electrics, machining, paintwork, upholstery and much more. I gained a City and Guilds diploma qualification in Vehicle Restoration. It was among the best things I've ever done. I learned skills and know-how that would have taken a lifetime to acquire working alone in my garage, and I also gained some lifelong friends.

In late 1996 the restoration course was in the future, and I was reading with increasing excitement about the book. Being that time of year, I made it plain to everyone that the book would be a very welcome Christmas present – and my better half obliged.

Over the holiday I read the book three times, from cover to cover. The first thing to sort out was whether I could do it, as I didn't want it to end up as another unfinished project. I reviewed my strengths and weaknesses.

I was able to weld and I had a decent welding set, after the restoration work, but I needed to make sure my welding was of a sufficiently high standard. The mechanical work didn't look too taxing to me. I'd changed engines and gearboxes a few times on my various wrecks, so I felt reasonably confident about that. Other things – like the glass reinforced plastic (GRP) work, upholstery, painting and the electrics – were more of a worry, but I banked on getting help from my friends and relatives. As it turned out this was readily given. If you ask around, you're sure to find someone who can help. More of that later.

While I was looking for a local welding course to improve my skills, the Restoration Diploma course came up. Problem solved. I made up my mind and went for it.

I needed a donor car and some steel, and my mate Dave was able to help on both counts. His father–in–law had a Mk4 Cortina I could have. All I had to do was go and collect it, which was fine except the car was in Wales and I was in Yorkshire. Dave and I decided to make a holiday of it, staying in Pwllheli for a couple of days and then driving back, with me following Dave's car in the Cortina. We hit the motorway and the engine dropped a valve rocker. After fishing out the offending item we carried on, with me in the now three-cylinder Ford, over the Pennines and back home.

Obtaining the steel was an interesting story. I'd been looking around for steel box section for quite a while in all the places that were suggested in the book, when Dave said, "I know where there's a blacksmith with a load of steel." So, off we went. The place was a proper old-fashioned blacksmith's yard with a scrap pile 30ft across and 10ft high! The proprietor (who was, quite appropriately, an old-fashioned blacksmith) told us we could have as much of his scrap as we wanted for a tenner. It was hard work loading up, and the van barely

made it back home, but I made the chassis and many other things and I've still got loads left.

Early in 1997 the build started and I became aware of the Locost Car Club, and in particular the Yorkshire group. My first visit was in April that year, and I've barely missed a meeting since. They're a brilliant bunch of blokes, generous to a fault (except for getting a round in!) and so knowledgeable about cars that sometimes I'm in awe.

Over time I've become more and more involved with the club, and I now edit the club newsletter and I'm the Vice Secretary as well as the Technical Advisor. The Locost community spirit is very special and I see it more as a brotherhood. A clan of like-minded, practical people, who want to help their fellow builders, via the internet, through the club or at kit car shows and meetings throughout the year. The club has members world-wide and over 20 UK meetings take place each month. If there isn't a meeting near you, you could always start one – there are builders in every county of the UK.

My build progressed quite slowly because I was at college most of the time, but the facilities for making things were excellent, and I was able to compare notes with two of the tutors who were also building Locosts. The moulds for the

▲ Trevor Davis's amazing all-aluminium bodywork.

◄ This immaculate car shows the standards that have been achieved by enthusiasts.

glassfibre wings were made there, and the tutors and I shared the work and the costs. As the college had a full-size wheeling machine I was also able to use this to make my nose cone from aluminium. This sounds quite impressive until you learn that I had to fill and paint it before I could fit it to the car. Club member Trevor Davis's car (see photo) is panelled entirely in aluminium and shows what can be done if you have the necessary skills. His car really is a work of art and was named 'Locost of the year'.

My chassis was soon welded up and I remember thinking that she was almost finished. Hmm – not quite. As with any job of this type, it was the finishing that took the time. I included a heater, a fully-trimmed interior, a full windscreen and a lockable boot – all things that took time but added nothing to the driving experience.

The new Haynes Roadster is as simple as possible, which not only saves building time but also keeps the cost down. As you'll see in Chapter 11 on the interior, the Roadster is fitted with the minimum instrumentation necessary to pass the SVA test – a speedometer with odometer, a brightsix module for the warning lights and switches for the lights and horn. I'd advise you to keep your car as simple as this, maybe with the addition of temperature and fuel gauges for peace of mind. I've seen cars with stereo systems and thick pile carpets, even one with neon lights under it (!) but none of these things is noticed when you're driving. It's supposed to be a pure driving experience – all the extras just add weight.

When my original car was finished, the DVLA gave me the donor car registration, as it was completed before the new obligatory SVA test came into force. These days you may get an age-related plate – the same registration year as your donor but not the donor registration itself – if you can prove that most of the mechanical parts came from your donor car, which is what we did with the prototype Roadster. If you can't, you'll get a 'Q' registration, which is fine but you can't replace it with any other private plate should you wish to, as it indicates a car of indeterminate age. If you use all new parts you will be allocated a new, current, registration number. You can use one 'reconditioned' major component (usually the engine) and still get a new registration, but you must keep every receipt and bill. The DVLA will need substantial proof that all the parts (including the chassis) are new.

These days I use my car as much as I can – club meetings all around the north in the summer, an annual trip to Le Mans for the 24-Hour race, and track days and sprints.

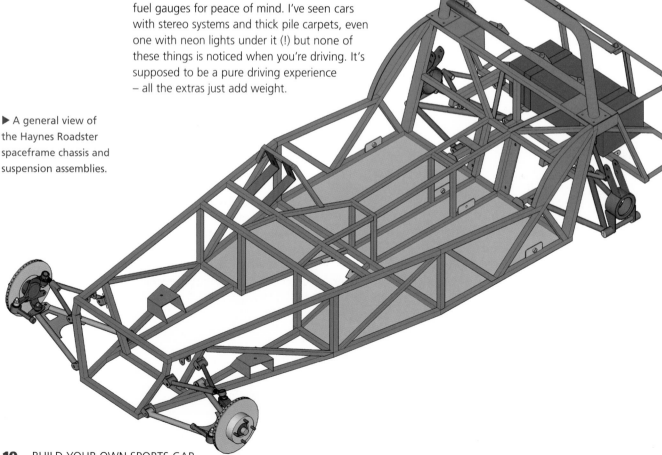

▶ A general view of the Haynes Roadster spaceframe chassis and suspension assemblies.

Cars like the Roadster are the natural successors to the great British tradition of 'special' building, which dates from the dawn of motoring. Even some of the first cars were taken apart and made to better suit their owners' purpose. The first mass-produced car, the Model T Ford, was made in every possible configuration, from farm tractor to racing car. In Britain the Austin Seven chassis had special bodies fitted to it from its inception. The building of 'specials' received a boost in the aftermath of the Second World War, when war surplus materials were readily available and cheap, including many an aircraft fuel drop-tank that became a sleek car body.

This flurry of activity spawned the fledgling kit car industry, initially as aluminium or GRP bodies to fit standard chassis. As production cars moved towards unitary construction, the kit car companies began to supply their own chassis to take donor car parts. These cars were popular until purchase tax was imposed, which eroded the cars' large price advantage. The market then began to develop a reputation for poor quality – both in the manufacture and standard of construction – much of it well deserved. Happily this has largely been cured by government legislation, including construction and use regulations, the MoT test and the SVA. Today's kit cars are, almost without exception, very well engineered and finished. The price paid for this advance is that the kit car is no longer a cheap way to get the sports car you want. The Haynes Roadster, though, fills the need.

The main advantage of building your own car, as opposed to the kit car, is that the cost can be spread over as long a time as you like. There's no lump sum to pay up front like there is for a kit. And I find that scouring the autojumbles and wheeling and dealing with friends and acquaintances is half the fun!

All cars of this type are basically very simple, but the Haynes Roadster is technically quite advanced. The spaceframe chassis has been designed using stress analysis software to ensure rigidity. The suspension has been developed in conjunction with Martin Keenan of MK Engineering (Martin has been building, racing and developing cars and motorcycles for many years, and his 'Indy' sports car is one of the bestselling kit cars ever made) and has been designed to eliminate bump steer and provide handling and roadholding at least the equal of cars costing many thousands of pounds more. Cheaper and better – it's a win–win situation!

▲ £200-worth of very tidy Sierra donor car. It was a shame to break it!

COULD YOU DO IT?

Why not? The skills involved are not difficult to master and may be learned locally in most cases; donor cars are getting cheaper by the day; and the help and support available these days is impressive. No garage? Cars have been built in back gardens, under a tarpaulin and in the garden shed!

Speaking of donor cars, it's virtually impossible to find MkII Escorts any more, and the Cortina uprights are very difficult to track down and expensive when you find them, bizarrely sometimes more expensive than complete cars! This book uses more readily available donor cars, with the additional benefit that these donors give your car independent rear suspension for better ride and comfort.

THE DONOR CARS

Rear wheel drive (RWD) cars are the exception these days. Front wheel drive (FWD) cars are cheaper and easier to produce, hence their proliferation. In my opinion, RWD is the ideal set-up, freeing the front wheels for steering duties and the rears to propel the car. People who have grown up with FWD are often staggered by the handling prowess of RWD cars like ours.

Amongst recent cars that have RWD are the Ford Sierra, Mazda MX-5, the BMW 3 series (E30 and E36), and the Mercedes 190 range.

■ Ford Sierra

The Sierra is the successor to the Cortina, with much of the same running gear, although it varies in two areas important to our build. First, the live axle of the Cortina is replaced by a differential fixed to the body and trailing-arm suspension units with separate springs and dampers. We will replace these items with a double wishbone set-up with coil-over spring/damper units. The rear hub is bolted to a new fabricated upright. Second, the front suspension uprights are different, with a MacPherson strut mounting at the top. To convert this to twin wishbones, we need to make (or have made) a 'mushroom' adapter.

The standard engine is the Ford Pinto, in 1.3, 1.6, 1.8 and 2.0-litre capacities, sometimes known as the SOHC (single overhead cam) engine. It's quite a tall engine, and some builders have increased the height of the chassis to compensate, but my car has this engine in a standard height chassis, with just the air filter sticking through the bonnet. Reducing the depth of the sump and moving the oil filler cap to the rear of the rocker cover also give additional clearance. Alternatively, you could always source a different engine if you think the height will be a problem.

A few Sierras had the CVH (compound valve hemispherical head) engines in 1.6 and 1.8-litre capacities, or the 2.0-litre DOHC (double overhead

cam) engine. These engines don't seem to be very popular with builders – the CVH because of the lack of cheap tuning equipment, and the DOHC because of its physical size (bigger than the Pinto in all dimensions). If you use these engines you will have to make different mountings as detailed in Chapter 6.

At the time of writing, there were over 75,000 Sierras still in use on UK roads, so the Sierra is likely to be a popular and plentiful donor for several years to come.

Many of the parts from the Sierra can be adapted for use in the Roadster (see Chapter 3).

■ BMW 3-series
The E30 and E36 BMW 3-series models were well-built sturdy saloons. As with the Sierra, the BMW has all-round independent suspension that we can use, with modifications, for the Roadster. The front suspension requires a modification to the suspension strut, as the standard upright isn't tall enough. The four-cylinder engines are tall, like the Pinto, while the six-cylinder engines are not so tall, but they are heavy.

■ Mazda MX-5
One of the world's most popular sports cars, the MX-5 is sold world-wide under the names of Eunos and Miata. Again, the suspension set-up is independent and needs some modification. The standard engine is compact and powerful.

▼ The wheels and steering column-mounted switchgear are the only outwardly visible traces of our Sierra donor. *(John Colley)*

◀ If you don't like 'bad-hair days', you probably don't want one of these... *(John Colley)*

■ **Other donors**
Throughout the book, usually at the end of each chapter, there is advice on making parts from other sources fit our chassis.

A NOTE ON DIMENSIONS
The car has been designed by computer (actually, by me working the computer, but you get my drift) using the metric system. All my working life in engineering I've used metric units, and all the dimensions in this book are in millimetres. A conversion table is printed below if you wish to convert to imperial measurements, but as a guide, one inch equals 25.4 millimetres. This is a precise measurement, but please don't ask me for any other precise imperial measurements – all that 5/32nds of an inch stuff makes my head hurt!

1 millimetre (mm)	1mm	0.03937in
1 centimetre (cm)	10mm	0.3937in
1 metre (m)	1000mm, 100cm	1.0936yd

1 SKILLS REQUIRED

I suppose that if you've been interested enough to buy this book you will already have some of the skills required to build your own car. Many people become quite accomplished amateur mechanics by necessity. In your youth, when the only car you can afford is an old banger which you have to maintain yourself, you tend to learn certain skills to keep mobile. This usually leads to one of two outcomes: either you develop an interest for 'tinkering' which stays with you forever more, or you resolve, as soon as you can afford it, to buy a car which is never going to require you to lift the bonnet! I dare say that the former applies to you.

None of the skills called for in the building of your car is technically difficult, but you will need to develop tenacity. There's always that period when you start to learn a new skill when you think you are never going to be able to do it, and the temptation to give up is quite strong. But, if you stick at it you may well surprise yourself. Practice makes perfect, and even the best welder in the world had never picked up a torch at one stage. Skills can be learned from advice given in books, or even over the internet, but there's no substitute for proper personal tuition. You'll learn so much quicker this way.

▶ **Fig. 1.1** Your new welding skills will come in handy for other projects too!

WELDING

I learnt to weld the hard way by buying a welder and practising until I was confident enough to work on a car, in the process building up a large pile of very poorly welded scrap. I wouldn't recommend this method. The buzz word of the age is 'education', and there are more and better courses available now than there have ever been. Many of these courses include welding.

As I said, proper tuition will reduce the time it will take you to become competent. Locating a local course shouldn't be difficult. Try Learn Direct (http//:www.learndirect.co.uk) who have a national database of courses available, or you could call your local council or technical college. Many of these courses will be free or available at a reasonable cost.

The method best suited to welding your chassis is MIG welding. Other possible methods are gas welding, arc welding or TIG welding. TIG welding produces beautiful welds in the right hands, in both steel and aluminium, but unless you're lucky enough to have access to TIG welding equipment the cost involved will generally rule this method out – good TIG sets cost thousands of pounds.

Gas welding is inconvenient for the home builder. The gas bottles (oxygen and acetylene) must be hired and the lines and torches bought, and Health and Safety is a particular issue since leaking gas can cause an explosion (if you're using this method and suspect a leak, take the bottle back to the supplier immediately). Also, gas cylinders can go off like a bomb if caught in a fierce fire, so all combustible material must be removed from the entire area when gas welding. Special gas-welding goggles, or a gas-welding mask, must be used, along with gloves and protective clothing. The gas bottles are heavy (although you can get small portable sets) and, of course, the techniques are more difficult to master than for MIG welding. The main disadvantage of gas welding is heat build-up. The weld is formed by the melting of the welding rod into the joint, consequently the weld gets very hot, and this may cause distortion. If you decide to use gas welding you should try to minimise the effects by welding on one side of the chassis and then move to the corresponding joint on the opposite side of the chassis. One advantage that gas welding has over the other methods is that it doesn't require an electricity supply and can be used in remote locations.

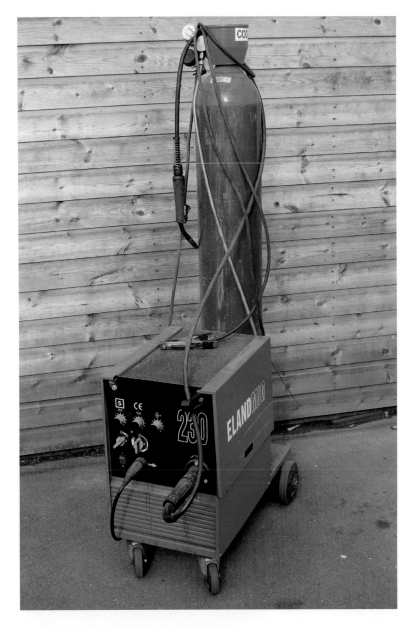

▲ Fig. 1.2 A typical industrial MIG welder, complete with gas bottle.

Arc welding is at first glance a tempting option. The sets are very cheap when viewed against the price of a MIG set, and the welding method appears to be similar. In arc welding, flux-coated welding rods are used. The flux acts in a similar way to the gas in MIG welding, shielding the weld from impurities, but it remains on the surface of the weld and needs to be removed with a 'chipping' hammer. This, of course, adds to the time required to make the weld. An arc-welding mask must be used along with heavy gloves and protective clothing. Great care must be taken to protect yourself and others from the effects of electric arcs, both in arc and MIG welding. ANY exposure of the eyes to the searing light of an electric arc can cause serious eye damage, and skin can be burned – never weld with bare arms, for example.

It takes longer to learn how to use an arc welder correctly, but the most important disadvantage for us is that arc welding is not very suitable for the thin tubes we will be using – even on a very low power setting it's likely that the welds will 'blow through'.

MIG welding has revolutionised welding. The skills required to make good strong welds are easily learnt, and the sets themselves are cheap enough to be affordable by the DIY user. Sets can also be hired, but if you do this you will need to be more organised. The lengths of steel should be cut, clearly labelled and stored logically so that the process becomes not unlike building a construction kit. Depending on your skill level, the chassis can be tacked together in one or two days and the entire chassis welded in around a week to ten days. I've seen with my own eyes a chassis fully welded in a day, and I know people who've taken seven or eight years!

For MIG welding, a proper MIG-welding mask or helmet must be used along with heavy gloves and protective clothing. As with arc welding, all bare skin must be covered to prevent ultraviolet light burns.

MIG welding works by completing an electrical circuit via the MIG wire and the earth lead of the welder. The earth lead is attached to the workpiece, and pressing the trigger activates the nozzle on the torch to produce a flow of gas (usually carbon dioxide or a carbon dioxide/argon mix) and starts the wire feed motor. The wire is

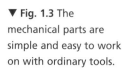

▼ **Fig. 1.3** The mechanical parts are simple and easy to work on with ordinary tools.

fed from the welder into the torch and out to the work piece. When the wire touches the work the circuit is completed, the metal being earthed to the welder via the earth lead, and an electric arc is struck.

The wire and the edges to be joined melt into the weld pool and are both shielded from impurities and cooled by the gas coming out of the nozzle. Releasing the trigger halts the wire feed and the shielding gas, thereby ending the process.

Better welds are produced by pushing the weld away from you, ie, starting at the left side of a weld directly in front of you and working left to right with the nozzle pointing to the right. This may seem unnatural at first, as it would appear easier to start at the left side and have the nozzle pointing to the left. By angling the nozzle the other way the weld progresses in the way that the wire is coming out of the torch and produces a less 'blobby' weld than would be the case (caused by extra wire being pushed into the weld pool) if the 'natural' way is used.

Prior to commencing any welding in anger, the machine has to be set up to weld the gauge of steel you're using. Wire feed speed, gas flow and current flow (power) are the usual adjustments available, but you should refer to the manual that came with your welder. The ideal weld is said to be produced when the sound is like frying bacon. Personally I don't like my bacon that well done, but you get the idea! I'd recommend using some scrap box section to practise making the type of weld required to build the chassis, and subjecting them to the club hammer test – if the steel tears before the weld breaks then the welds are pretty strong. Some welds benefit from a little tidying up with an angle grinder, but you must be careful not to weaken the weld by removing too much material. If your welds call for a lot of grinding, then you need more welding practice!

MECHANICAL SKILLS

As I mentioned before, many of us have picked up car mechanics piecemeal as we've needed to repair our own vehicles, and the skills needed to build the Roadster aren't extensive or specialised, and may be acquired locally. The Haynes manual for the donor car is an ideal place to start, as probably the first thing you'll do is strip the donor car. Other books and websites that might be of use are listed in Appendix 2.

Take care in choosing your donor car. You can't expect it to be 'as new', of course, but you do

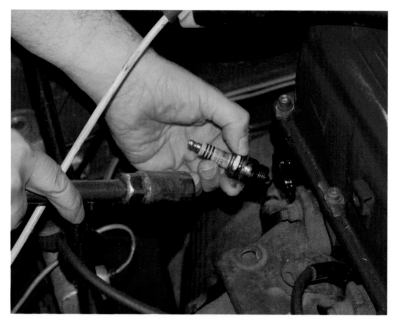

need to be sure the basics are serviceable. Take a test drive and make sure that the brakes pull up squarely, and that the engine sounds reasonable and shows no sign of blue smoke on the over-run. Does the car jump out of gear? Can you hear rumbling from the transmission or wheel bearings? All these things might cause you trouble or expense – probably both. Buying a non-runner is usually cheaper, but at least try to find out any known faults – even so, you'll be relying on the vendor to be candid.

It's a real temptation to be over-enthusiastic when stripping the donor car. Before you start, make a list of the things you need from it, using Chapter 3, and work around the car taking things off logically, labelling everything and, possibly, taking photographs of how things fit together. Don't trust your memory, it may be some time before you put things back together.

Don't forget that you're not alone. Others are building similar cars, and help is available via owners clubs and the internet.

BODYWORK
The Roadster bodywork is reasonably simple and easy to form. The aluminium panels can be cut with tin snips from new sheets, or salvaged metal, using the patterns in Chapter 8, and all are easily formed without special tools. Glassfibre work is also covered in Chapter 8. It's not difficult, but it can be messy and great care must be taken when dealing with the chemicals involved. Many people will want to buy the GRP panels from the manufacturers of similar kit cars. Bargains are still to be had, particularly if you're prepared to put some work in repairing and painting damaged panels. New GRP panels are available from MK Engineering.

PAINTING
The space frame is best treated with a rust-inhibiting primer and a top coat. You can obtain chassis paint, but many people have their own favourites. I use a red oxide primer and household gloss. This is cheap, of course, and has the added advantage that the paint is quite flexible when dry, making it more resistant to stone chipping. You can spray-paint your chassis if you have the facilities, but as there's more 'space' than tubes it can be very wasteful of paint. If funds allow, your chassis can be powdercoated – this is a tough finish which is electrostatically sprayed as a powder onto the chassis, and then baked. The finish is very durable but it's important to touch

▲ **Fig. 1.4** Tony Skelding of Bodicraft applies the top coat to the prototype car.

up any chips as water can work it's way under the finish and become trapped, causing rust. The aluminium panels can be left as they are. Bare aluminium has a very attractive sheen to it and can be kept in good condition with a quality metal polish, or it can be lacquered to preserve the finish. If you intend to paint your bodywork, you'll find more details in Chapter 14.

UPHOLSTERY
There's no real need to do any elaborate trimming work to your car. Seats from small hatchbacks will often be of the right size to fit our type of car, and they will simply bolt in, possibly without the original subframe. The Rover Metro has a seat subframe which is quite compact and might be suitable. Another option would be to modify the rear seat from a production car, and in Chapter 11 I've also included a pattern for the production of a 'sports' seat which requires none of the professional upholsterer's skills. Interior side-panels, if you require them, can be made from hardboard, plywood or aluminium covered in vinyl or carpet, and the floor can be covered with rubber matting or heavy-duty car carpet. Many prefer the look of bare aluminium inside the car, sometimes even making the floor from aluminium sheet, bonded and riveted on.

2 TOOLS AND EQUIPMENT

The most important items you will need aren't tools at all. As with any such enterprise, it's vital that you use the appropriate protective equipment and clothing. I find well-fitting cotton overalls do the trick. You certainly shouldn't wear anything which can become entangled in any sort of machinery, and that includes jewellery. I've seen a very nasty burn injury caused by shorting out a spanner onto a wedding ring – be very, very, careful.

Steel-capped boots will protect your feet from dropped heavy objects. When welding, all skin should covered, and heavy gloves and the appropriate goggles or mask should be used. Never, for example, use gas welding goggles for MIG welding – serious eye injuries could result. Heavy gloves or gauntlets should also be used for any grinding, drilling or cutting operations, along with clear goggles, in good condition, to protect your eyes.

▶ **Fig. 2.1** Ideal workwear – a cotton boiler suit. *(Draper Tools)*

▲ **Fig. 2.2** Stout gloves are essential. *(Draper Tools)*

▼ **Fig. 2.3** Goggles like these will protect your eyes from sparks and dust. *(Draper Tools)*

▼ **Fig. 2.4** You won't need a large trolley jack. One like this 2-tonne jack will suffice. *(Draper Tools)*

Try to keep your work area tidy. Where possible, avoid trailing wires from power tools as they may cause you to trip and fall. Make sure that all inflammable materials are removed from any area where welding or grinding are to take place, and a dry-powder fire extinguisher (for both liquid and electrical fires) is a sensible precaution, as is a first-aid kit. Ensure that there is adequate ventilation when using paints or other hazardous substances (refer to the manufacturer's guidelines).

It's easier to work on the chassis if it is held at a convenient height, either on axle stands or on trestles, but make absolutely sure that they are solidly enough constructed to take the weight, especially as you add components. Never work under a car, or even a chassis, supported only by a jack.

Remember, think safety at all times. Don't try to cut corners or do any job without the necessary protective equipment.

The tools and equipment required to build your car are not exotic, and if you've maintained your own car you'll probably have many of them already. The largest single item required is a welder. This can, of course, be borrowed or hired. When buying a second-hand welder always ask to see it working. As mentioned in the previous chapter, if you are well organised you can minimise the cost of hiring. If all the lengths are cut and shaped, and stored in a logical order, you can follow the construction guide like a manual for flat-pack furniture. Although, at first glance, the chassis looks quite complicated, so long as you work to the plan it's not too difficult.

Other items that might be better borrowed or hired include engine cranes and any specialist tools needed for dismantling or assembly. The cost of buying such things for a single job are prohibitive. The other tools you require might already be in your workshop. Any power tools purchased second-hand should be checked over by a qualified electrician before use.

Wire brushes, either wooden-handled or drill-mounted, are ideal for cleaning donor parts. An old toothbrush can be used for cleaning intricate parts, and a supply of clean rags makes the job easier.

▲ **Fig. 2.5** Substantial axle stands make working under a car much safer. *(Draper Tools)*

▼ **Fig. 2.6** A typical industrial MIG welder. *(Draper Tools)*

▶ **Fig. 2.7** A selection of wire brushes. The manual brush incorporates a scraper. *(Draper Tools)*

TOOL KIT

When buying tools, the very cheapest might be a false economy. The cheap 'market quality' tools might last long enough to do the job, or they might not. If you buy two or three lots of the cheap tools you'll probably pay the same as for one reasonable tool and, as a bonus, the more expensive tool will be fit for further service. Actually, tools don't need to be new. You can buy them second-hand from autojumbles, car boot sales and from adverts in local papers. Bargains can be found if you look out for well-known makes, and inspect them carefully before purchase.

As a minimum, you will need a metric socket set in sizes 8mm to 24mm, a set of ring spanners and open-ended spanners in the same sizes, or a combination set of open/ring spanners. It can be of benefit to have two of the more popular sizes (generally 10mm, 13mm, 15mm and 17mm) in case you need to hold a bolt while undoing the nut. Sometimes you can use mole grips, or an adjustable spanner for the same purpose.

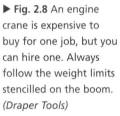

▶ **Fig. 2.8** An engine crane is expensive to buy for one job, but you can hire one. Always follow the weight limits stencilled on the boom. *(Draper Tools)*

◀ **Fig. 2.9** A simple
socket set like this is
sufficient for our needs.
(Draper Tools)

▲ **Fig. 2.11** Colour-coded
screwdriver handles help
you reach for the right type.
(Draper Tools)

Welding clamps of differing types will be useful, as will small and large spring clamps, trigger action and magnetic clamps.

You'll need a selection of screwdrivers, in both crosshead and straight types. One of each type in small, medium and large sizes will suffice. When dismantling, a selection of cold chisels will be handy for chopping out sections for access.

Ideally you should have a good selection of different hammers for different jobs – heavy ones for dismantling suspension (and testing your welds!), etc., medium ones for general tasks, a planishing hammer for bodywork tasks and a hide or plastic mallet for delicate parts.

For cutting, you will need a hacksaw and a junior hacksaw, along with tin snips, and for cleaning up metal you will need files in various grades of flat, round and triangular shapes. An angle grinder is invaluable for this sort of work, removing material quickly to be finished with the files and/or a wire brush. Angle grinders are probably the most dangerous tool in the workshop. Make sure you wear your protective equipment, and protect yourself and others from sparks. The sparks can mark glass, paint or GRP, so protect or remove any such items from the area.

Various types of pliers will be needed – at least one long nose type, a standard type and

▼ **Fig. 2.10** A selection
of hammers and mallets.
(Draper Tools)

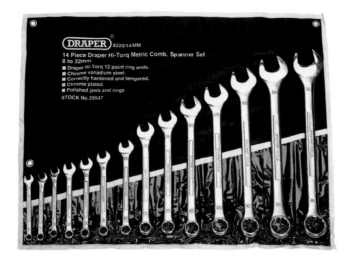

▲ **Fig. 2.12** Combination ring and open-ended spanners in a convenient plastic roll. *(Draper Tools)*

▲ **Fig. 2.13** A good hacksaw will be invaluable. *(Draper Tools)*

▼ **Fig. 2.14** A set of pliers, including long-nosed types and side cutters. *(Draper Tools)*

other gripping devices, such as water-pump pliers, and the aforementioned mole type grips will also be required. Side cutters and wire strippers are needed for electrical work.

I would say that a bench vice with at least a 125mm jaw is vital, as is an electric drill (a cordless one is probably best as you can work anywhere with it, but the regular type will suffice). A drill press or a stand for your drill is useful to have, but if you're careful you can use your ordinary drill.

ENGINEERING PROCESSES

Marking out for cutting is a vital stage of construction and should be done with great care. Remember the old adage: 'measure twice and cut once!' You will need a centre punch, scriber, set square, long steel ruler, or tape, and a short steel ruler. Engineer's blue dye and ordinary correction fluid can help to make scribed marks clearer. A set square or adjustable square, including a protractor, should be used to ensure that cuts are at the correct angle; and remember to allow for the thickness of the blade when marking and cutting.

Holes should always be marked accurately and centre punched to prevent the drill wandering. Always use a pilot drill for any holes over 3mm in size, and work up to the required size in stages. Sheet metal of 16swg or less can be cut with tin snips. Standard snips cut with the waste to the left and left-handed snips cut with the waste to the right. I find the type known as 'aviation snips' produce the cleanest line.

Sheet can also be cut using a hand or drill-mounted 'nibbler'. The hand version removes a 2mm strip which comes out of the top of the nibbler. You must, of course, allow for this waste in your marking out. The drill-mounted version removes small half circle shapes and can produce a very clean cut.

Another way of cutting aluminium sheet is to use a heavy-duty craft blade to score the material on one side and then carefully bending the sheet until it fractures along the line. This method is best suited to short cuts.

Filing is an art in itself. The old-fashioned 'fitters' could achieve fantastic results using progressively finer files. It's easier these days to use the angle grinder to get a reasonable line, finishing with the files and emery cloth, or wet and dry paper, where necessary. Files should only be used with a handle, as without one

▼ **Fig. 2.15** A bench vice is vital. This one includes a small area behind the jaws to act as an anvil. *(Draper Tools)*

▶ **Fig. 2.16** A cordless drill is a boon when working on different parts of the car. Try to get a spare battery so that you can have one charging whilst the other is in use. *(Draper Tools)*

◀ **Fig. 2.17** An angle grinder is a useful tool to own. It has no peers for removing metal quickly, but it must be handled carefully – it can cause serious injury. *(Draper Tools)*

there's a real risk of pushing the tang of the file through your hand.

Grinding and drilling should be done at the bench vice where possible, observing all the safety advice above. With the drill, besides drilling holes, you can use grinding stones, abrasive flap wheels, wire brushes and polishing attachments.

One useful addition is a flexy drive, which allows you to drill holes, or carry out any of the other processes in a confined space. Wire brushes and cutting and grinding discs are available for angle grinders, as are flexible sanding discs. The accessories for the grinders are more aggressive in their action than the drill-mounted ones, so great care must be taken not to remove too much material, particularly when dressing welds. Never force a grinding or cutting disc, if it fragments the pieces can cause serious injury.

Sometimes two hands aren't enough, and this is where clamps come in useful. Welding clamps come in various types for holding metal in place, and it's probably best to buy a set as you may well need each combination. Mole grips can also be used in certain situations. When constructing the chassis, magnetic welding clamps can be invaluable, particularly the right-angle types, for example to hold chassis verticals in place for tacking.

Plastic spring-type clamps can be used for temporarily holding bodywork or trim whilst drilling holes, as can the trigger-type clamps.

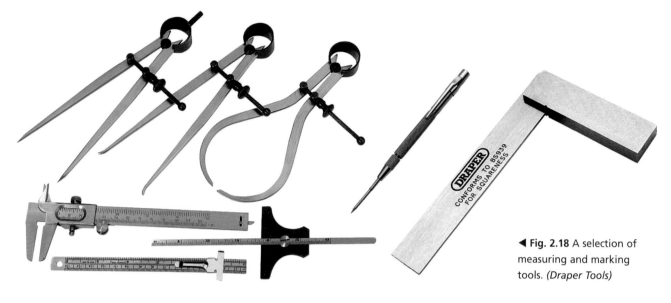

◀ **Fig. 2.18** A selection of measuring and marking tools. *(Draper Tools)*

▲ **Fig. 2.19** Aviation snips and Gilbow type tin snips are used for cutting aluminium and thin steel sheet.

▼ **Fig. 2.20** A set of welding clamps. These clamps come in a bewildering selection to suit almost any welding job. *(Draper Tools)*

Remember to protect the surface of any bodywork that is clamped. Your vice can also be used for holding material to be drilled, cut or filed.

There are a few methods required for joining materials together. The first and most obvious is welding, which we covered in the previous chapter.

For joining dissimilar materials you will need mechanical fixings, and riveting will be the method most used. A simple hand riveter is sufficient, although the 'lazy tongue' type makes the job easier, and the use of an electric or air riveter makes it easier still.

The process of riveting is simple. The most common rivet sizes are 2mm, 3mm and 4mm, although smaller and larger ones, as well as ones in imperial sizes, are available. They also vary in length. A good general-purpose size is 3mm by 10mm long. This is the size used to secure the Roadster's aluminium panels.

Most rivet guns come with interchangeable heads to allow the different sizes to be used. A hole of a precise size to suit the rivet being used is drilled through both items to be joined, and the rivet is pushed through with the shank of the rivet in the gun. As pressure is applied to the handles in a simple riveter, or by the action of the mechanism, the flattened base of the rivet is drawn towards the riveter, expanding the sleeve so that it presses the two items together. At a pre-set point the shank shears, leaving the rivet in place holding the items very firmly together. A rivnut tool works in a similar way but leaves in place a threaded insert for a setscrew or bolt to be used to secure a component or panel.

Light duty fixings, such as for interior panels, can be made using self-tapping screws. It's important to drill the correct sized hole to match the screw size.

Various adhesives and sealants can be used. For example, bathroom sealant is good for sealing the cockpit, and impact adhesive for making trim panels, etc. Polyurethane adhesive/sealant has many applications. It forms a remarkable bond that is difficult to break without damaging the components involved, so use it carefully! This type of adhesive is used as the only fixing on the front wings of some kit cars which are similar to ours – it's very strong.

▲ **Fig. 2.21** Plastic-handled files rarely lose their handles, unlike the wood-handled ones. *(Draper Tools)*

▲ **Fig. 2.22** Always wear protective equipment when using grinding stones – there's a chance they may shatter. *(Draper Tools)*

▲ **Fig. 2.23** Ratchet-type clamps such as this have soft jaws and are useful for temporarily holding body panels in position. *(Draper Tools)*

▲ **Fig. 2.24** A 'lazy tongues' type riveting tool. This is considerably easier to use than the type illustrated in Fig. 2.25. *(Draper Tools)*

▶ **Fig. 2.25** A hand-held riveting tool and a selection of rivets. *(Draper Tools)*

3 PARTS AND MATERIALS

Finding a donor car is probably the best starting point, although you probably won't need any parts from it for a while. If you're pushed for space (as most of us are) you'll find it difficult to store a chassis as well as the donor car which, when stripped, will take up the space of around three cars. Not an ideal domestic situation, believe me.

This book describes the building of a car based on parts from a Ford Sierra, but throughout I'll give hints and tips for using other donors with a similar set-up. Whichever car you pick for the running gear, it should be rear-wheel-drive with independent rear suspension.

Sourcing a donor car need not be difficult, as long as you keep your eyes open. Because of the downturn in the price of scrap, most dealers will charge around £30 for collecting old cars, and your kind offer to take the car off the owner's hands for nothing will seem positively generous!

A good course of action would be to scan the 'breaking and salvage' section of your local free advertisement paper, or to place an advert in the wanted section. Many local councils have a car collection service. A number of people I know have found their donors this way, although one or two have had to take their spanners down to the yard and remove everything themselves on site! When taking this route it's best to emphasise the 'recycling' aspect. Most of the energy that is used by a car in it's lifetime is in it's manufacture, and by re-using car parts you are recycling and saving the planet. Gives you a warm glow doesn't it!

You may be able to place an ad in your local

shop or garage. Also, try getting to know your local MoT tester who might be prepared to tip you off if a suitable car becomes available. It could be that someone you know has, or knows of, a suitable car. Ask around – you never know. Another alternative is to source a complete car, or the necessary parts, from a scrapyard. If you use this method it will be more expensive as the yard needs to make a profit. If money is no object, then you can buy a complete donor package – check out the kit car press.

Because this is a budget build, try to buy a running car on which you can test the drive train. Make sure that the engine, gearbox, front uprights and rear axle/final drive assembly are serviceable. (The braking and steering must be overhauled.) If you're unsure, take along a friend who knows about cars. Don't forget to haggle if necessary, and remember that MoT failures aren't really worth anything to the general public.

A friend of mine found a donor by chance. Seeing a car with a flat tyre and grass growing around it in someone's front garden, he enquired and found that it was an MoT failure because of welding to the rear sub-frame mounts and front inner wings. This, of course, was not a problem for his purposes, but he kept it in mind as a bargaining point when it came to agreeing a price. As it happened, though, when he asked the price the lady threw him the keys and said, "I'll be glad to see the back of it!" The next day he arrived with a trailer and winch and put the keys in the ignition to release the steering lock. Just out of curiosity he gave the key a twist. It started! He drove the car up onto the trailer and whisked away his bargain.

STRIPPING THE DONOR CAR

Proper organisation of your workspace is vital. Try not to put heavy components where they could fall or be tripped over and, where possible, drain all fluids and dispose of them responsibly. Your local council dump will advise – most have oil tanks for used oil. Use a barrier cream and/or gloves when handling used oil, as it can be carcinogenic. A power washer is useful for initial cleaning of non-electrical components. I used a large fence post preserver bucket and paraffin for the cleaning. Use a wire brush to clean off road dirt and oil. The paraffin leaves a slightly oily finish which protects the parts, but must be cleaned off if you intend to use paint as a finish on the parts. Home blasting-cabinets are available and make a great job of removing grime, rust and old paint, but you must make sure that any oilways, bearing surfaces or electrical components are protected from damage. Be sure to store the parts in a way that will not cause deterioration and won't be a hazard as you work. Metal racking is probably best – it's sturdy and easy to keep clean.

The appropriate Haynes manual would be a good purchase, not only for the dismantling and rebuild, but also for any reconditioning you wish to do.

Be methodical as you strip the donor. Where possible, put nuts, bolts and screws back onto the component you have removed. Bag and label small components – you might know exactly what they are and where they go today, but will you in two years' time? If necessary, mark larger components with a paint marker or correction fluid. Having removed the loom and electrical equipment, re-attach the components to the wiring where you can, and label the wires using masking tape and a marker pen. Make the writing clear and large, as it tends to deteriorate in the garage environment. This belt and braces approach ensures that you know which wire goes where when it comes to reassembly. If you have the facilities, take photographs of the parts in-situ as a further aid. Keep a written log of your expenses and keep receipts, particularly if you intend to get a new or donor age-related registration number.

THE PARTS REQUIRED FROM THE DONOR CAR

■ Engine

Including all ancillaries – starter motor, alternator, manifolds, distributor, carburettor. If your Sierra has fuel injection, you can use it, but the plenum chamber will stick up through the bonnet, unless modified. It might be easier to find an inlet manifold and carburettor from a non-injection Sierra. Modifications will be required to the fuel system and a new petrol tank will need to be made (see Chapter 7).

▼ **Fig. 3.1** Choose the best donor car you can afford and, if possible, take a test drive before you buy.

Gearbox

Including clutch assembly and mounting brackets. Early Sierras are fitted with a four-speed box, later ones with a five-speed. The four-speed transmission tends to give better acceleration, the five-speed better fuel economy and lower noise output. Both gearboxes are interchangeable, using the appropriate clutch components and flywheel spigot bearing.

- Brake master cylinder
- Windscreen washer system, if required
- Exhaust pipe and silencer
- Wheels, including tyres and nuts
- Rear brake proportioning valve
- Clutch, handbrake, speedometer and accelerator cables
- Handbrake lever
- Instrument cluster
- Steering wheel and column assembly, complete with ignition lock and switch gear
- Battery (if in good condition)
- Wiring loom and switches
- Ignition coil
- Horn
- Fuse box and all necessary relays and flasher unit
- Fuel pipe
- Seat belts (if in good condition and assuming you're not fitting harnesses)

Some parts shouldn't be re-used, particularly braking and steering wearing parts. Everything else you removed should be inspected very carefully to ensure that it is serviceable. If you're not certain that the parts are usable, get them checked by a professional mechanic or electrician.

RECONDITIONING

Braking system

Check that the front discs are not warped or cracked and that the callipers have full movement and aren't leaking. Also check the drums on the rear brakes for wear and the wheel cylinders for leakage and free movement. You will need to replace any suspect parts of the braking system. Scored rear drums can be re-faced by an engineering shop, but only if sufficient material remains. If they've been re-faced before, the surface may be too thin to have it done again. As a matter of course, brake pads and shoes should be replaced, unless obviously new and unworn, and you will be fitting new flexible and rigid brake pipes.

Starter motor

Check the pinion is free to move and that the teeth are in good condition, and lubricate with light oil. Make sure that the electrical connections are secure, and check that the motor operates by connecting it to a good battery.

▼ Fig. 3.2 A Ford Sierra rear axle assembly. Yours will probably look like this, too, but you can work wonders with a wire brush and a little elbow grease!

■ Exhaust

My first exhaust was built using suitably modified donor parts. This will do the job but perhaps isn't cosmetically ideal. Exhaust centres can be a good source of alternative parts. Check their scrap bins, but ask first! Specialist suppliers can sell you all the parts you need if you want to build a new system for yourself, and complete ready-made systems are available from MK Engineering.

■ Wiring loom

The Sierra loom, depending on the model, can be very complicated. You won't have electric windows, air con, interior lights or a heated rear window, so much of the loom can be removed. At a basic level it's easier to remove all the loom bindings and trace the wires to the components that you need. Place the electrical items approximately where they will be in the finished car and remove all the wires that you don't need. Wiring looms for our type of car can be bought from MK Engineering – this isn't a cheap option but it will be quicker.

PARTS FROM OTHER SOURCES

■ Steering rack

Use a Ford Escort Mk II steering rack, new or second-hand. Your local motor factors will be able to get you a standard one and, because of the Escort's continued popularity in rallying circles, you can get racks in various ratios from the specialist rally supply companies. (I used a 2.9 turns lock-to-lock rack and this seems to be ideal.) Obtain the rack mounting rubbers and clamps too.

■ 2x Steering rack extensions

These can be bought from MK Engineering or made by any competent machine shop from the diagram in Chapter 5.

■ 2x New Sierra track-rod ends

■ 2x New Ford Transit drag-link ends

(Lockheed part number TA298 or equivalent) Ensure that you get two components of the same part number, the right-hand threaded ones. It would be usual to buy one of each hand for use on the Transit. These form the top ball-joints on the front suspension.

■ 2x Austin Maxi lower balljoints

(Unipart part number GSJ 188 or equivalent)

■ 4x Coil-over dampers

Front and rear dampers are 13in open and 9in closed with a 25mm solid extension at the top. Suggested spring rates 350lb per inch front, 200lb per inch rear. Other sizes of damper can be accommodated by altering the bracket positions on the chassis. Suitable dampers available from MK Engineering.

◀ **Fig. 3.3** A Ford Escort Mk II steering rack and aftermarket aluminium rack clamps.

■ 16x polyurethane bushes
See Chapter 5 for details.

■ SVA compliant lighting
If you have the SVA manual you can use the positioning diagrams. Any lighting needs to be E-marked and securely fitted. Requirements are two front headlights (which should include side lights), red rear lights, brake lights, reflectors, indicators front and back with side repeaters. A high intensity rear fog lamp should be fitted on the centreline or offside of the car.

■ Seats or adaptable back seat
Many small hatchbacks have suitable seats, or you can adapt a rear seat as shown in Chapter 11.

■ Radiator
The Sierra radiator is too wide to fit in the nosecone. An alternative needs to be sourced from a modern small hatchback. These are more efficient, size for size, and are easily able to cope with a 2.0-litre engine. The Nissan Micra, Renault Clio and Volkswagen Polo radiators are suitable.

■ Electric fan
Where applicable, you must remember to remove the belt-driven cooling fan from the engine as there probably won't be room for it. You need a fan that you can use in the original orientation to the car you take it from. One that sits in front of the radiator and blows air through is probably best. A very nice cast aluminium one is fitted to the Citroën BX range.

If fitting a windscreen you will also need a windscreen wiper motor, cable, wheel boxes and wipers from a Rover Mini. The later ones are preferred as they are two-speed. Ensure that they meet the SVA requirements of 45 cycles per minute and that they self park out of the driver's view.

In addition, a small heater can be fitted. Those from a Rover Mini and a Volkswagen Polo are suitable, but you need to decide at an early stage if you're going to fit a heater, as modifications to the bulkhead will be necessary.

OTHER MATERIALS REQUIRED
Refer to Appendix 1 for dimensions and patterns of manufactured steel components

■ Rectangular hollow steel sections:
- 25 x 25mm square 16swg
- 19 x 19mm square 16swg
- 51 x 25mm 16swg

- Round steel tube:
  - 19mm diameter 16swg
  - 25mm diameter 16swg
  - 28mm external diameter x 22mm internal diameter
  - 33.7 diameter x 2.6mm
- Seamless steel tube:
  - 25mm diameter
  - 19mm diameter
- Round steel bar stock:
  - 20mm, 26mm, 30mm
- Round steel pipe:
  - 5-inch external diameter x 65mm long
- Steel sheet:
  - 16swg
  - 1mm
  - 3mm steel plate offcuts
  - 5mm steel plate
  - 10mm steel plate
- Steel strip:
  - 41 x 3mm, 25 x 3mm, 13 x 3mm
- Steel or aluminium tube, petrol resistant rubber hose and clips for fuel tank filler
- Aluminium sheet:
  - 1.2mm half hard
- 25mm aluminium capping strip
- Rubber strip 30 x 2mm
- New rigid brake pipe and fittings
- Flexible front and rear brake pipes for the donor car
- New brake pads and shoes
- Hardboard or thin ply, sponge and vinyl for interior panels, if required
- Sealant
- Paint materials as required
- Glassfibre materials, if making your own panels
- Assorted fixings, including rivets (3 x 10mm), nuts (locking and plain), bolts and setscrews, clips and self-tapping screws

In addition, if you're fitting a full windscreen you'll need some aluminium U-shaped extrusion for the frame and glass cut to your pattern, carrying an approved BS kite mark applied by the glass manufacturer. Note that this cannot be applied by the glass supplier, even if the glass itself complies.

FINDING THE STEEL

As I said in my introduction, I was lucky to get all the steel I required for £10. You might be lucky too. Many fabrication companies have piles of off-cut steel that they have to pay someone to

take away, so it's worth asking such firms if you can have a rummage. They might not let you get the steel yourself because of health and safety concerns (this also applies to the exhaust centres), but if you give them a list of materials, they might oblige. If your steel is from different places, ensure that it's all the same thickness, or use similar-sized tubes in the same locations on each side of your frame to ensure the chassis flexes in the same way on both sides. Think laterally about the sources of materials. Who might use that material and consequently have some left over? For example, I was unable to find seamless steel tube in the local engineering shops or even the steel stockholders. Asking around, I discovered that one of the biggest users of seamless tube are hydraulics manufacturers. A few quick phone calls got the tube sorted. Of course, you can buy new steel from a stockholder if all else fails.

OTHER MATERIAL SOURCES

Van and truck breakers can be a good source of aluminium sheet. Luton-type vans usually have large aluminium sheeted sides. I'd advise some sort of powered metal shear or cutter as it's a hard job by hand, but not impossible (take some friends along – many (sore) hands make light work!)

A great source for other parts is the autojumble. Think of a car boot sale with nothing but car parts and you've got it. To me, much of the fun in building the car was mooching around jumbles looking for that elusive bargain. We used to make a family event of it, although the wife and kids sometimes got a faraway look in their eyes! Things like shock absorbers, lights and glassfibre parts are often to be found at these events, as well as new brake parts and pipe and fittings. Parts for reconditioning and servicing are usually cheap too. Look out for events in magazines and newspapers.

Scrapyards aren't the treasure trove they used to be. Until a few years ago they were literally yards full of scrap cars, and you wandered in with your tool kit, took what you wanted to the owner (whilst avoiding his massive, oily dog) got a price and walked away with it. Not any more. The traditional scrappy has been forced out of business by EEC directives on fluid disposal, etc., and has been replaced by the 'dismantler'. These concerns still have a yard but they don't let you in. Instead, you go into their office and tell them what you want and they fetch it from the warehouse. This is great for most people, but not for the scavenger

Fig. 3.4 Coil-over shock absorbers suitable for the Roadster, from Protech (left) and Dampertech (right).

Fig. 3.5 You'll need a radiator like this one from a Renault Clio or similar. Also visible in this picture are the electric fan and the expansion bottle for the cooling system.

► **Fig. 3.6** A typical scrapyard scene – mind the dog!

Ford has made things easier for us in one important way. All Ford engines, from the 1960s up to today's Zetec-based Duratec engines, share the same gearbox/engine bolt pattern. But, on the very latest Mazda-developed Duratecs it's been changed. Shame!

■ **Ford Pinto SOHC**

This is the engine we have used for the car described in this book. Usually free with the donor car, it will either have a four-speed Type E or a five-speed Type 9 RWD gearbox. The five-speed box can be fitted to any Pinto by changing the flywheel spigot bearing and clutch components to the five-speed type. This engine was manufactured in 1.3, 1.6, 1.8 and 2.0-litre versions, and there was an American 2.3-litre engine which was never sold in the UK.

A host of tuning parts are available. Some Pinto engines are suitable for unleaded petrol – all those with cylinder heads originally equipped with fuel injection are, and so are those marked M, MM, N, NN (1.6 litre), S, SS (1.8 litre) and P, PP, R, RR (2.0 litre). The marks will be found adjacent to No. 4 spark plug on the head. The Cosworth 16-valve turbocharged engine was a development of this engine, although you won't see many Sierra Cosworth donors!

■ **Ford CVH**

This engine was fitted to some 1.6 and 1.8 Sierras with the five-speed Type 9 gearbox. Relatively few tuning modifications are around, but all these engines are suitable for unleaded fuel.

■ **Ford DOHC 8v**

This is the second of the alternative engines fitted to the Sierra from 1989. It's a tall and heavy engine not popular with the tuners, although a 16-valve version was fitted to the Escort RS2000. This engine will be mated to the later MT75 gearbox, which is larger than the Type 9 and may require some modification to the transmission tunnel to fit.

■ **Ford Kent crossflow OHV**

Originally fitted to the Anglia and Mk I and Mk II Escorts, this engine is highly tuneable, but it's now very old technology. They would originally have been fitted with a four-speed gearbox, but the five-speed Type 9 box fits very nicely, although some clutch parts need to be mixed and matched. As standard, these engines are

who needs to 'find a part to do the job' not a part from a particular car. My own car has parts from Alfa Romeo, Jaguar, Rover, Fiat, Citroën, Porsche, Vauxhall, Volkswagen and, of course, Ford. Sometimes you can get over the threshold of the yard, but they're so afraid of the health and safety aspects that it's not likely. You can find out what other builders have used via the club or on the internet forums, and then visit the dismantler and buy. Prices have increased because of the legislation, but the upside is that the returns policy has improved. The old policy involved that dog I was talking about.

Other sources include wanted ads for parts in the local papers (as you may have done for your donor car) and, of course, word of mouth. Ask around your friends and relatives. I discovered that my cousin used a firm that cuts glass for plant (forklifts, diggers, etc.) – result, one free windscreen.

It's more difficult to source things like separate round instruments these days, and the book shows you how to use the donor car's instrument panel, suitably modified. Some cars that are still around in the scrapyards have round instruments – the Skoda saloons and Porsche 924s come to mind. New round individual instruments are available, and sometimes these come up second-hand. Although they're generally robust, check carefully any second-hand instruments. Again, autojumbles are a good source.

ALTERNATIVES – ENGINES AND GEARBOXES

Because the engine space in the Roadster is quite large there's potential for choosing from a wide range of different power units. The main stumbling block, though, is the need for a rear-wheel-drive (RWD) gearbox but, as we'll see, this need not be an insurmountable problem.

unsuitable for unleaded fuel, but you can either use an additive to the fuel, or have stainless steel exhaust valves fitted.

■ Rover K-series
Small and light, these engines are used by many specialist car manufacturers as well as Rover. Available in 1.1, 1.4, 1.6 and 1.8-litre capacities in both 8-valve and 16-valve versions. As standard it comes with a transverse gearbox, but bell housings and adapter plates are available to fit a Ford Type 9 gearbox. All engines are designed to run on unleaded fuel. They have a reputation for head gasket problems, but this is mostly down to poor maintenance and servicing.

■ Rover V8
Originally a Buick design, this has been the engine of choice for specialist manufacturers requiring a light and powerful V8 engine. A good donor would be the SD1 Rover which comes with a RWD gearbox. Unfortunately, these are usually automatics, but manuals can be found. Late model original Range Rovers may have engine capacities up to 4.5 litres. Post 1980 engines are suitable for unleaded fuel.

■ Fiat twin-cam
A jewel of an engine – immensely tuneable and with a big following – produced in 1.3 to 2.0-litre capacities and used in Alfa Romeo models as well. It was last used in RWD form in the Fiat 131 Mirafiori. Adapter plates are available to fit the Ford Type 9 gearbox. You'll have to use an additive, or convert it to hardened valve seats, to run on unleaded fuel.

■ Vauxhall XE
A very popular 16-valve engine used in Astras, Cavaliers and Calibras. A tuner's favourite in 2.0-litre form. A five-speed gearbox from an Opel Manta or Vauxhall Carlton/Senator with RWD will fit and, as usual, adapters for the five-speed Ford gearbox are available. These engines were designed for unleaded fuel.

■ Toyota 4AGE
A small and light engine, very popular with kit car builders. The combination of light weight and good power output make it an ideal choice. Most applications of this engine are transverse, i.e. FWD, or mid-engined RWD as in the Toyota MR2. A T50 RWD gearbox from a Corolla or Celica can be fitted, but these are becoming increasingly rare. Again, bespoke bellhousings and adapter plates save the day.

■ Motorcycle engines
Increasingly popular, these engines combine light weight and remarkable power for their capacity. They are literally at the cutting edge of engine technology. A six-speed sequential gearbox is part of the complete package you would get from a donor bike. This can be linked by rods or cables to a gear lever or Formula One style steering wheel paddle system. All this leads to optimal performance on track, but the powerplant has downsides for road use. The first is the lack of a reverse gear. You might think that you can manage without, but it becomes seriously irritating when parking and manoeuvring. This can be overcome by the fitting of a reverse box (usually in the transmission tunnel) which is operated by a lever or switch, but all this adds weight and leads to a certain amount of power loss, not to mention the extra cost.

Another factor to consider is the amount of gear changing involved when driving a bike-engined car on the road, and the 'buzzy' nature of the exhaust, which can be seriously wearing on a long journey. Having said all that, the thrill of a bike-engined car in the right environment is seriously addictive. See the alternatives section in Chapter 6 for motorcycle engine fitting suggestions.

ALTERNATIVES – REAR AXLE
The type of final drive we need is secured to the bodyshell of the donor car and the driveshafts and hubs are attached using trailing or semi-trailing arms. The method of differential attachment varies from vehicle to vehicle. The Sierra, for example, has through-bolts which locate into the underbody, but the MX-5 has a large rubber-mounted subframe. Some differentials are fixed through the top and others through the sides of the casing.

To use an alternative rear axle, it's necessary to fix the differential on the centreline of the car and level with the output end of the gearbox using plates similar to the Sierra-based version. Placing the differential in position in the chassis, measure carefully to the structure and make plates to support it. It's vital that the plates are strong enough as the forces involved are high. See Chapter 5 for rear upright modifications.

4 MAKING THE CHASSIS

The chassis looks very complicated at first glance, but broken down into stages it's a simple process not unlike the construction kits of our youth. In Appendix 1 you will find the dimensions for every tube and plate, including illustrated details where angled cuts, etc., are required. Some people like to cut all the steel in one go, but I'd advise against this. Although the drawings in this book are very precise, it's better to cut each piece as it's needed, so that it can be tried in place and filed or ground to a tight fit. As an exception to this, tubes which are the same but on opposite sides of the chassis (BR5 and BR6, for example) should be cut together to ensure uniformity.

▶ **Fig. 4.1** The building board supported on a metal table – note the stiffening timbers beneath the board.

▼ **Fig. 4.2** The basic setting out dimensions for the bottom rails of the chassis.

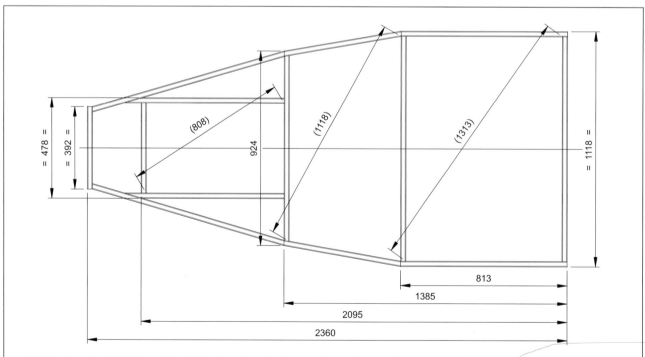

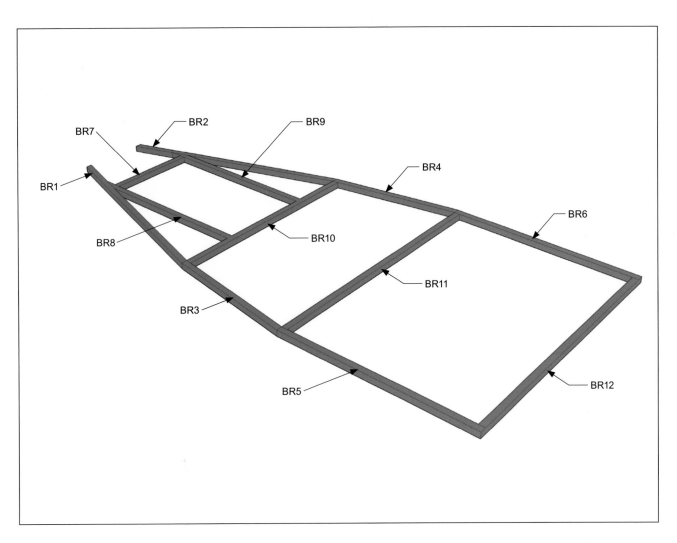

BR7
BR2
BR9
BR1
BR4
BR6
BR8
BR10
BR11
BR3
BR5
BR12

LAYING THE FOUNDATION

The chassis does not require a jig, but you will need a true flat surface, and one that can be marked out accurately with a pencil or marker pen. This excludes most garage floors or any concrete surface, and marking out with chalk cannot ever be anywhere near accurate enough, as chalk lines will be 2mm thick at least! The chassis made for this book was built on a 2440 x 1220mm sheet of 12mm plywood. To keep the sheet flat a frame of 75 x 50mm timber was glued and screwed to the underside. Select your timber carefully; a bent support frame won't keep the ply flat. Some builders paint the board with white emulsion paint to make the lines stand out.

The board should be marked out with the lines as shown in Fig. 4.2. A steel straight edge and a fine marker pen are probably best. It's important not to make the lines too thick because you must ensure that the initial tubes are in the right place – they are the foundation of your chassis. Once the lines are drawn and checked,

▲ **Fig. 4.3** The main bottom rails of the chassis.

▼ **Fig. 4.4** Wooden blocks fixed to the baseboard to ensure correct alignment.

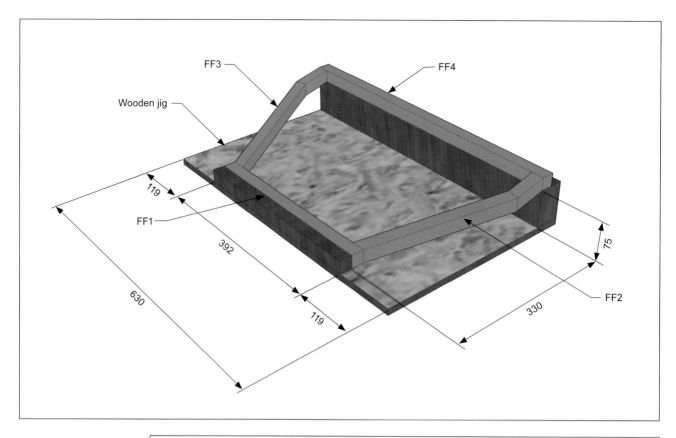

FF3

FF4

Wooden jig

FF1

119

392

630

119

75

330

FF2

▲ **Fig. 4.5** The wooden jig required to construct the front frame of the chassis.

▶ **Fig. 4.6** The dimensions of the components for the front frame.

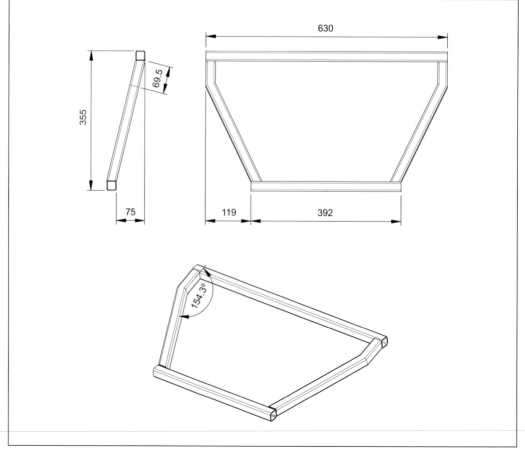

630

69.5

355

75

119

392

154.3°

40mm pieces of 25 x 15mm of timber can be screwed alongside the lines as shown in Fig. 4.4. These will help keep the tubes in alignment when tack welding and prevent the tubes being moved inadvertently while working around the chassis.

The tubes BR1 to BR12 form the base level of the chassis – see Fig. 4.3. Cut the tubes as shown in the drawings in Appendix 1 and trial fit them between the wooden blocks, trimming the tubes to fit if necessary. Accuracy at this stage will pay dividends later. Make the junctions between tubes as close as possible to aid the welding process. Use the check dimensions on the plan to ensure accuracy.

When you're happy with the fit of these tubes, tack weld them together, working on one side of the chassis and then the other to minimise any distortion. No tubes should be fully welded at this stage – a short tack weld is sufficient to hold the tubes. Check that all the tubes are flush to the board when you have finished welding. Should any tube not be flush, grind off any tack welds as necessary and make the tube flat to the board and weld again.

THE FRONT FRAME

The front frame should be built up next, and a simple wooden jig can be constructed, as in Fig. 4.5, to make the task easier. FF1 and FF4 are straight cut pieces of 25 x 25mm box section – 392mm long for FF1 and 630mm long for FF4 – see Fig. 4.6. FF2 and FF3 require a wedge to be taken out and the tube bent and welded to suit. The wedge should not go through the bottom face of the tube and the tube should be bent and welded as shown in Appendix 1. Place the tubes in the jig and clamp in place where possible, and tack weld.

ATTACHING THE UPRIGHT TUBES

The uprights U3 to U6 should be attached to the chassis next – see Fig. 4.7. Note that U4 and U5 have an angle on the top face as shown in Appendix 1. Magnetic welding clamps are useful for holding the uprights for tack welding. Failing this, hold a square against the upright as you weld, and check the uprights are vertical when tack welded. Note that U3 and U6 are aligned with the outside of tubes BR3 and BR4 respectively.

The front frame can now be fitted, FF1 should be lined up with the front edge of the building

▼ Fig. 4.7 The second stage of chassis construction.

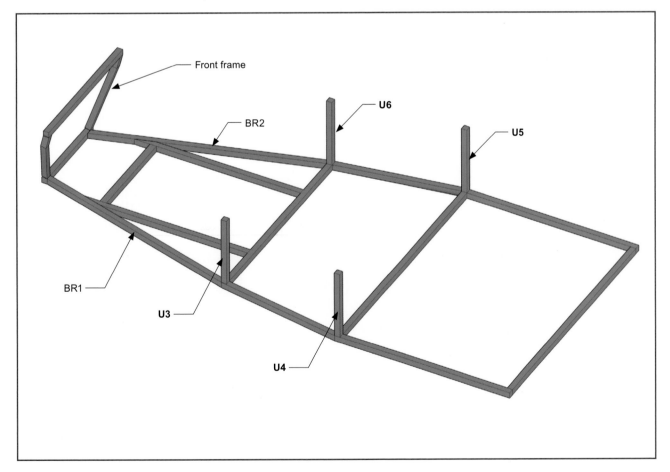

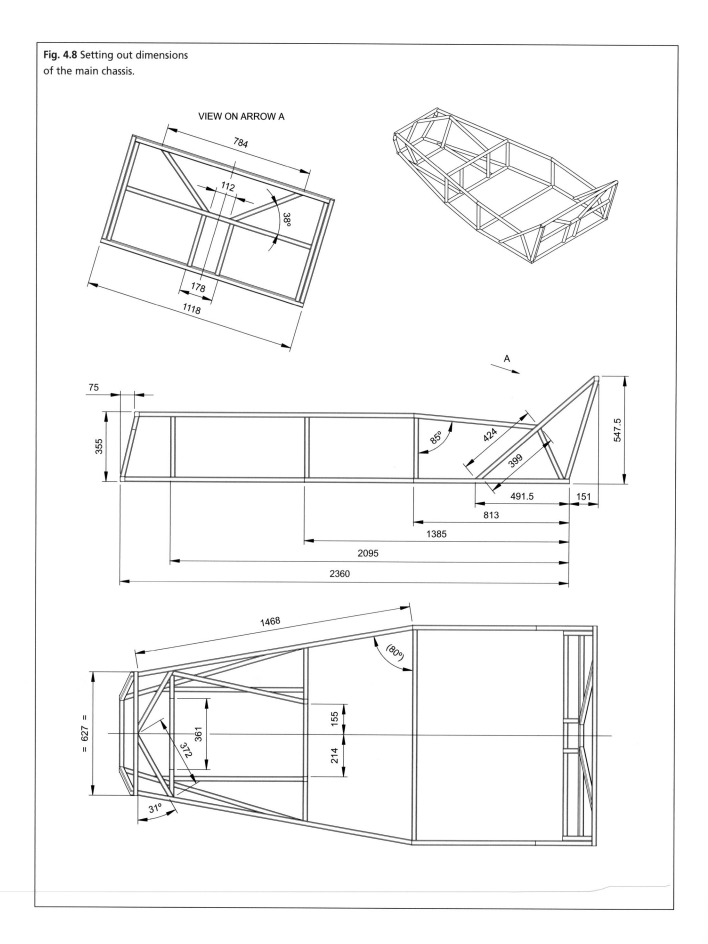

Fig. 4.8 Setting out dimensions of the main chassis.

VIEW ON ARROW A

784

112

38°

178

1118

75

355

A

85°

424

399

547.5

491.5

151

813

1385

2095

2360

1468

(80°)

627

155

361

372

214

31°

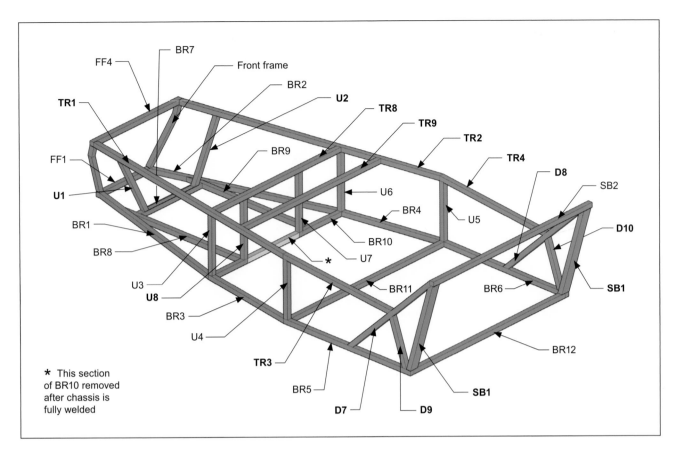

* This section
of BR10 removed
after chassis is
fully welded

board. The ends of FF1 line up with the ends of tubes BR1 and BR2. Clamp FF1 to the board ensuring that the front face of FF4 is 75mm behind the front face of FF1 (this should be the case if the front frame was built on the jig, and FF1 is clamped flat to the board – see Fig. 4.8).

SECOND STAGE CHASSIS CONSTRUCTION

TR1 and TR2 should be cut next, the outside being lined up with the outside front corner of U4/U5 and either end of FF4 – see Fig. 4.9. Tack weld to the uprights and FF4. TR8 fits vertically above BR10 between U3 and U6. TR9 fits behind TR8, with a 195mm gap between the tubes. Tack weld both in place. Front suspension uprights U1 and U2 should be fixed next, noting that they are placed square to rail BR7 at the bottom. The top front corner of the upright is aligned with the outside of the rails TR1/TR2. See Fig. 4.10.

Next, add uprights U7 and U8, the portion of rail BR10 between these uprights should be removed, after the chassis is fully welded, to allow access for the gearbox. Cut the four rails SB1 and weld them together in pairs. These could be replaced by single lengths of 50 x 25mm box section if you can obtain it.

The two SB1 assemblies should be supported and welded at either end of rail BR12, as shown in Fig. 4.9. SB2 is welded to the tops of the SB1 assemblies, ensuring that the ends line up with the outside of the chassis. Cut rails D7 and D8 and tack in position between the SB1 assemblies and BR5 and BR6 respectively. TR3 and TR4 can now be placed and tacked between TR1/D7 and TR2/D8 and D9 and D10 fit between D7/BR5 and D8/BR6 respectively.

▲ **Fig. 4.9** The second stage of chassis construction.

▼ **Fig. 4.10** Correct alignment of the junction of TR1/U1. TR2/U2 similar, handed.

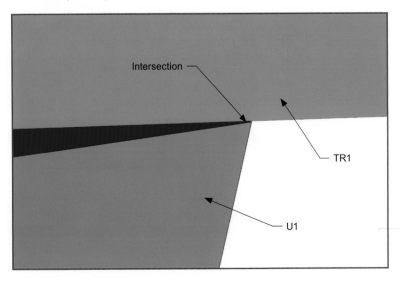

Intersection

TR1

U1

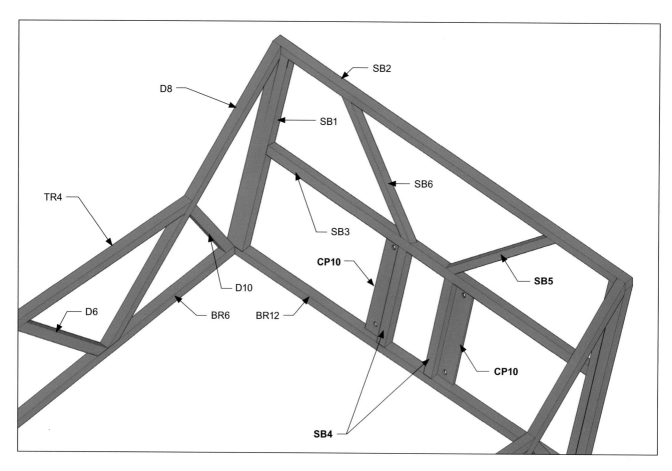

▲ **Fig. 4.11** Chassis side and seat back rails.

Tack weld SB3 between the two SB1 assemblies, as shown in Fig. 4.11, and using the check dimension shown in Fig. 4.15. Cut rails SB4 and tack in position between BR12 and SB3. Plates CP10, for location of the differential, are positioned on the outside of these rails and should be tacked in position in line with the rear edge of the SB4 rails. The seat back bracing pieces SB5 and SB6 can then be tacked in between SB2 and SB3.

Cut and tack rails TR5, TR6 and TR7 in place in the engine bay area – see Fig. 4.12.

The side bracing should be added next, noting the positioning of the diagonal braces in relation to the other rails. This involves cutting rails D1 to D6 and tacking them in place.

The chassis should now be rigid enough to be moved carefully forwards approximately 750mm to enable the rear section to be made. It may be necessary to remove some of the wooden blocks to let the chassis sit flat on the board.

REAR SUSPENSION FRAMEWORK
The next stage is to construct the frames supporting the rear suspension – see Fig. 4.13. Cut rails RS1, RS2 and RS3 and place flat on the

board, check for square and tack together to form the lower frame. Similarly construct the top frame from rails RS4, RS5 and RS6. Rails RS7 RS7a, RS8 and RS9 should be tacked to the under side of the RS4/RS5/RS6 frame, lining up the rear corners at either side. Place the lower frame RS1/RS2/RS3 in position on rail BR12 ensuring that the frame is set centrally on the chassis and 3mm from the front edge to accommodate the two plates CP1. Support the other end of the frame 25mm from the board with off-cuts of 25mm box section. Tack the frame and the end support plates CP1 (x2) to BR12.

Cut the vertical rear frame support rails RS10 (x2) and tack in place vertically at the rearmost corners of the RS1/RS2/RS3 frame. The RS4/RS5/RS6 frame sits on the top of the RS10 uprights at the rear end. RS7 and RS7a are tack welded to the underside of rail SB3. The end of rails RS7 and RS7a are filled using plates CP2. Bracing rails RS11 and RS12 are positioned between SB3 and the rear corners of the RS4/RS5/RS6 frame.

Chassis plates CP3 and CP4 – see Fig. 4.14 – should be added next, ensuring that you've remembered to weld on the four captive 8mm nuts, RS15 and the shock absorber bracket to the

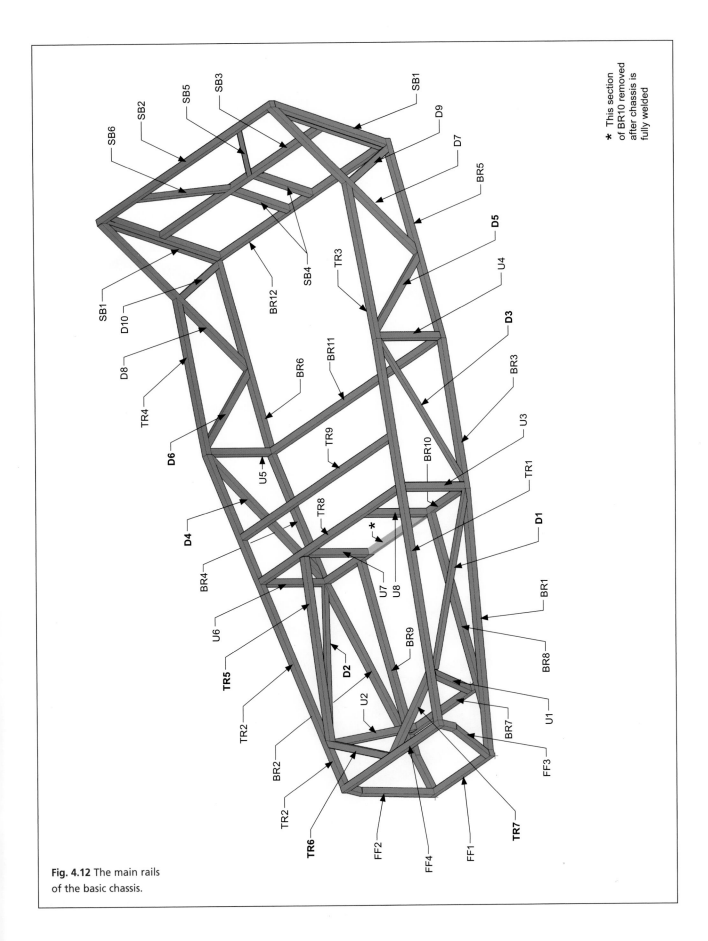

Fig. 4.12 The main rails of the basic chassis.

SB3

SB5

SB2

SB6

SB1

D9

D7

BR5

SB1

D10

D8

TR4

D6

BR12

SB4

TR3

BR6

BR11

U4

D5

D3

BR3

U5

TR9

BR10

U3

TR1

D4

TR8

D1

BR4

U6

U7

U8

BR1

TR5

D2

BR9

BR8

TR2

U2

U1

BR2

BR7

FF3

TR2

FF2

TR6

FF4

TR7

FF1

* This section
of BR10 removed
after chassis is
fully welded

underside (see Appendix 1). The nuts, box section and the bracket should be fully welded as access is very difficult when the other rails are added. These plates line up with the outer and front edges of rail SB2 and the holes for the roll bar attachment are closest to the outside. The SB1 assembly is completed by adding plates CP5, CP6 and CP7, noting that the hole in CP6 is placed to the inside, lining up with the shock absorber bracket on plate CP3/CP4 – this is the access hole for the bolt for the top of the shock absorber. CP7 is tacked to CP3/CP4 and CP6 with the long diagonal facing downwards to be welded to rails D12 later.

Now add short pieces RS13 to the rear faces of rails RS10, 85mm above the baseboard, and tack rail RS14 across these pieces, lining up with the outside of the chassis.

The next pieces required are the rear panel tubes, RP1 and RP2. These are formed from 19mm round steel tube, bent as shown in Appendix 1. The easiest way to form these tubes is with the help of a friendly local plumber. Their tube forming gear will make short work of the job. Alternatively, you could bend them a little at a

time using a vice. This is quite likely to kink the tube, but the kinks will be on the inside and, it is hoped, will be covered by the rear panel.

Tack RP1 to the ends of RS14 and confirm the vertical check dimension in Fig. 4.15. Rails D11 link RS14 and plate CP6. Tack these in place next. RP2 fits in a similar way to RP1 to the face of rails D11 and can be held in place by cutting and profiling the ends of rails RP3. When you're satisfied that RP2 is correctly positioned, tack the RP3 rails in place, along with RP2.

Add bracing rails D12 and D13 next. The lower end of D12 lines up with the end of rail RS4/RS5 and the top is welded to CP7 and SB2. D13 is butt joined to the lower end of D12 and profiled on to RP1 at the rear.

Add the fuel tank supports, plates CP8, between RS14 and RP1, touching the inside face of RP3 at the rear, and parallel.

Roll bar support plates CP9 are tacked to the underside of rail RP2, positioned with the cut-out around RP3. Add gusset plates CP25 between plates CP9 and the RP3 rails to complete the assembly.

▼ **Fig. 4.13** The rails forming the rear suspension area of the chassis.

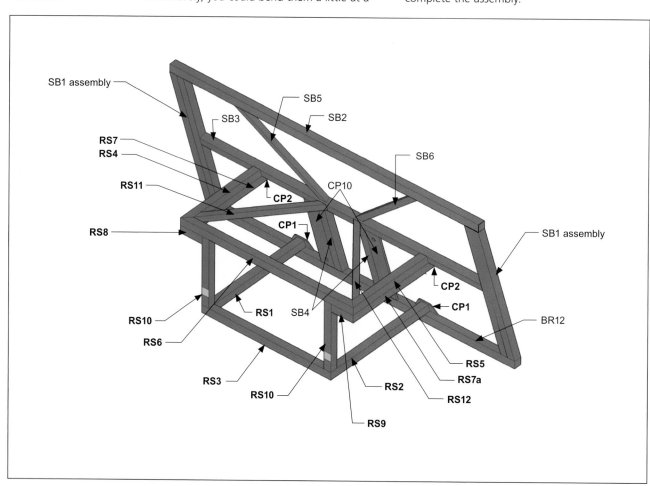

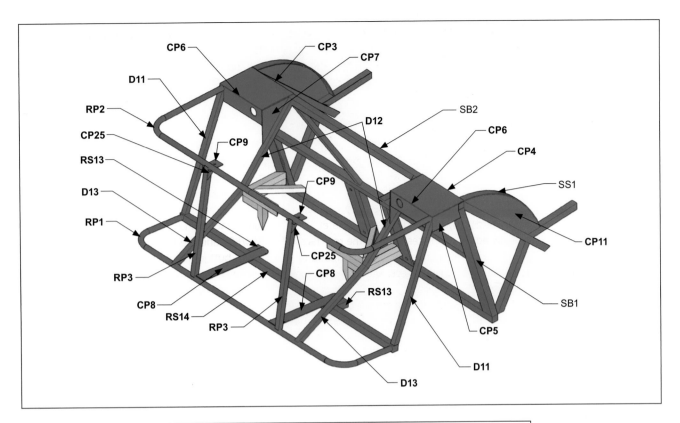

CP6 — CP3 — CP7

D11

RP2

CP25

RS13

D13

RP1

RP3

CP8

RS14

CP8

RP3

CP9

CP9

CP25

CP8

D12

RS13

SB2

CP6

CP4

SS1

CP11

SB1

CP5

D11

D13

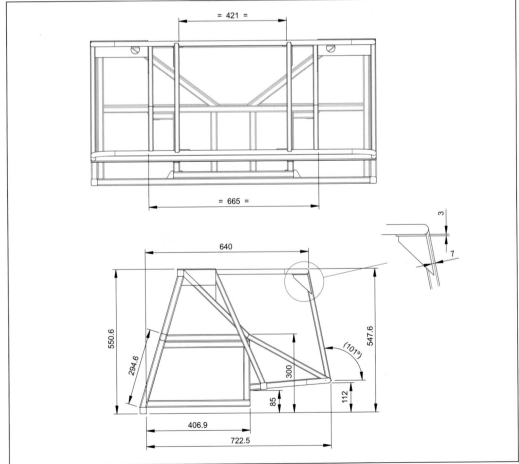

= 421 =

= 665 =

640

3

7

550.6

294.6

547.6

(101°)

300

85

112

406.9

722.5

▲ **Fig. 4.14** Rails in the rear chassis area.

◄ **Fig. 4.15** Arrangement of the rear suspension and rear panel area.

The curved side supports, SS1, are made from 25 x 3mm steel strip bent as shown in Appendix 1. The top edge of these is lined up with the top of SB2 and the bottom rests on TR3/TR4. Plate CP11, of 1mm steel sheet, is tacked into the space to the outside of SS1 to complete this area.

TRANSMISSION TUNNEL

Adding the transmission tunnel gives extra strength to the chassis. Cut rails TT1, position on the baseboard, and tack as shown in Figs. 4.17 and 4.18. TT2 and TT3 are placed between BR10 and BR11. Verticals TT4 and cross piece TT5 should be tacked together flat on the board and checked for square, then positioned on top of the TT1 rails, against the rear face of BR11, and tacked. Verticals TT6 should be tacked to TT1 as shown in Fig. 4.17. Rails TT7 connect the TT4/TT5 frame and SB3, and cross piece TT8 bridges the two assemblies, lining up with the TT6 verticals.

TT9 and TT10 fit vertically above TT2 either side of TR9, and likewise TT11 and TT12 fit vertically above TT3, again either side of TR9. This alignment is important to ensure that the transmission tunnel panels fit without problems.

▲ **Fig. 4.16** A general view of the rails at the rear of the chassis.

▼ **Fig. 4.17** The rails of the transmission tunnel area.

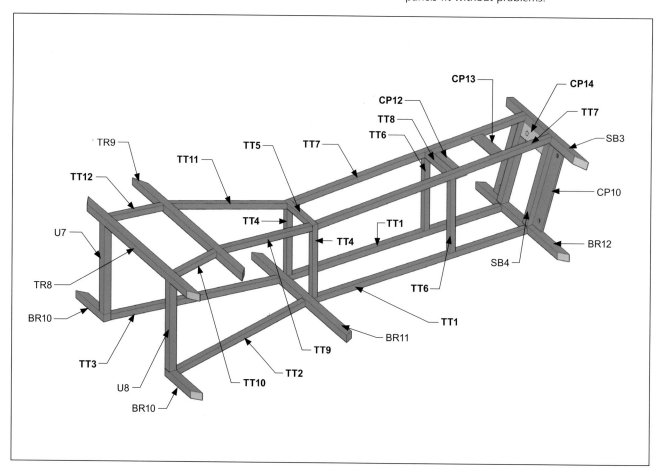

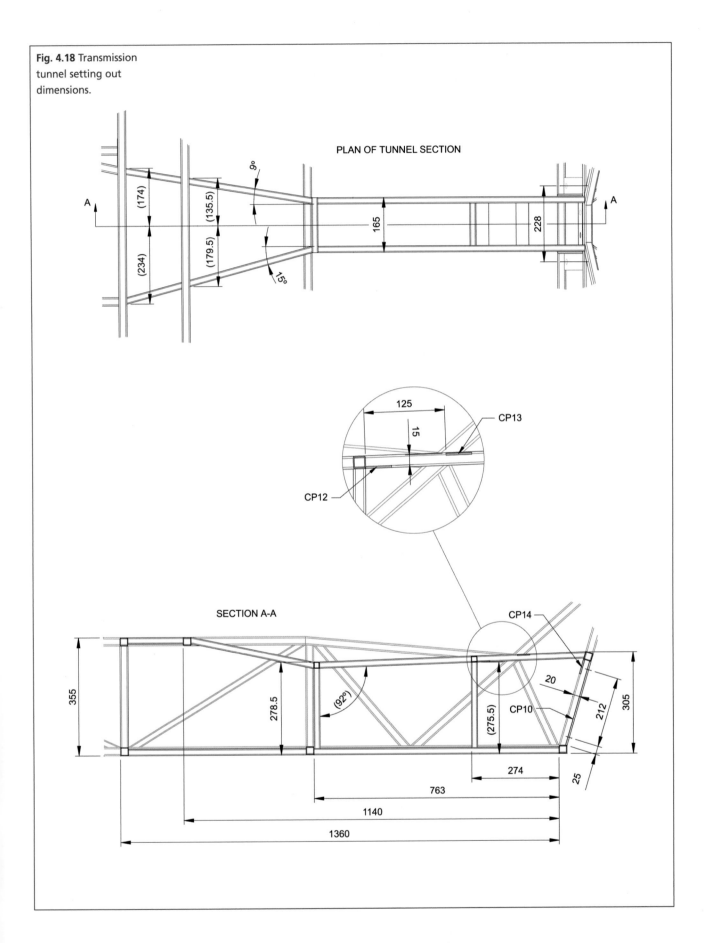

Fig. 4.18 Transmission tunnel setting out dimensions.

PLAN OF TUNNEL SECTION

(174)

(135.5)

9°

(234)

(179.5)

15°

165

228

A

A

CP13

15

125

CP12

SECTION A-A

CP14

355

278.5

(92°)

(275.5)

CP10

20

212

305

274

25

763

1140

1360

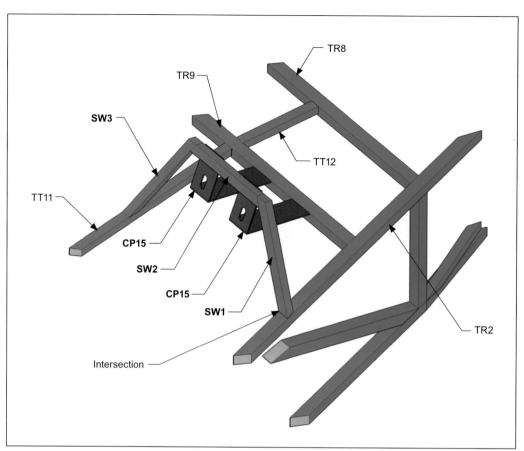

▶ **Fig. 4.19** The steering wheel support frame.

▼ **Fig. 4.20** Dimensions of the steering column support frame.

TR8

TR9

SW3

TT12

TT11

CP15

SW2

CP15

SW1

TR2

Intersection

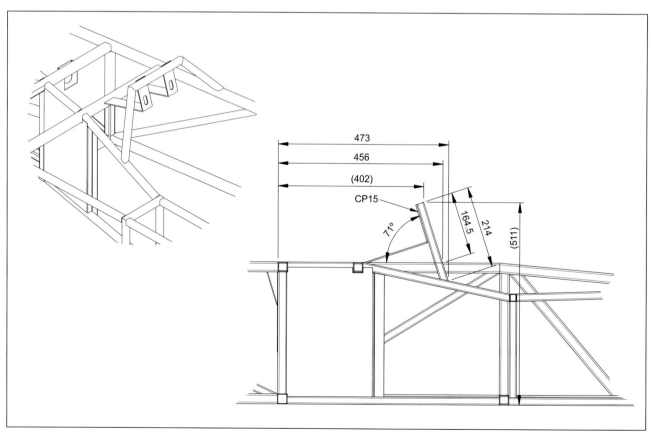

473

456

(402)

CP15

71°

164.5

214

(511)

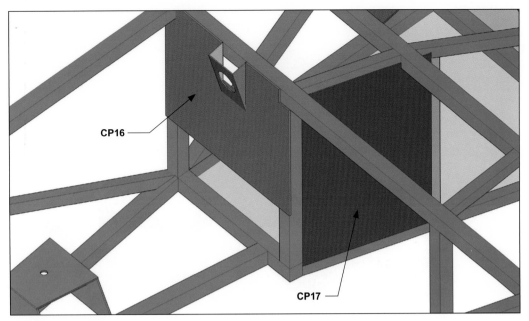

◀ **Fig. 4.21** The panels required in the driver's footwell area.

CP16

CP17

▼ **Fig. 4.22** Setting out dimensions for the front wishbone and shock absorber brackets.

HANDBRAKE AND STEERING COLUMN SUPPORTS

Handbrake support plates CP12 and CP13 are next. CP12 fits flush with the bottom of the TT7 rails, against the back edge of TT8. CP13 sits between the TT7 rails, 12mm from the bottom and 125mm behind TT8 – see Fig. 4.17.

The handbrake guide plate CP14 is tacked onto the SB3 and SB4 rails at the rear of the transmission tunnel.

The steering column support frame is made from rails SW1, SW2 and SW3. Again these should be assembled flat on the board, the angles checked and the rails tacked together. The frame should be positioned as shown in Figs. 4.19 and 4.20, with plates CP15 tacked in place to complete the assembly.

Two steel plates need to be attached to the chassis in the driver's footwell area at this stage – see Fig. 4.21. Plate CP16 forms the top of the driver's bulkhead and the lower support for the steering column, and for protection plate CP17 is positioned on the gearbox side of the driver's footwell – outside, to give an extra 25mm of space.

SUSPENSION BRACKETS AND LOWER SEAT BELT ANCHORAGE

The next job is to locate and tack all the suspension and shock absorber brackets – four wishbone brackets front and rear and an upper shock absorber bracket at the front on either side. The rear upper shock absorber bracket, you will remember, is already attached to

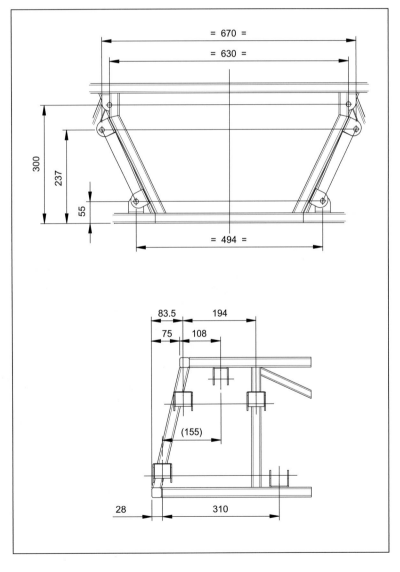

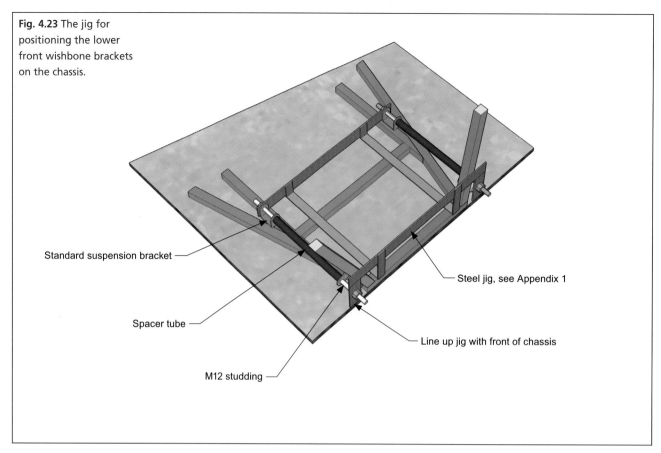

Fig. 4.23 The jig for positioning the lower front wishbone brackets on the chassis.

Standard suspension bracket

Spacer tube

M12 studding

Steel jig, see Appendix 1

Line up jig with front of chassis

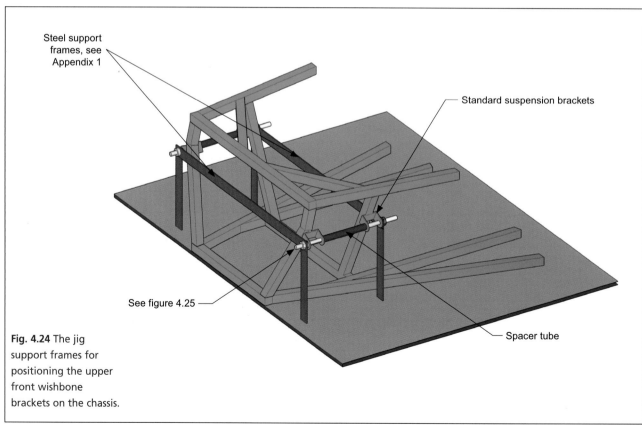

Steel support frames, see Appendix 1

Standard suspension brackets

See figure 4.25

Spacer tube

Fig. 4.24 The jig support frames for positioning the upper front wishbone brackets on the chassis.

plates CP3/CP4. For the front, the two simple jigs shown in Figs. 4.23 and 4.24 will ensure proper alignment of the wishbone brackets. The shock absorber bracket should be aligned as shown in Fig. 4.22.

At the rear, the bottom wishbone brackets attach to rails RS1 and RS2, and the rear upper wishbone brackets are tacked to the underside of rails RS7/RS8, positioned as shown in Figs. 4.26 and 4.27.

Seat belt bottom anchorage plates CP18 need to be attached to rails BR5, BR6, and both TT1 rails – see Fig. 4.28. The plates are positioned 140mm from the respective junctions with rail BR12. The CP18 plates on rails BR5 and BR6 should be tacked flush with the inside of the rails with the captive 7/16ths nut on the outside.

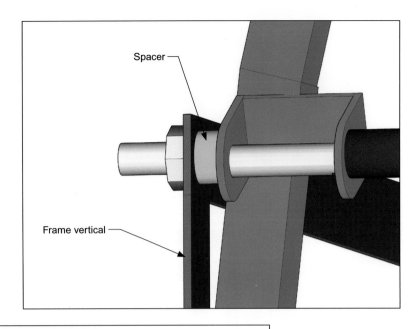

▲ Fig. 4.25 Detail for positioning front upper wishbone brackets.

◀ Fig. 4.26 Setting out dimensions for the rear wishbone and shock absorber brackets.

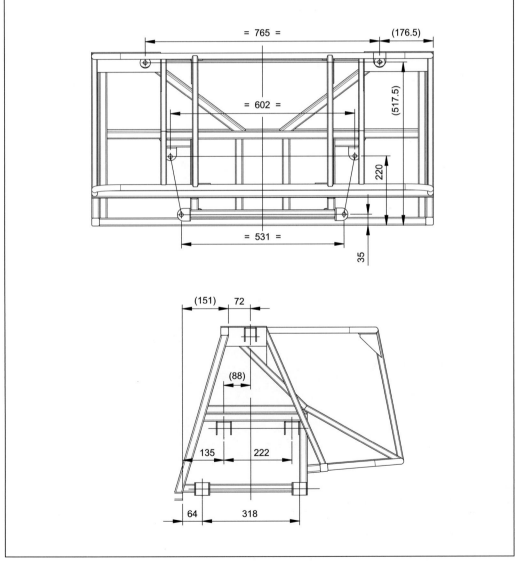

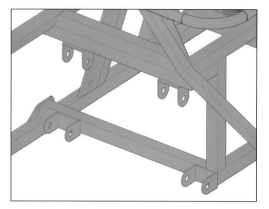

▶ **Fig. 4.27** Positions of rear wishbone brackets.

The CP18 plates on the TT1 rails should be positioned with the plate flush with the outside of the transmission tunnel (i.e. facing into the seating area) and with the captive nut on the inside of the transmission tunnel.

Tack the headlight supports (see Fig. 4.29) to TR1 and TR2. The centre of the support lines up with the centre of the front upper shock absorber bracket. The support can be made using round or square tube, but it's worth sourcing some oval, if you can, as it makes for a much neater job.

▶ **Fig. 4.28** lower seat harness bracket positions.

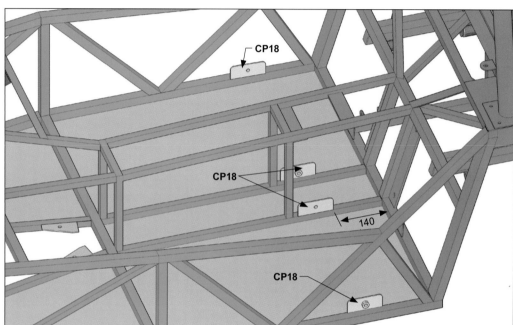

CP18

CP18

140

CP18

▼ **Fig. 4.29** The headlamp supports.

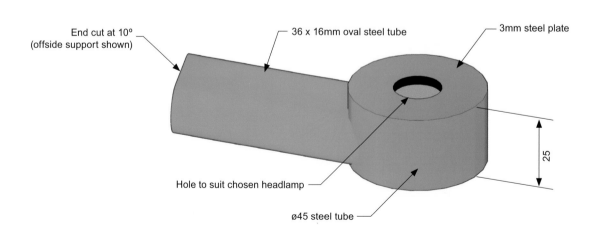

End cut at 10°
(offside support shown)

36 x 16mm oval steel tube

3mm steel plate

25

Hole to suit chosen headlamp

ø45 steel tube

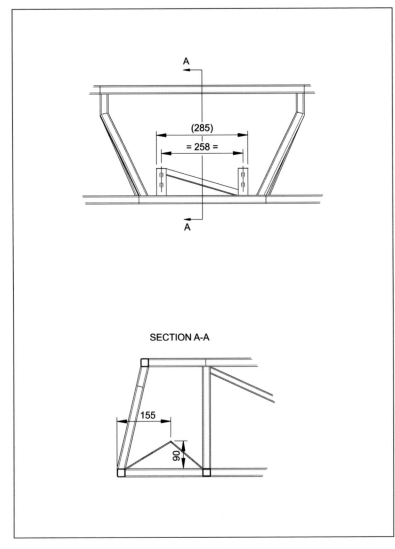

A

(285)

= 258 =

A

SECTION A-A

155

90

◀ **Fig. 4.30** Dimensions and arrangement of the steering rack supports.

▼ **Fig. 4.32** Flexible brake line support on upright U1.

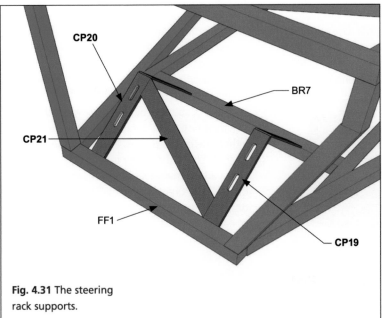

Fig. 4.31 The steering rack supports.

CP20

BR7

CP21

FF1

CP19

MOUNTS FOR STEERING RACK, RADIATOR AND NOSE CONE

The steering rack mounts consist of plates CP19, CP20 and CP21 – see Figs. 4.30 and 4.31. Tack the longer arms (containing the slots) of CP19 and CP20 to the back upper edge of FF1, and the shorter arms to the front upper edge of BR7. Plate CP21 forms the diagonal brace between plates CP19 and CP20.

Tack small plates CP22 to FF1 and FF4 to accommodate your chosen radiator, and tack plates or brackets in position to hold the top and bottom of your nose cone. If you don't have these parts to hand when making your chassis they can be attached later, either by welding or rivnuts.

Brackets (CP23) for the flexible brake pipes should be added at the front on uprights U1 and U2 under the top wishbone mounts, and at the rear on rail RS14 on the rear face, 240mm from either end.

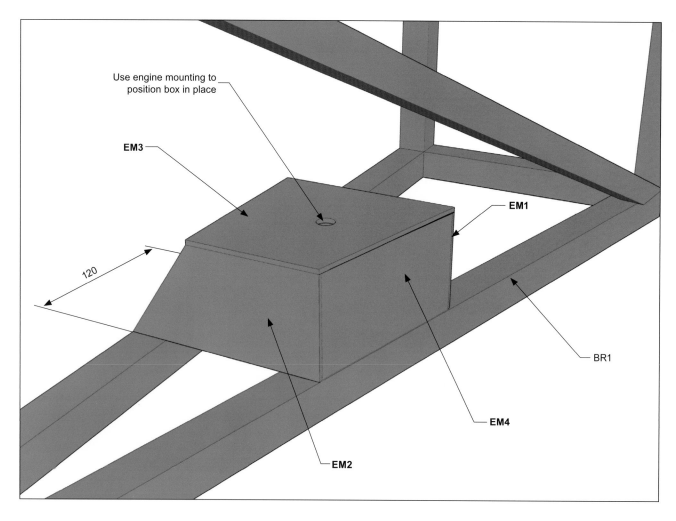

Use engine mounting to position box in place

EM3

120

EM1

BR1

EM4

EM2

▲ **Fig. 4.33** The nearside engine mounting for a Sierra-based car.

▶ **Fig. 4.34** A nearside engine mounting in situ.

ENGINE MOUNTS AND FLOOR

The engine mountings are a simple box made from 3mm steel plate with a hole to receive the Sierra cast engine mountings. Cut plates EM1 to EM4 and tack together. Use a locking nut to fasten the assembly to the outer engine mounting stud on the cast Sierra mounting, through the hole in plate EM3, ensuring that the assembly is in the correct orientation and noting that the offside mounting is similar, but handed. Tack weld the fabricated assembly to chassis rails BR1/BR8 and BR2/BR9.

The mounts detailed in Fig. 4.33 are for the Sierra-based car with the SOHC Pinto engine and standard engine mountings. Other engines will need different mounts to be fabricated (see Chapter 6).

The chassis must be now fully welded. To minimise distortion, try to weld alternately on either side of the chassis, and allow the welds to cool. Check that every tube is fully welded. There are so many welds that it's easy to miss one or two. Check systematically by working down the list of tubes and checking both ends of each. Your chassis' integrity depends on all the welding being done!

The floor of the car can be cut from the roof of the donor car or from sheet steel. The chassis should be placed on the roof or sheet and marked around. Cut the floor out and tack to the underside of the bottom rails.

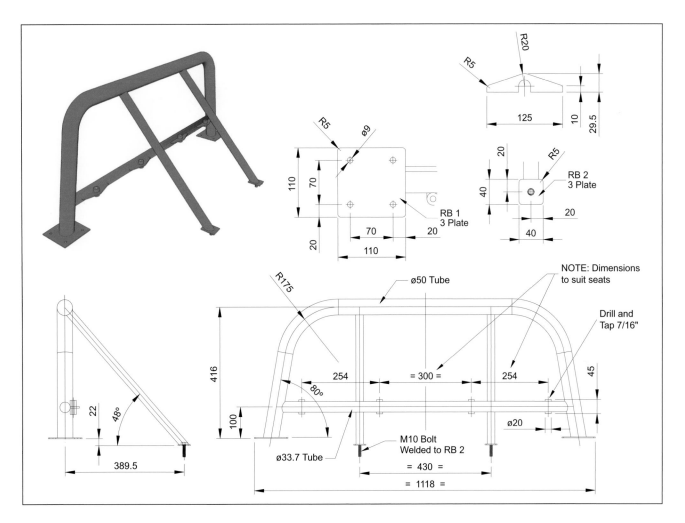

ROLL BAR

The roll bar carries the top seat harness mounts, and because of this it must be solidly constructed. The main hoop of the roll bar must be bent using a hydraulic bending machine, using thick-walled (preferably seamless) 50mm diameter tube – see Fig. 4.35. Try local engineering companies for material and facilities to do the bending. It's not acceptable to use, for example, exhaust tubing. Although it's easier to fabricate, it's simply not strong enough, either for the seat harness mounts or to offer you any protection should the worst happen and you roll the car. When you have the main tube fabricated, cut the plates RB1 and tack to either end of the hoop.

Temporarily fit the hoop to plates CP3/CP4 on the chassis. Make plates RB2 and using the bolt welded to the underside, attach to plates CP9. Cut the rear roll bar stays from 30mm diameter seamless steel tube approximately 575mm long. Profile the ends to the main hoop at the top and cut the bottom of the stays at an angle to fit plates RB2, and tack together. The seat harness

bar is made from 33.7mm seamless steel tube. Cut to length and profile the ends to fit the roll bar main hoop and tack in place.

The harness brackets are made from 3mm steel plate – see Fig. 4.36. Tack these in place as shown. The roll bar can now be fully welded. Complete roll bar assemblies are available from MK Engineering.

▲ Fig. 4.35 Dimensions of the roll bar and upper harness attachment points.

▼ Fig. 4.36 The brackets required for the seat harnesses on the roll bar.

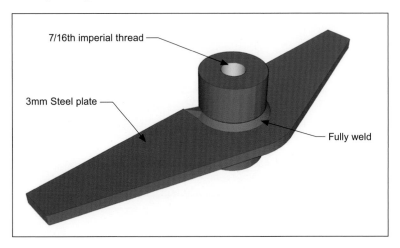

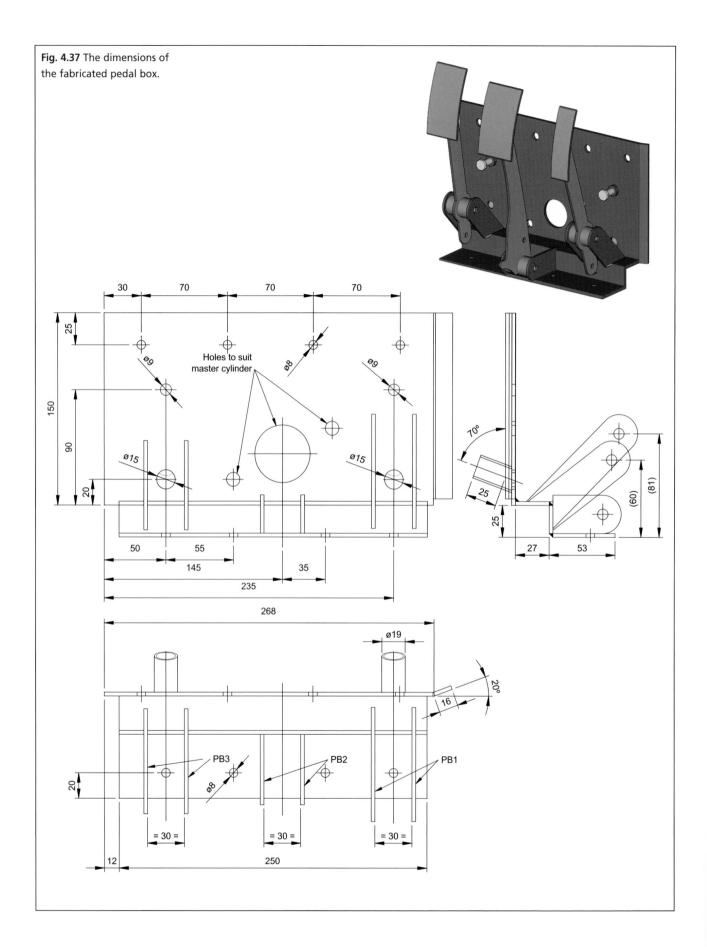

Fig. 4.37 The dimensions of the fabricated pedal box.

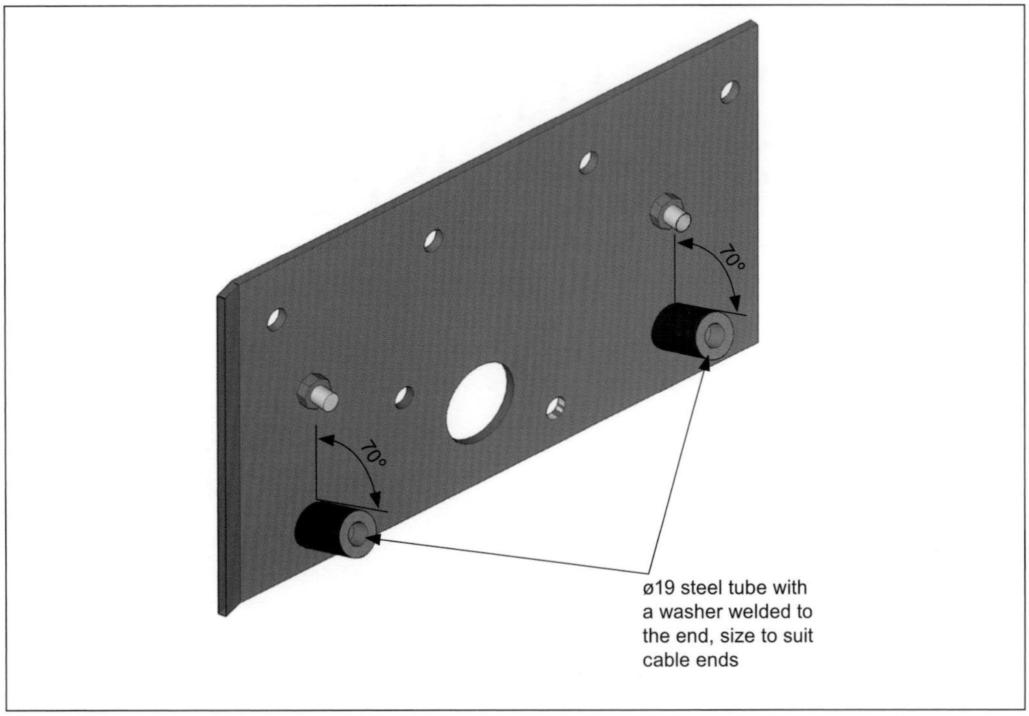

◀ **Fig. 4.38** View of the rear of the pedal box.

ø19 steel tube with a washer welded to the end, size to suit cable ends

PEDAL BOX

The pedal box is built as a separate unit, bolted into the driver's footwell. The box itself is made from pieces of 3mm steel plate welded together (see Fig. 4.37). Tack all the pieces together and then fully weld. Position plates PB1, PB2 and PB3, tack in position and fully weld when you've tried the pedals in position.

Two tubes of 19mm diameter steel tube should be welded to the back of the pedal box, angled to provide a smooth path and end support for the cables for accelerator and clutch – see Fig. 4.38.

Dimensioned drawings for the pedals can be found in Appendix 1. Weld the foot pads and the bush tubes to the pedal shafts after you've bent the pads to the radius of the pedal shaft. The brake pedal includes an adjustable stop at the front. An 8mm hole should be drilled in the floor directly beneath the stop. Fasten an 8mm bolt into the hole with a locking nut on either side of the floor, to facilitate adjustment. The clutch and accelerator pedal have similar stops in the upright part of the pedal box.

22mm diameter x 30mm long acetal bushes with an 8mm hole are used in the pedal pivots along with 8mm bolts and locking nuts. Forward stops, PB4, should be secured to the clutch and accelerator pedals, using the pedal pivot bolts and adjusted to prevent the pedals moving forward. Temporarily fit the pedal box in place

and mark the positions of the eight fixing holes (four in the floor and four in plate C16), remove the pedal box and drill the holes. Bolt the box in position using M8 bolts, washers and locking nuts. The pads of the pedals need to be covered in non-slip material to satisfy the SVA inspector, either rubber or an abrasive material. I used 80 grit emery paper.

▼ **Fig. 4.39** The pedal box installed.

The suspension units for the Roadster need to be fabricated with great care. Your safety depends on the integrity of these components. Set out the dimensions with attention to detail and, if you are not absolutely confident in your welding ability, take them to a professional welder to complete them. All these parts will be available from MK Engineering.

The wishbones are mounted using polyurethane bushes as shown in Fig. 5.2. The bushes have a stainless steel inner tube, which can be pressed into the centre when the bushes are in the bush tube using a vice or light press. These bushes are available from MK Engineering.

To ensure that the parts are correctly aligned, use jigs such as the ones illustrated for each of the wishbones and the rear upright parts.

All the wishbones are made from seamless tube.

▲ **Fig. 5.1** A general view of the front suspension.

▶ **Fig. 5.2** A suspension bush. Two required per bush tube, with one inner stainless steel tube.

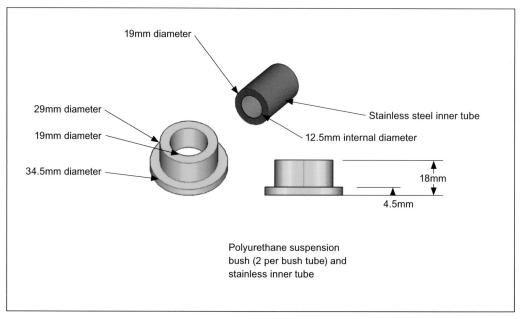

19mm diameter

29mm diameter

19mm diameter

34.5mm diameter

Stainless steel inner tube

12.5mm internal diameter

18mm

4.5mm

Polyurethane suspension bush (2 per bush tube) and stainless inner tube

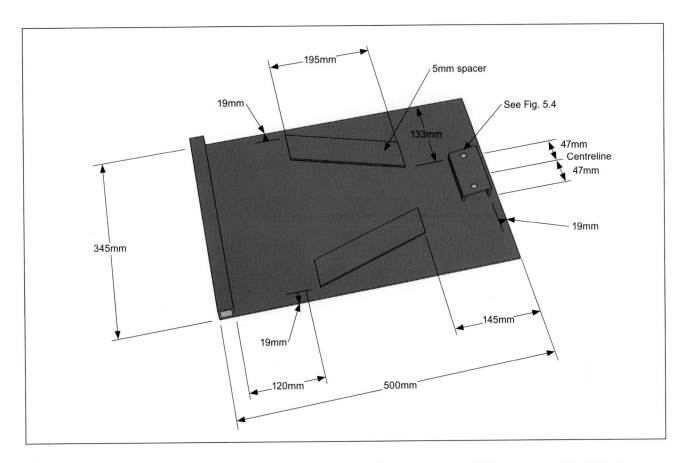

FRONT LOWER WISHBONE

The jig shown in Fig. 5.3 is constructed from steel plate. Provided that the dimensions are used faithfully, the jigs could be made from wood if you are more confident with it. The lower wishbones are not handed, you should make two wishbones using this jig.

The base plate is 3mm steel sheet 345 x 500mm with a length of 25 x 25mm box section, 345mm long, tack welded to one of the 345 long edges. The 5mm spacers are used to support the main tubes and should be tack welded in the position shown. The plate support bracket (Fig. 5.4) can be made by fabricating

▲ **Fig. 5.3** The jig required to construct the front lower wishbones.

◄ **Fig. 5.4** The frame used to support the bottom plate of the front lower wishbone.

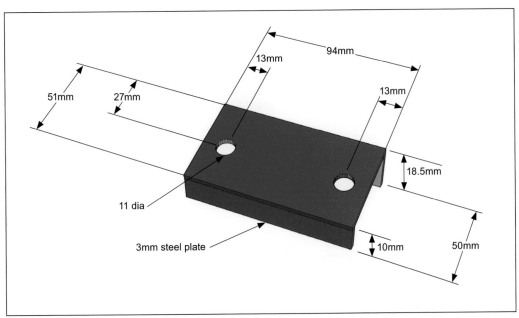

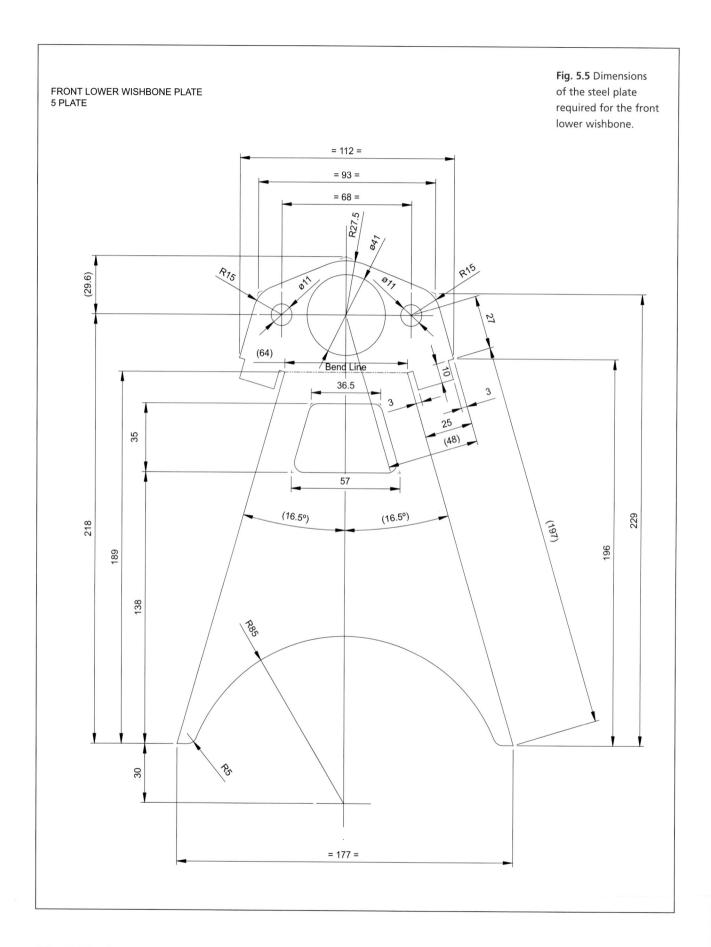

FRONT LOWER WISHBONE PLATE
5 PLATE

Fig. 5.5 Dimensions of the steel plate required for the front lower wishbone.

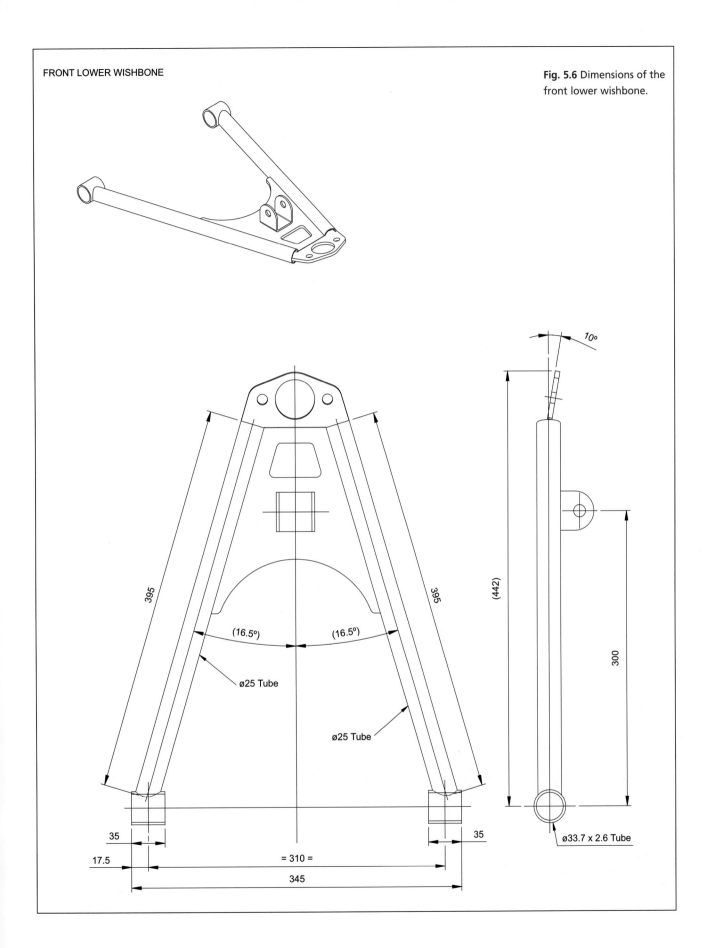

Fig. 5.6 Dimensions of the front lower wishbone.

395

395

(442)

(16.5°)   (16.5°)

ø25 Tube

ø25 Tube

300

10°

35   35

17.5

= 310 =

345

ø33.7 x 2.6 Tube

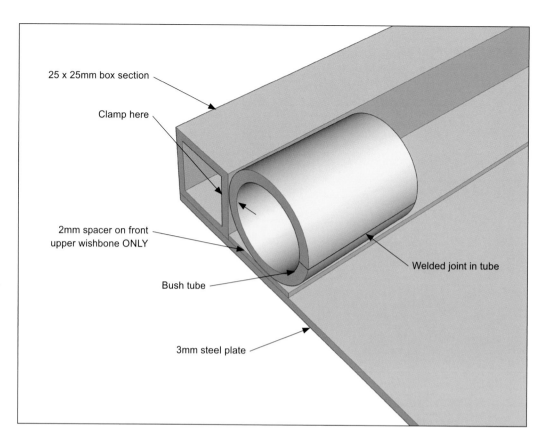

▶ **Fig. 5.7** Method of clamping the bush tubes into the jig.

25 x 25mm box section

Clamp here

2mm spacer on front upper wishbone ONLY

Bush tube

Welded joint in tube

3mm steel plate

three pieces of steel together or by bending a single piece. It is important that the height, angle and the hole spacing are checked and confirmed before fabrication of the wishbone begins.

The wishbone plate should be cut as shown in Fig. 5.5. It's perhaps easier to make a pattern and get these parts laser cut, or buy them from MK Engineering.

▼ **Fig. 5.8** The front lower wishbone in its jig.

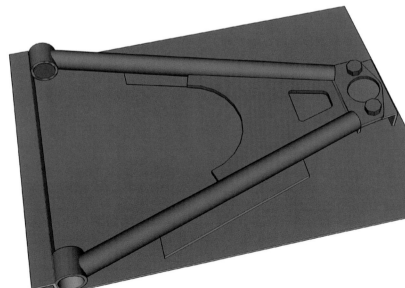

If you make the plates yourself, be sure to make the bend in the plate 10°. The Maxi ball joint can be used to check the dimensions for the hole spacings are correct.

When complete, the wishbone plate should be fixed using nuts and locking bolts to the plate support bracket on the jig.

Two standard bush tubes are fixed to the box section, as shown in Fig. 5.7, using mole grips or clamps.

The tubes should be positioned so that the joint in the bush tube faces away from the box section. This ensures that the joint is within the welded area when the wishbone is complete.

The main wishbone tubes are made from 25mm seamless tube, and should be carefully profiled to fit in the jig as shown. It's important that the tubes are a very good fit to the bush tubes and the plate.

Tack the bush tubes, main tubes and plate together, and ensure that all dimensions remain correct. When you're happy that all is well, fully weld the components together, welding alternately on either side and top and bottom. In this way you should minimise any distortion.

Weld a shock absorber bracket in the position shown in Fig. 5.6.

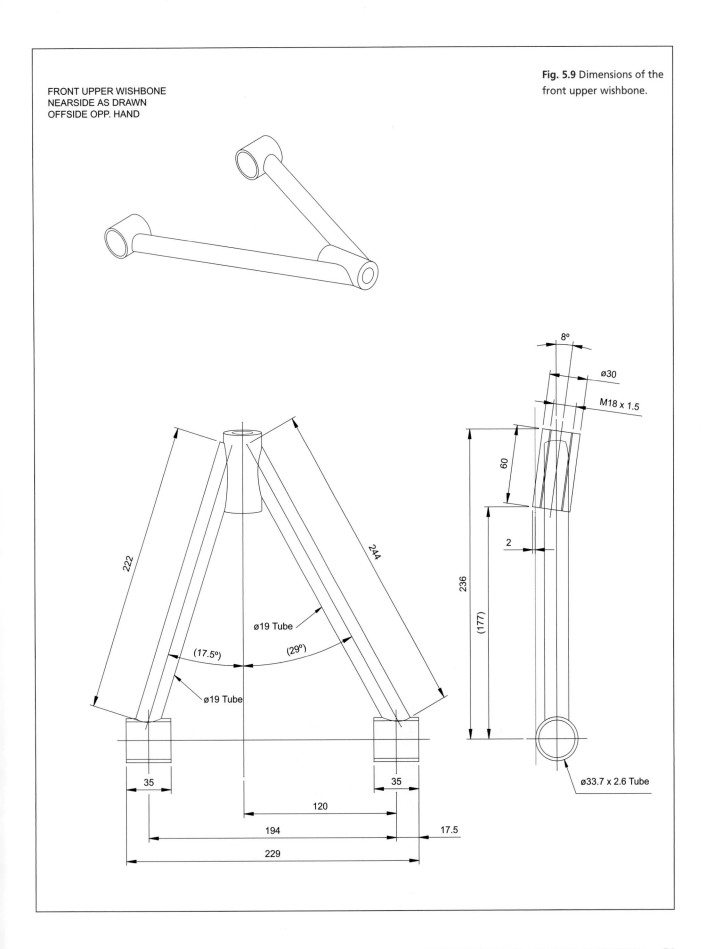

FRONT UPPER WISHBONE
NEARSIDE AS DRAWN
OFFSIDE OPP. HAND

Fig. 5.9 Dimensions of the front upper wishbone.

ø19 Tube

ø19 Tube

(17.5°)

(29°)

222

244

35

35

120

194

17.5

229

8°

ø30

M18 x 1.5

60

2

236

(177)

ø33.7 x 2.6 Tube

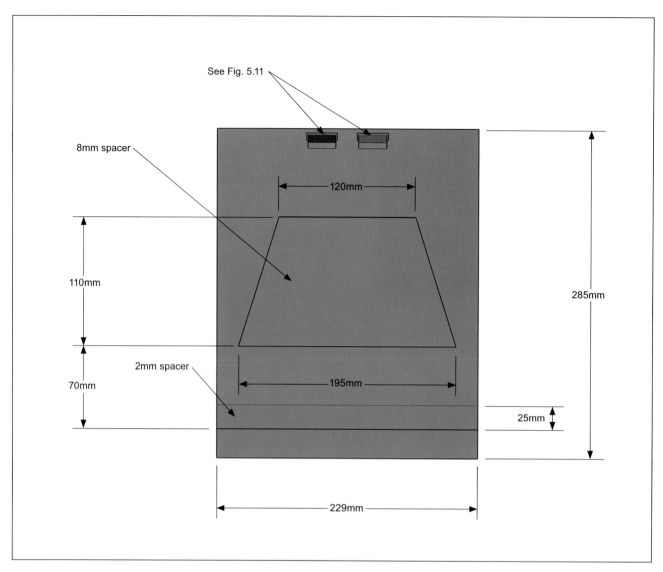

See Fig. 5.11

8mm spacer

120mm

110mm

285mm

2mm spacer

70mm

195mm

25mm

229mm

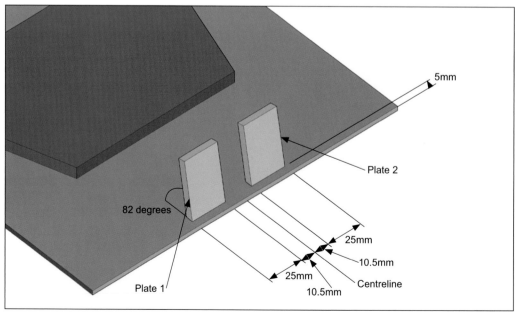

▲ **Fig. 5.10** The jig for the front upper wishbone (plan).

▶ **Fig. 5.11** Detail of the bush support plates for the front upper wishbone jig.

5mm

Plate 2

82 degrees

25mm

10.5mm

25mm

Centreline

Plate 1

10.5mm

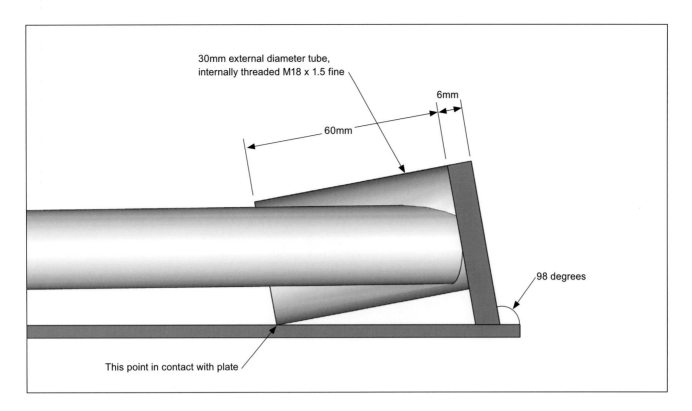

30mm external diameter tube,
internally threaded M18 x 1.5 fine

6mm

60mm

98 degrees

This point in contact with plate

FRONT UPPER WISHBONE

The front upper wishbones are different either side of the car, but they can still be made using a single jig – see Figs. 5.10 and 5.11.

The jig is made from 3mm steel sheet 285 x 229mm with a 229mm long piece of 25 x 25mm box section tacked to one of the 229mm long sides. The 8mm and 2mm spacers should be tacked on and the 25 x 6mm plates are positioned as shown in Fig. 5.11.

The construction of the upper wishbone is similar to that of the lower wishbone, with the main tubes from 19mm seamless tube, but note that the threaded insert is positioned as shown in Fig. 5.12. You will need to make one wishbone using plate 1 and one using plate 2, as shown in Fig. 5.13. Tack and weld as above. When fitted, the longer arm of the upper wishbone is placed to the front of the car.

▲ **Fig. 5.12** Detail showing how the threaded inserts are positioned on the front upper wishbone jig.

Fig. 5.13 Make both wishbones in this jig, as shown.

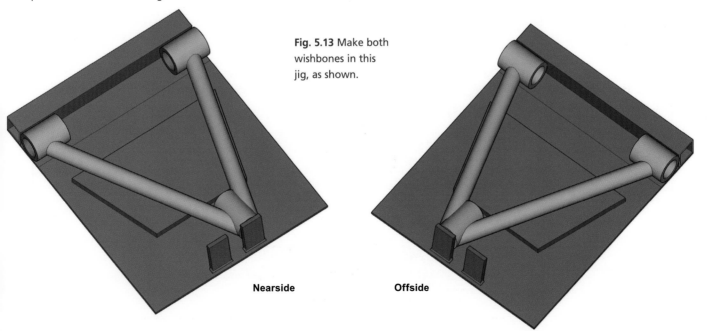

Nearside

Offside

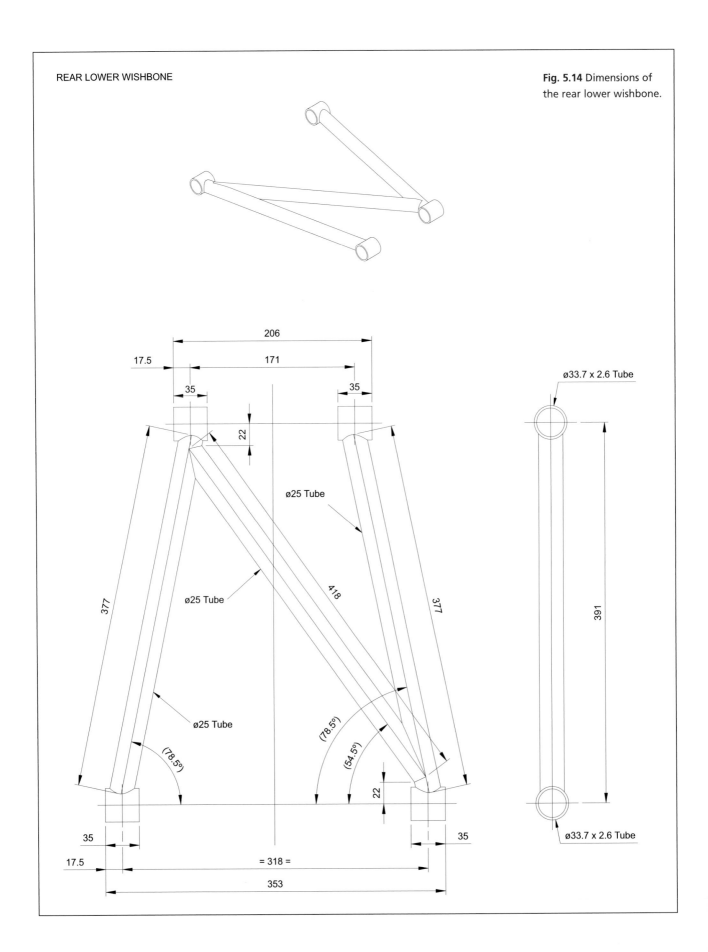

Fig. 5.14 Dimensions of the rear lower wishbone.

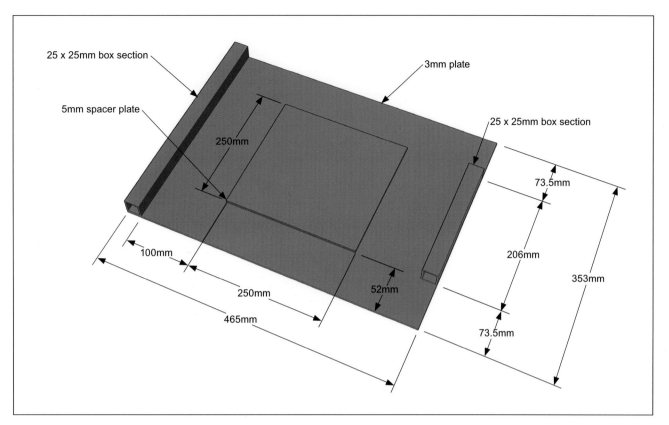

25 x 25mm box section

5mm spacer plate

3mm plate

25 x 25mm box section

250mm

100mm

250mm

465mm

52mm

73.5mm

206mm

73.5mm

353mm

REAR LOWER WISHBONE

The rear lower wishbones are handed but can be made in a single jig because one is a mirror image of the other, make two as shown and then invert one for fitting, see later in this chapter for orientation.

The jig is, again, made from 3mm steel plate 475 x 353mm with 25 x 25mm box section positioned on either side and the spacer plate in place as shown in Fig. 5.15.

Four bush tubes are clamped to the box sections in the usual way and the main tubes from 25mm seamless tube are profiled to the sides of these tubes.

The cross brace is profiled to the main tubes as shown, and the wishbone fully welded.

▲ **Fig. 5.15** The jig required for constructing the rear lower wishbones.

▼ **Fig. 5.16** The rear lower wishbone in its jig.

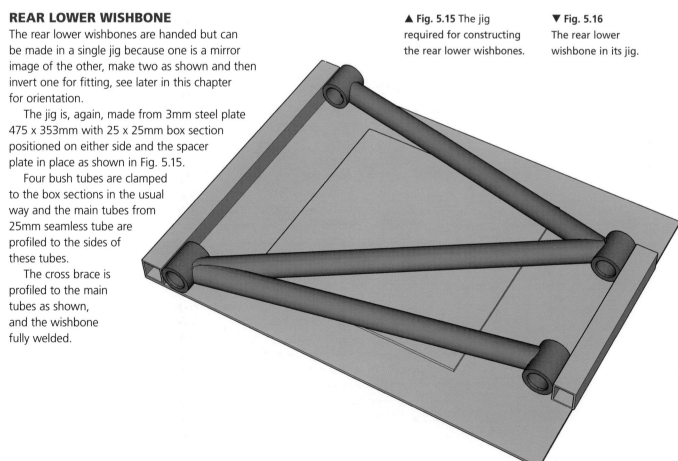

Fig. 5.17 Dimensions of
the rear upper wishbone.

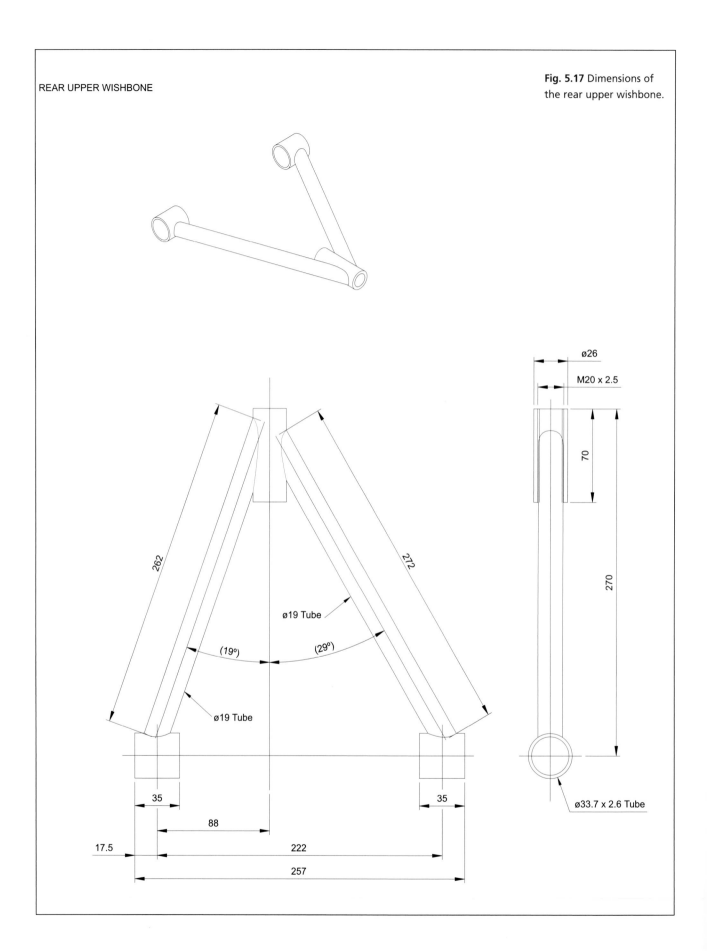

ø26

M20 x 2.5

70

270

262

272

ø19 Tube

(19°)   (29°)

ø19 Tube

ø33.7 x 2.6 Tube

35   35

88

17.5

222

257

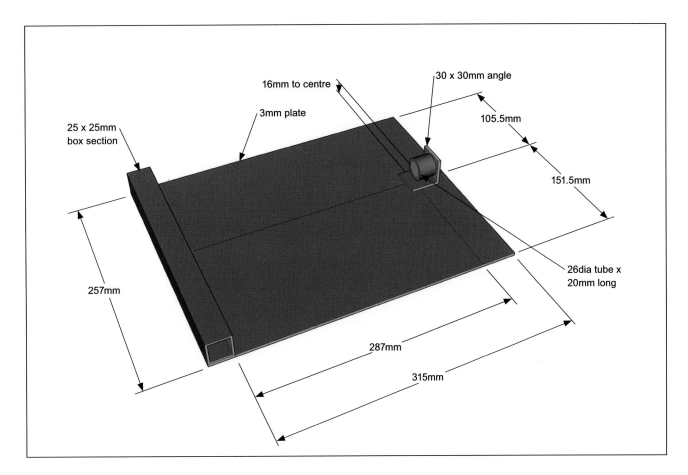

25 x 25mm box section

16mm to centre

3mm plate

30 x 30mm angle

105.5mm

151.5mm

26dia tube x 20mm long

257mm

287mm

315mm

REAR UPPER WISHBONE

Again the rear upper wishbone is handed, but you can make both wishbones in the same jig and invert one.

The jig of 3mm steel plate measures 257 x 325mm, with a section of 25 x 25mm box section 257mm long, tack welded to one edge. A steel 30 x 30 mm angle (or bent plate) should be positioned as shown in Fig. 5.18. Tack weld to the front of the angle a piece of 26mm diameter tube or bar, 20mm long to match the threaded insert of the wishbone.

As with the other wishbones, clamp two bush tubes to the 25 x 25mm box section and position the threaded tube on to the 26mm diameter tube with a clamp.

▲ **Fig. 5.18** The jig required for constructing the rear upper wishbones.

◀ **Fig. 5.19** The rear upper wishbone in its jig.

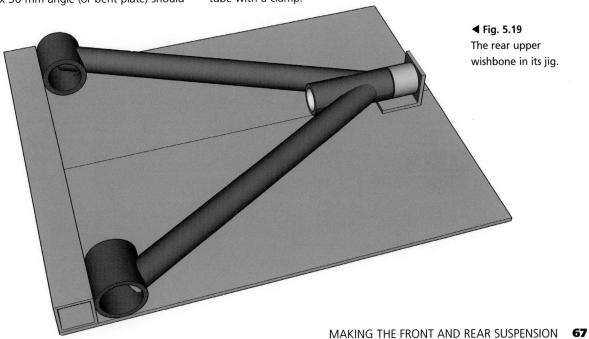

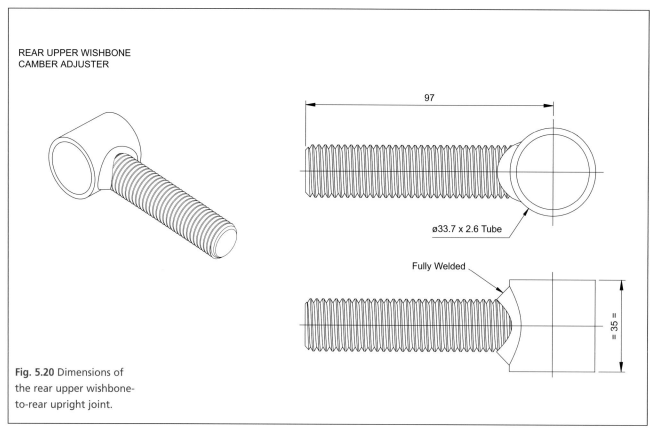

REAR UPPER WISHBONE
CAMBER ADJUSTER

97

ø33.7 x 2.6 Tube

Fully Welded

= 35 =

Fig. 5.20 Dimensions of
the rear upper wishbone-
to-rear upright joint.

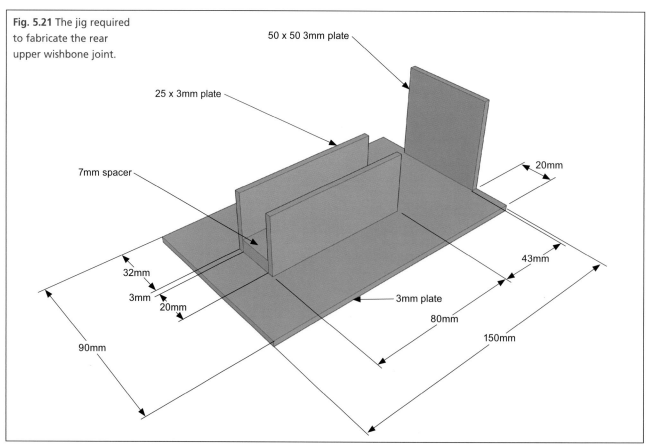

Fig. 5.21 The jig required
to fabricate the rear
upper wishbone joint.

50 x 50 3mm plate

25 x 3mm plate

7mm spacer

20mm

32mm

3mm

20mm

43mm

3mm plate

80mm

90mm

150mm

Profile the main tubes, of 19mm seamless tube, to the threaded insert and the bush tubes; tack, check and fully weld.

The top rear wishbone is connected to the rear upright using a fabricated joint as shown in Fig. 5.20. For accuracy, this should be fabricated using a jig similar to that shown in Figs. 5.21 and 5.22.

Tack the bush tube to the bolt or threaded rod, check for square and fully weld.

REAR UPRIGHTS

The rear uprights carry the Sierra rear hubs and link the top and bottom wishbones and provide a location for the lower end of the rear shock absorber.

The jig is shown in Fig. 5.25. The 12mm internal diameter tube RU6 is positioned as shown. The pipe we used had an outside diameter of 19mm, which meant we used a 9mm spacer on the lower tube – the important dimension is to the centre of the tube. Adjust the thickness of the spacer to ensure that the centre of the tube is 18mm above the baseplate. To position the upper tube, make a template as shown in Fig. 5.26 from paper or card and transfer to two pieces of thin ply.

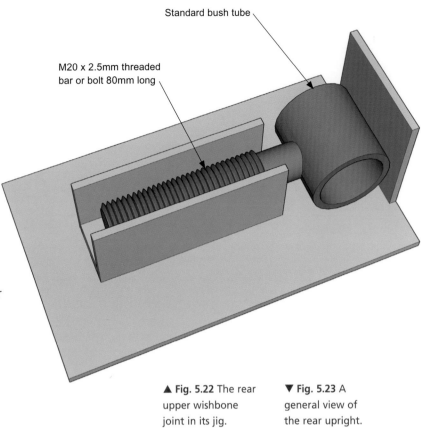

Standard bush tube

M20 x 2.5mm threaded bar or bolt 80mm long

▲ **Fig. 5.22** The rear upper wishbone joint in its jig.

▼ **Fig. 5.23** A general view of the rear upright.

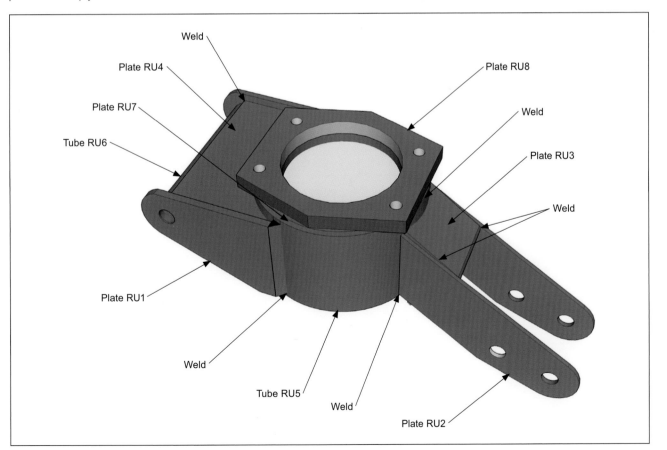

Weld

Plate RU4

Plate RU8

Plate RU7

Weld

Tube RU6

Plate RU3

Weld

Plate RU1

Weld

Weld

Tube RU5

Weld

Plate RU2

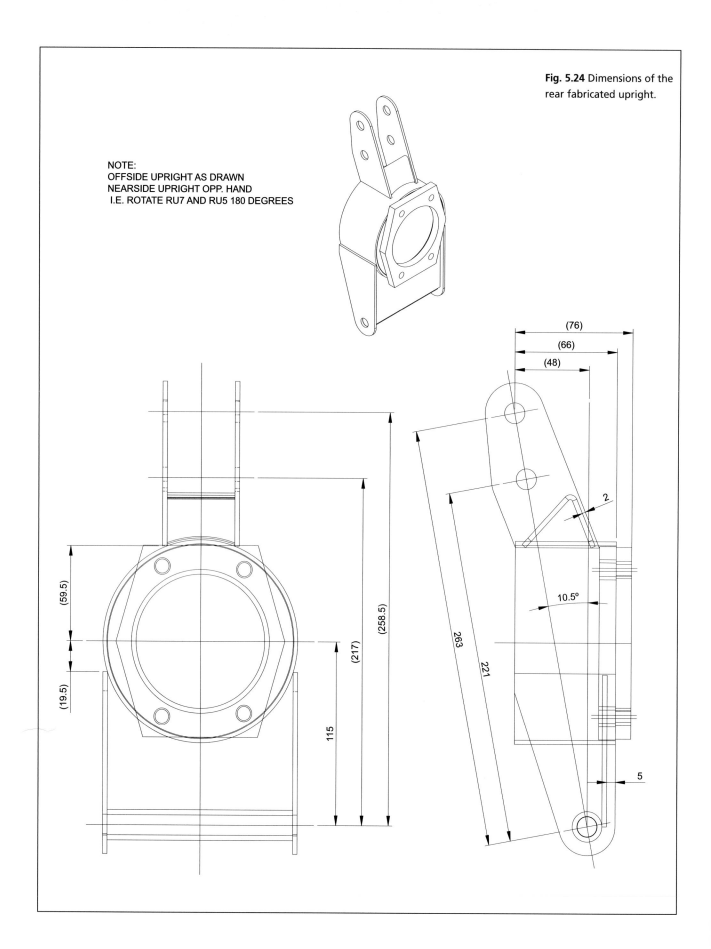

Fig. 5.24 Dimensions of the rear fabricated upright.

NOTE:
OFFSIDE UPRIGHT AS DRAWN
NEARSIDE UPRIGHT OPP. HAND
I.E. ROTATE RU7 AND RU5 180 DEGREES

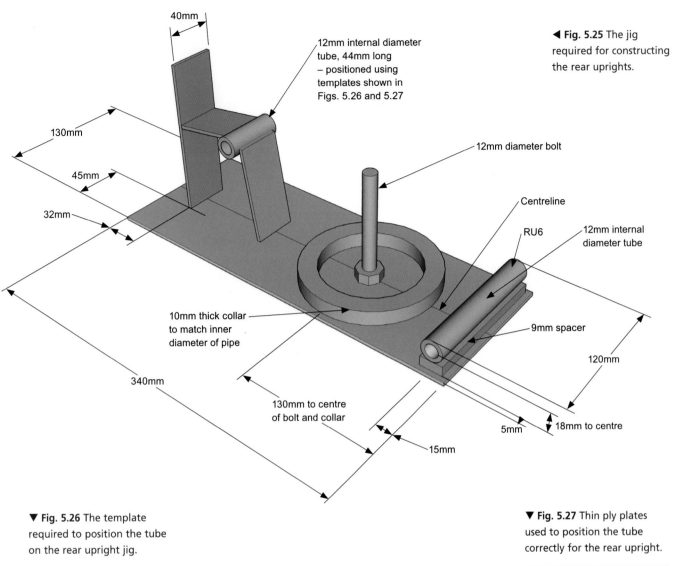

40mm

12mm internal diameter tube, 44mm long – positioned using templates shown in Figs. 5.26 and 5.27

◀ **Fig. 5.25** The jig required for constructing the rear uprights.

130mm

12mm diameter bolt

45mm

Centreline

RU6

32mm

12mm internal diameter tube

10mm thick collar to match inner diameter of pipe

9mm spacer

340mm

130mm to centre of bolt and collar

120mm

5mm

18mm to centre

15mm

▼ **Fig. 5.26** The template required to position the tube on the rear upright jig.

▼ **Fig. 5.27** Thin ply plates used to position the tube correctly for the rear upright.

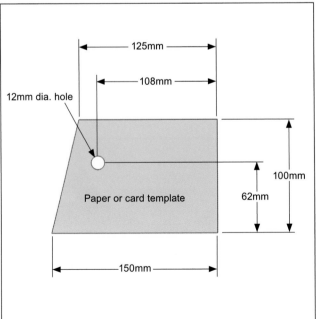

125mm

108mm

12mm dia. hole

100mm

62mm

Paper or card template

150mm

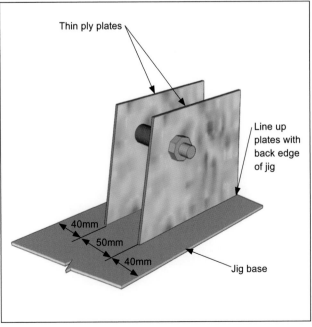

Thin ply plates

Line up plates with back edge of jig

40mm

50mm

40mm

Jig base

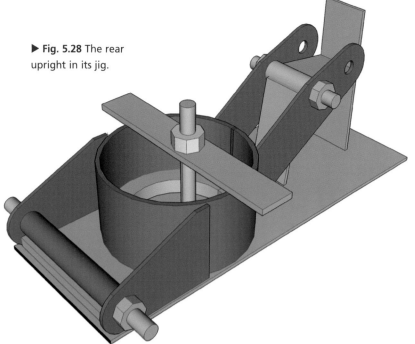

▶ **Fig. 5.28** The rear upright in its jig.

▼ **Fig. 5.29** Orientation of the rear upright plates.

Position on the rear upright jig with the tube fastened between them as shown in Fig. 5.27. Use pieces of 40 x 3mm steel strip to support the tube in place and tack weld.

Next, cut plates RU1 (x2 per upright), RU2 (x2 per upright), RU3 and RU4 (1 per upright) as shown in Appendix 1. The main body of the upright is made from a 65mm long section of 5-inch external diameter steel pipe, RU5.

Position the pipe over the collar and fix the RU1, RU2, RU3 and RU4 plates as shown, tack and fully weld when checked.

The circular plate RU7 must be drilled so that the holes line up with the bolts emerging through plate RU8. Plate RU8 is orientated differently for disc and drum-braked rear ends and is drilled and tapped to make the bolts that hold the Sierra hub to the upright – see Fig 5.29. The hole spacings and sizes are the same for both types.

Fully weld the plate flush with the edge of the steel pipe, both inside and out.

PUTTING THE SUSPENSION TOGETHER

The wishbones are fitted using polyurethane bushes. These bushes have a stainless steel inner tube which can be pressed into the centre, when the bushes are in the bush tube, using a vice or light press. Starting at the front put all the bushes into the bush tubes in each wishbone.

The Maxi ball joint should be secured to the bottom front wishbone using the nuts and bolts that come with the joint (be sure to use locking nuts), then the wishbone can be attached to the chassis using a 12mm grade 8.8 bolt and nut through each bracket and bush tube.

The Transit drag-link end should be screwed into the threaded insert in the front top wishbone,

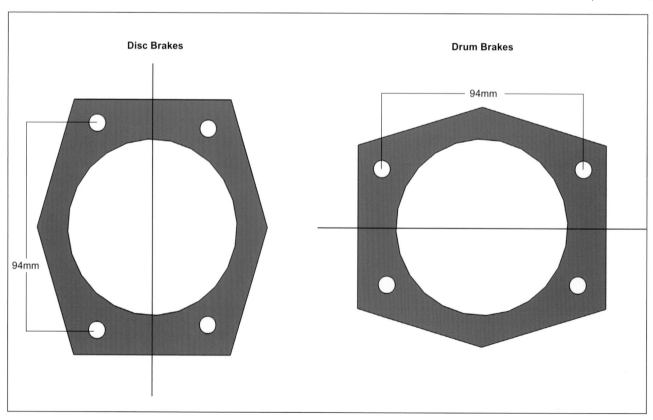

Disc Brakes

Drum Brakes

94mm

94mm

◄ **Fig. 5.30** The front upright mushroom.

to counter the anti-dive geometry of the Sierra suspension set-up. Camber can be adjusted by screwing the drag link in and out of the threaded insert in the wishbone.

The hole at the bottom of the Sierra upright must be machined (reamed) to accept the taper on the Maxi ball joint. This job is best entrusted to an engineering workshop, or modified uprights can be obtained from MK Engineering.

The Sierra upright/mushroom insert assembly can now be fixed between the Maxi ball joint and the Transit drag-link end. Don't finally tighten the ball joints or mushroom/upright joint, as you'll need to unfasten them to attach the front mudguard stays (see Chapter 8). Fit the shock absorber between the bracket on the lower wishbone and the corresponding bracket on the chassis, beneath the headlamp bracket.

The rear wishbones need the bushes and inner tubes inserted into the bush tubes, four for the lower wishbone, two for the upper wishbone and one in each upper wishbone-to-rear upright joint. The lower wishbones need to be installed with the cross brace angled from outside rear to inside front on either side (two wishbones, you will remember, were made in the same jig – one is inverted for fitting). Again the wishbones are attached to the brackets with grade 8.8 M12

with its lock nut, and the wishbone can be attached. The longer arm of the wishbone is placed to the front – this sets the camber.

The 'mushroom' insert, as shown in Fig. 5.30, is used to replace the Sierra's suspension strut and to locate the taper of the drag link end. It's not worth trying to make these inserts, as they need to be precise and they're available quite cheaply at MK Engineering.

The insert must be tight in the suspension upright, with the hole at the front. On no account should the insert be used to alter the camber of the front suspension. The hole is offset

▼ **Fig. 5.31** Beginning to assemble the front suspension.

▼ **Fig. 5.33** Modifications
to the steering column
lower shaft.

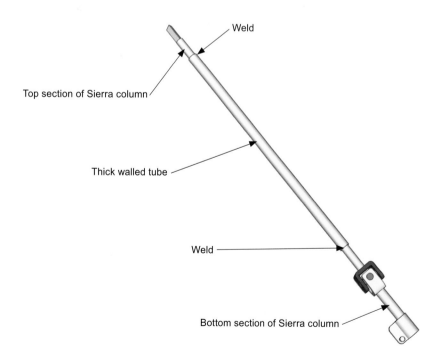

Weld

Top section of Sierra column

Thick walled tube

Weld

Bottom section of Sierra column

bolts and locking nuts, and the upper wishbone
joint is screwed into the upper wishbone with its
locknut in place. The wishbone joint is fixed to the
lower hole of the two in plates RU2 on the top
of the rear upright assembly, with an M12 bolt
and locking nut. The rear upright is secured to the
bottom wishbone using either a long 12mm grade
8.8 bolt or threaded bar to the same specification.

The shock absorber fits between the top holes
in the RU2 plates in the rear upright assembly
and the shock absorber bracket attached to the
underside of plates CP3/CP4 on the chassis. Install
the bolt in the top mounting through the hole in
plate CP6.

STEERING

The steering shaft of the Sierra is not long
enough to reach the steering rack of the Roadster,
so it must be extended.

The shaft should be cut in half in the centre,
and a piece of thick-walled tube obtained with an
inside diameter the same as the outside diameter
of the Sierra steering shaft. Fit the bottom end of
the cut steering shaft to the steering rack, and the
top end to the steering column and measure the
distance between the two. Add 120mm to the
length you measure and cut the thick-walled tube

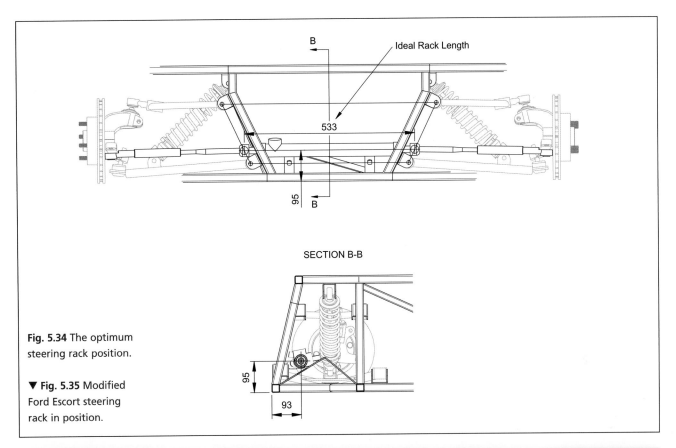

B

Ideal Rack Length

533

95

B

SECTION B-B

Fig. 5.34 The optimum steering rack position.

95

93

▼ **Fig. 5.35** Modified Ford Escort steering rack in position.

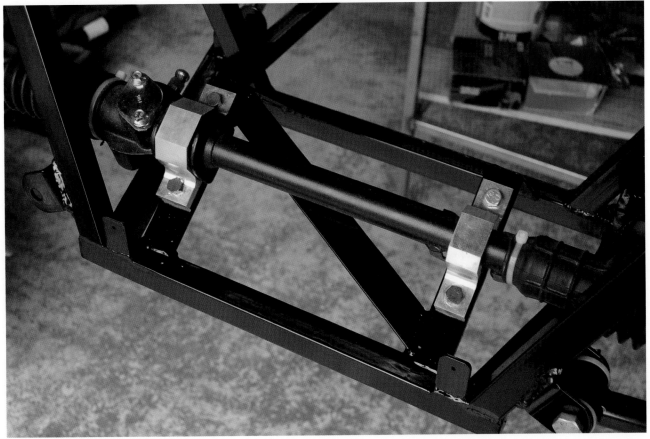

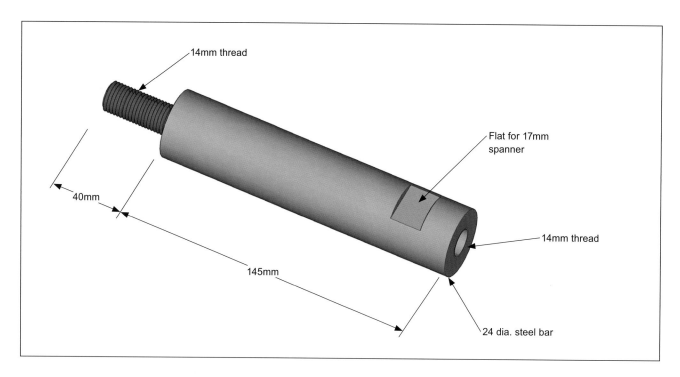

14mm thread

Flat for 17mm spanner

40mm

14mm thread

145mm

24 dia. steel bar

▲ **Fig. 5.36** The steering rack extensions.

to this length. The steering shaft ends should be pushed into the tube at either end by 60mm before being fully welded. There is an obvious safety issue here, and if you don't feel confident that your welding is sufficiently strong, then entrust the job to a professional. Fit the steering shaft, centre the steering rack and then put on the steering wheel at the straight-ahead position.

In the chassis section we made mountings for the steering rack, and the rack is attached using bolts and locking nuts with the original Escort clamps or after-market items. You will note that the holes are slotted, this is to give fine adjustment to the steering rack when setting the car up.

The Escort MkII steering rack needs to be extended using an extension as shown in Fig. 5.36. These extensions are also available from MK Engineering. NEVER try to extend track rods by welding. Not only is it dangerous, it's also an automatic SVA and MoT fail. Screw the extensions tightly to the track-rod ends and then screw the locknut onto the rack, followed by the extension/track-rod-end assembly. When the toe angle has been adjusted, lock the extensions with the locknut. Fit the track-rod-end tapers to the steering arms on the Sierra upright.

Although the Ford Escort steering rack is very close to the ideal size, for *absolute* precision, modifications to the rack are required. Fig. 5.34 shows the dimensions providing the optimum position for the steering rack. To achieve this,

the steering rack body must be shortened. This really isn't a DIY proposition, but any competent engineering company should be able to do the job for you. The 533mm dimension is between the balljoint centres of the track-rods.

ALTERNATIVES

FRONT SUSPENSION UPRIGHTS

Production cars have a bewildering array of front hub designs – but, of course, not all will be suitable for our Roadster. The Ford Cortina had a very useful upright, with a top joint that would take the Transit drag-link end as used with our Sierra-based car and the Maxi or standard Cortina bottom ball joint. The problem is that these are like hen's teeth these days.

When looking for alternative uprights you should endeavour to match the geometry set out in this book. Measure and set the joint positions. Uprights like the Cortina, with a hole in the top, can be milled to match the taper of the Transit drag-link end. If the top of the upright is of a similar design to the Sierra, an insert like the Sierra one detailed can be used. This replaces the MacPherson strut and provides a top location, connecting the wishbone and upright. If sufficient adjustment is possible you may be able to use the top wishbones as drawn. If not, you should lengthen or shorten them to match the upright and the geometry you have worked out. To optimise the geometry it may be necessary to relocate the joint further forward or back. To achieve this the jig should be altered to move the threaded bush to the required location, and the arms of the wishbone adjusted as necessary to support the bush properly. Extreme adjustments shouldn't be necessary and should be avoided.

Some uprights, such as those used on the E30 BMW 3-series, lack sufficient height to use a strut insert alone. In these cases a dummy strut can be manufactured to bring the height to match the height of the Sierra upright. A thick-walled tube of the same external diameter as the strut should be cut to length and internally threaded at the top. The top mushroom insert should be similar to the Sierra one, machined to take the Transit drag-link end, with a lower section threaded to match the top of the dummy strut. To assemble, the drag-link end should be attached to the insert with the appropriate locking nut and tightened to the correct torque. The tube should then be screwed up tightly to the insert. Finally, the dummy strut should be placed in the collar and the nut and bolt tightened to complete the assembly (see Fig. 5.37).

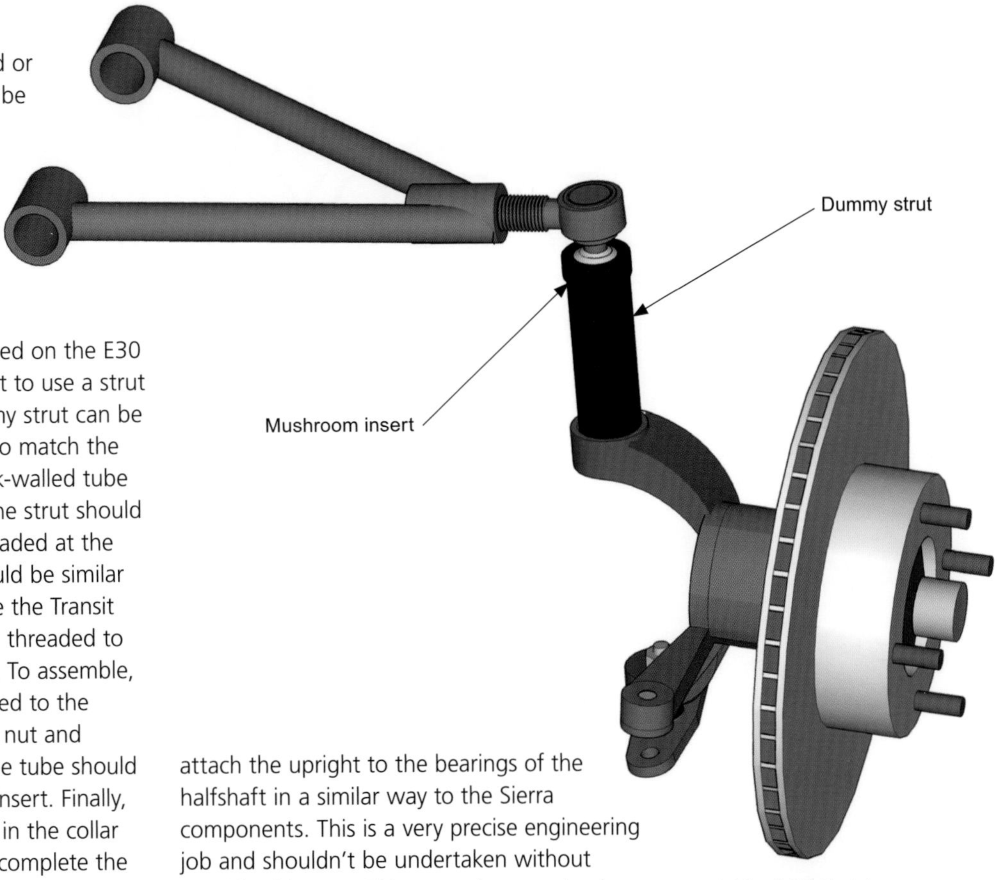

REAR SUSPENSION UPRIGHTS

Many RWD cars with independent suspension can be modified for use with this type of car.

Some uprights can be used as they come from the donor car by adapting the wishbones. A good example of this is the Mazda MX-5. The bottom fixing of the upright uses the same method as we've used, ie, a long bolt through two fixings on the bottom wishbone. The spacing of the bush tubes can be altered to suit.

The top fixing requires the fabrication of a different joint, as in Fig. 5.38. Basically, this is the same joint as we've used on the Sierra-based car, but using a suspension bracket instead of the bush tube. Maintain the geometry by altering the lengths of the wishbones as described for the front uprights.

Other types of upright are similar to the Sierra in that they have a bolt-on hub assembly. The fabricated upright can be altered to take account of the bolt centres and track differences.

If the hub is part of the trailing arm system of the donor car, then it will be difficult to use the hub. If you have access to a lathe, a hub-carrier can be turned up and attached to a plate to

Dummy strut

Mushroom insert

attach the upright to the bearings of the halfshaft in a similar way to the Sierra components. This is a very precise engineering job and shouldn't be undertaken without considerable care. This type of conversion has been done using the rear axle of the Vauxhall Carlton/Senator range, for example.

If you're contemplating using a different donor car, it's advisable to mock up the system and to carefully measure the donor parts to ensure that the wishbones and uprights can be fabricated and fitted in a similar way to the Sierra-based car.

▲ Fig. 5.37 Sketch of a dummy strut arrangement, used when your chosen upright isn't tall enough.

◀ Fig. 5.38 An upper rear wishbone joint, for use where a single bolt fixing is required for an alternative rear upright.

6 FITTING THE ENGINE, GEARBOX & BACK AXLE

Fitting the engine and gearbox is a major step, and one not to be taken too early in the build. The temptation is to stick the running gear in as soon as possible, to make the car look more complete. Avoid this if you can. Once the engine, gearbox and back axle are in position you've got the weight of a car to move about – a car unable to move under it's own power. It'll be heavy.

SUMP MODIFICATIONS

Because the Pinto engine is quite tall, it's a good idea to reduce the depth of the sump to provide additional ground clearance. Mark the sump at the point where it is level with the bottom of the gearbox bell housing (this is approximately 150mm from the top of the flange) and scribe a line around the sump at this level. Cut the bottom of the sump off along this line.

▶ **Fig. 6.1** An early trial fit of the engine and gearbox.

◀ **Fig. 6.2** The cut-down sump. Note the small cuts to allow oil to enter the extension.

◀ **Fig. 6.3** The sump and the 1mm steel plates required for the extension.

◀ **Fig. 6.4** Drawing showing sump modification.

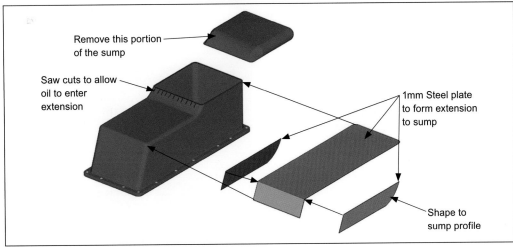

Remove this portion of the sump

Saw cuts to allow oil to enter extension

1mm Steel plate to form extension to sump

Shape to sump profile

You'll need three plates as shown in Figs. 6.3 and 6.4. Make a card template and cut the steel to the profile of the sump. These plates are used to restore some of the oil capacity lost by removing the bottom of the sump.

Clean up the areas to be welded and weld the plates onto the sump as in Fig. 6.4. Drill a 10mm hole in the bottom corner of the sump and weld a 10mm nut over the hole so that you can use a 10mm bolt as a sump plug. A copper washer will ensure a good seal.

Clean the sump with a wire brush, making sure that no debris remains in the sump. You can check for leaks by putting a small amount of thinners in the sump and placing it on some dry paper for a while. When you're sure it's not leaking, rub down and paint.

The oil pick-up pipe will need to be shortened by around 30mm to match the new sump depth – see Fig. 6.7.

Cut the pipe, re-weld and check the fit by re-attaching the pipe to the engine and trying the shortened sump in place. You should have approximately 5mm clearance. This can be checked by re-attaching the oil pick-up pipe and placing a ball of modelling clay on the bottom of the sump where the oil strainer will be. Temporarily

◀ **Fig. 6.5** The welded sump complete with extension.

◀ **Fig. 6.6** The completed sump with new sump plug.

◀ **Fig. 6.7** The cut-down and re-welded oil pick-up pipe.

fit the sump and the gasket and then remove. The modelling clay will show the clearance. It's important that the strainer is not right on the bottom of the sump, as oil starvation will result. If it's too high, the oil pipe may not be in the oil when cornering, again starving the engine of oil. Make sure you get all traces of modelling clay out of the strainer and the sump.

ENGINE MOUNTS
For a Sierra-based car the engine mounts as described in Chapter 4 should be used, along with the Sierra cast engine mounts. It will be necessary to place the engine and gearbox in place to ensure that the gearbox mounts are correctly placed.

A suggestion for a fabricated engine mounting for alternative engines is shown in Figs. 6.10 and 6.11.

▶ **Fig. 6.8** The Sierra gearbox mount separated from the crossmember.

▶ **Fig. 6.9** The offside gearbox mount.

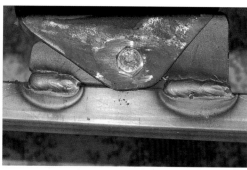

GEARBOX MOUNTS
The gearbox mount from the Sierra should be removed from the large crossmember by grinding off the rivets. The gearbox mounting plates GM1 and GM2 should be loosely bolted to the mount and the mount replaced on the underside of the gearbox with the rubber spacer in place. With the engine and gearbox in the correct position and the chassis raised on scrap 25 x 25mm box section, tack weld the mounts in place lined up with the top of rails TT2 and TT3. Remove the engine and gearbox and, fully weld the mountings to the chassis.

ALTERNATIVE ENGINES
For all other engine/gearbox combinations the following procedure should be followed. Place the engine and gearbox on the ground and support in the orientation that they will be in when the car is finished, and place the chassis over them, supported on scrap pieces of 25 x 25mm box section. Locate the engine-mounting holes or studs and fabricate a 5mm steel plate with holes to match their positions, either side of the engine. Fasten these plates to the engine.

Fabricate a 120mm long plate to bridge rails BR1/BR8 (nearside) and BR2/BR9 (offside) from 5mm steel plate, level with the centre of the engine-mounting plate (see Fig. 6.10).

Rubber mounts should be obtained, as Fig. 6.11. Ford Fiesta engine mountings are suitable, as are those from certain Land Rover models. A round mounting, about 100mm diameter and 50mm thick with a stud protruding 30mm either side, is about right.

Bolt the mount to the chassis plate and fabricate an 85 x 85 x 5mm square steel plate with a hole to suit the rubber mounting in the

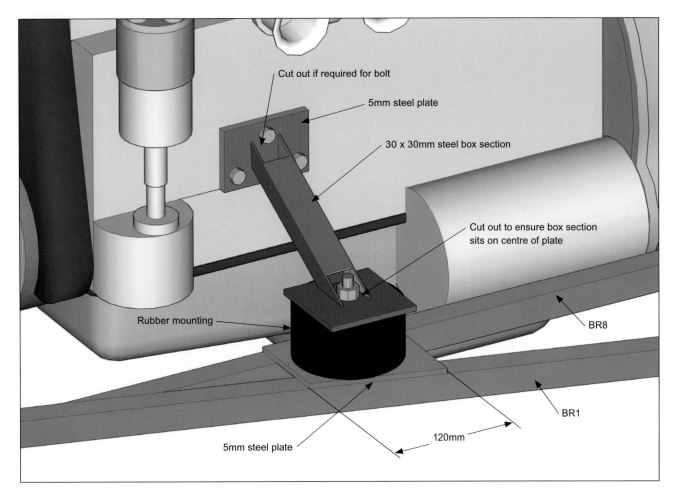

Cut out if required for bolt

5mm steel plate

30 x 30mm steel box section

Cut out to ensure box section sits on centre of plate

Rubber mounting

BR8

BR1

5mm steel plate

120mm

centre and fasten to the top of the mount. The two plates now need to be bridged using 30mm square box section or circular hollow section. Measure the distance between the 85 x 85mm plates and the engine mounted plate. Care should be taken to position the box section, or CHS, so that all the mounting bolts/nuts on the engine block can be fitted. A cut out will be required to the chassis end of the mounting to ensure that the box section sits over the centre of the plate so that the weight of the engine bears on the rubber mounting squarely. Tack the box section, or CHS, to the plates at the engine block and the top of the rubber mounting. Particular care should be taken to only tack the joint on top of the rubber mounting lightly as any excessive heat will damage the rubber. Remove the engine mounting and fully weld.

The gearbox mounts should be made once the engine is on the fabricated engine mounts and the gearbox is positioned centrally in the tunnel with the output squarely facing the differential. Obviously it's not possible to be precise about mountings for all gearboxes. In general, plates

should be fabricated to ensure that the gearbox is level and pointing directly at the rear-mounted differential, and that the mountings are at least equal in strength to the ones detailed for the Sierra gearbox mounts above.

Once the engine and gearbox mountings are fully welded, the engine and gearbox can be fitted. The traditional way is to lift the engine/gearbox assembly with a hoist, but it may be easier, with the engine and gearbox mountings removed, to lift the chassis over the engine and gearbox.

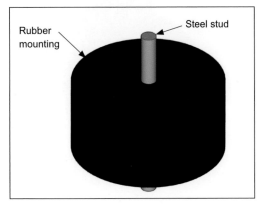

Rubber mounting

Steel stud

▲ **Fig. 6.10** A sketch of the engine mountings required for an alternative engine fitment.

◀ **Fig. 6.11** A typical rubber engine mount as required for an alternative engine fitment.

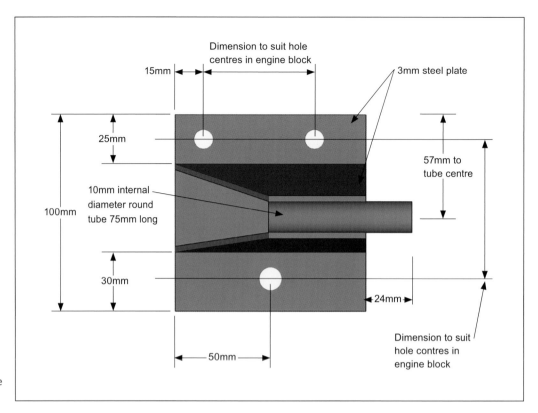

▶ **Fig. 6.12** The dimensions of the new alternator bracket.

Dimension to suit hole centres in engine block

15mm

3mm steel plate

25mm

57mm to tube centre

10mm internal diameter round tube 75mm long

100mm

30mm

50mm

24mm

Dimension to suit hole contres in engine block

▼ **Fig. 6.13** Vertical dimension to the centre of the round tube on the new alternator bracket.

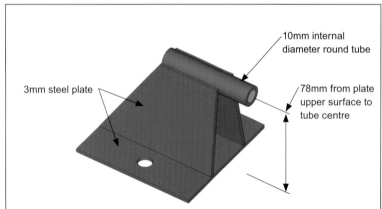

10mm internal diameter round tube

3mm steel plate

78mm from plate upper surface to tube centre

▶ **Fig. 6.14** The completed new alternator bracket.

Bolt on the engine ancillaries – starter motor, inlet and exhaust manifolds and carburettors or fuel injection. The alternator on a Sierra-based car will need to be lifted slightly to give sufficient room for the steering column, and a bracket which is suitable is detailed in Figs. 6.12–6.14. This bracket should be bolted to the engine block alternator mounting holes. Make the engine-mounting plate first as the mountings can vary in position from engine to engine.

EXHAUST SYSTEM
The exhaust system can be fabricated from parts salvaged from tyre and exhaust centres. Bends and suitable silencers are often to be found in their scrap bins. Ask nicely and they'll probably let you have some bits and pieces. Because of health a safety concerns, they probably won't let you look for yourself, but the guys at these places seem to be 'car people', and I've always found them more than helpful. A small donation for tea and biscuits might help too!

You'll need a silencer about 500mm long and various bends and straights. The sections should be welded together with the MIG welder. It may be easier to butt-joint the sections and weld a collar of mild steel around

Exhaust Silencer

Rubber mounting

3mm Steel plate
fixed to chassis

the joint. This will increase strength and help to make it leak proof. When it's complete, a good wire brushing and a coat of very-high-temperature (VHT) paint will tidy it up.

Fix a bracket with a hole to take a rubber mounting (the one normally used for Rover Mini exhausts is ideal) to the underside of the chassis. Attach a plate to the top of the mounting and tack the silencer to this top plate. Remove the silencer and fully weld the plate (see Fig. 6.15). Alternatively, complete exhausts, or all the parts to make an exhaust, are available from MK Engineering.

RADIATOR

The radiator from the Sierra is unsuitable because of it's size, and a smaller alternative should be found. I used a radiator from a 2000 model Renault Clio. This is very compact and has the advantage of an attached electric fan. If you buy the radiator and fan separately, make sure when fitting them to your car that the fan is in the right place, ie, in the same orientation as on the original car. A fan on the front of your radiator blowing air forward will do very little for your cooling! It is possible to reverse the direction of some fans but it's not as simple as

▶ **Fig. 6.16** An exhaust silencer in position.

▼ **Fig. 6.17** The radiator from a Renault Clio. This view also shows the electric fan and the cooling system expansion bottle.

swapping the wires around, and it's probably best to get one that goes with the radiator. I managed to get my fan behind the radiator (as it is in the Clio), but check you have enough space to do so.

The rest of the cooling system comprises an expansion bottle and the hoses to connect the various parts together. On the Pinto engine, the hose which used to go to the heater should be re-routed to the rear of the inlet manifold – unless, of course, you intend to fit a heater. Suitable heaters can be found in the Rover Mini range and the Volkswagen Polo (mid-'90s models). Fitting a heater will require some thought at the planning stage, as the bulkhead and the under dash area may need to be re-worked. Put the heater in place and see what might need to be altered.

The expansion bottle needs to be positioned as high as possible to prevent air locks in the system. A suitable tank is fitted to the Rover 200 range of cars. The connections on the expansion bottle should be made to the bottom hose (larger pipe) and thermostat bypass (smaller pipe).

PROPSHAFT

A propshaft will need to be fabricated, using the front and rear joints of the donor car. In the Roadster it is possible to use the 'rubber doughnut' type of front joint, as opposed to the more difficult to obtain universal joint type. This is because the differential is solidly mounted to the chassis and there is not much movement of the shaft, compared with a live axle car.

To make the shaft, cut the front and rear joints from the donor propshaft. Using a grinder,

▲ **Fig. 6.18** The differential fitted to the chassis. Note that in this photo the top mounting bolts for the differential assembly have not been fully tightened.

▼ **Fig. 6.19** The DM1/DM2 assembly fitted to the Sierra rear differential.

carefully clean up the joints. Place the front joint in the end of the gearbox, leaving 20mm of the splined shaft exposed between the front of the joint and the gearbox (this is to prevent contact between the two if the engine moves). Attach the rear universal joint to the differential flange and measure between the rear of the front joint and the forward flange of the rear universal joint. Cut a piece of thick-walled tube to this dimension and fit the joints to it. If you use a universal joint at the gearbox end, ensure that the yokes of this joint line up with the yokes of the rear universal joint. A good stiff fit is ideal for the joints into the tube, and either fully weld or, if you have any doubts about your own welding, take to a competent welder to complete. Incidentally, look after the rear joint to differential flange bolts – they are an odd size and difficult to replace.

DIFFERENTIAL ASSEMBLY

The differential/rear axle assembly can be fitted next using fabricated brackets made from plates DM1 and DM2. Weld the two plates fully at 90° to each other. Offer the brackets up to the differential, and secure with either long bolts or grade 8.8 steel threaded bar, complete with locking nuts at either end. Using a trolley jack, lift the differential until the holes in brackets DM1/DM2 line up with the holes in chassis plates CP10 and secure with M12 bolts and locking nuts. The driveshafts are fitted by sliding them through the rear uprights and securing the hub assembly to the rear upright using M8 bolts.

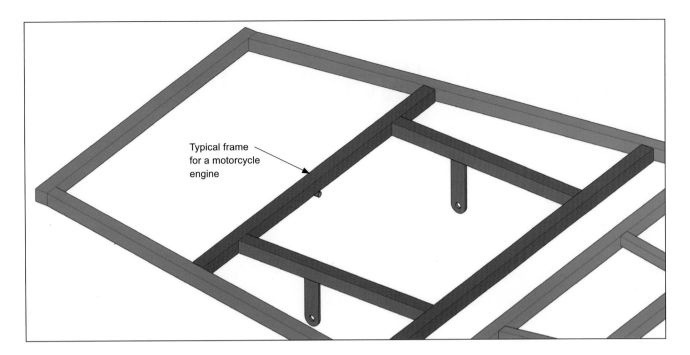

Typical frame
for a motorcycle
engine

MOTORCYCLE ENGINES

The fitting of a motorcycle engine is becoming more and more popular, and it's not difficult to see why. These engines are at the pinnacle of engine development. High revving, powerful and light, they come complete with a sequential six-speed gearbox – a heady mix. If you're in the market for this kind of motive power, you will need the complete engine, the wiring loom and the instruments from the donor bike. A word of caution: some engines come from stolen bikes, so buy from a reputable bike breaker, and be suspicious of missing or defaced engine numbers. If you're found in possession of such an engine it will revert to it's original owner and you might have to prove that you weren't the one who stole it!

Bike engines are usually hard mounted. This means that they are bolted solidly to the chassis. This will require the making of what is known as a 'cradle'. This is a frame that carries the engine in the engine bay of the car.

The sprocket of the bike is replaced by a sprocket adapter which enables you to fit a propshaft.

You will need to support the engine in place with the sprocket adapter lined up in all planes, and facing squarely the flange of the rear-mounted differential. This is most important. The flanges of the sprocket adapter and differential must be in line to prevent vibration and possible failure, which could cause injury.

The mounting points from the bike frame

should be obvious. These need to be tied into a frame bolted to the top of the engine bay (see Fig. 6.20).

One disadvantage of the motorcycle engine is the lack of a reverse gear. It's easy to underestimate the need for reverse, and up and down the land at club meetings you'll see the spectacle of people grunting and sweating as they push a perfectly serviceable vehicle from a parking space!

A reversing box can be bought which fits in the transmission tunnel, with a short shaft coming from the engine to the box and another one going to the differential. This is worked using a lever or switch on the tunnel top. If no reverse box is used, the propshaft should be of the split type, ie, with a centre bearing, like the Sierra donor prop.

Gearchange mechanisms for bike-engined cars can be mechanical or electronic. The simplest one is probably a gearlever linked by rods and pivots, or rod ends, to the gearchange on the bike gearbox. Pushing the lever forwards or backwards changes the gear up or down. A variation of this is the 'paddle shift'. Levers (or paddles) behind the steering wheel, again via metal rods, change the gears. Cable systems are sometimes used, but they tend to be difficult to set up.

Electronic systems usually use buttons on the steering wheel to activate a two-way electronic solenoid fitted to the bike gearchange lever.

▲ **Fig. 6.20** Typical modifications to the front upper chassis for the fitment of a motorcycle engine.

7 MAKING A FUEL TANK

The fuel tank detailed here will fit into the space between the rear suspension mountings and the rear panel, leaving space above for luggage. The tank can be made in mild steel or aluminium. Obviously an aluminium tank will be lighter, but you will need to use gas or TIG welding equipment. If there's a welding company near you, you may be able to get them to weld the tank after you have constructed it.

Some production car tanks may fit in the space available. If you can gain access to a breaker's yard with your tape measure, you may find one to suit. My own car uses a tank from a Vauxhall Chevette saloon. Note this is from the saloon not the hatchback. In the Chevette it sits between the back seat and the boot, hence it hadn't been exposed to the weather and is in 'as new' condition. It's a taller tank than the one

▼ **Fig. 7.1** The fuel tank in place in the chassis.

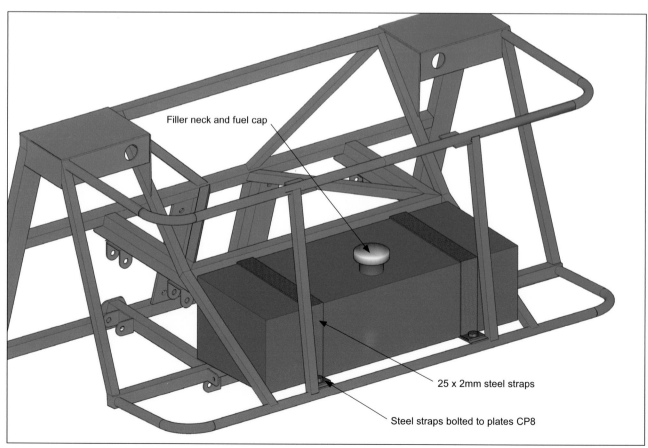

Filler neck and fuel cap

25 x 2mm steel straps

Steel straps bolted to plates CP8

shown here, filling most of the space between the differential mounting and the back panel, almost up to the level of rail RP2. Other tanks that have been used include those from a Triumph Spitfire and a Mini van.

The tank is made from a piece of steel or aluminium 866 x 610mm, as shown in Fig. 7.2. The sheet can be bent in the manner shown in the bodywork chapter, but a metal folder makes the job much quicker and easier. Allowances for the bends have been made in the dimensions shown. Two end-plates should be made as shown in Fig. 7.3.

The tabs on the outside of the plates should be bent in opposite directions at 90 degrees for either end. The baffle is essentially a third end-plate with the corners removed. You will need a piece of tube of a size to suit your filler cap, and some petrol resistant rubber tube if you intend to mount the filler on the rear panel. You'll also need to obtain a collar of metal for use with your sender unit, if fitted. This disc needs to be drilled and tapped to suit the sender fixings, and the centre hole should be large enough to allow the float to pass through. You can save quite a bit of time (and money) by not having a fuel gauge at

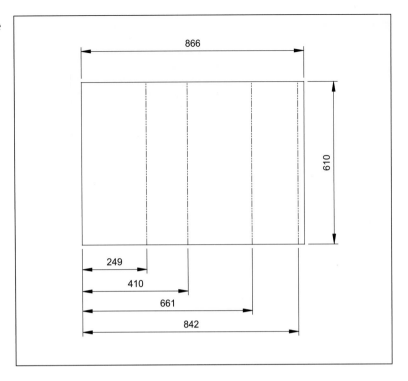

▲ **Fig. 7.2** The material required for the main part of the fuel tank.

▼ **Fig. 7.3** The fuel tank end-plates and baffle.

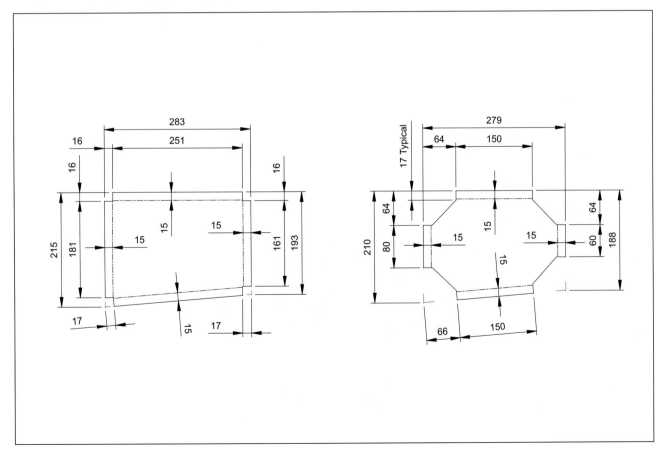

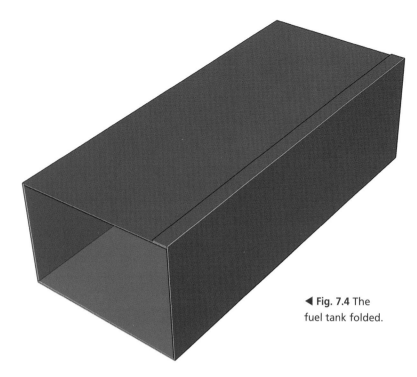

◄ **Fig. 7.4** The fuel tank folded.

as fuel can pass freely from either side of the tank, the baffle merely reduces fuel surge when cornering.

The collar for the sender should be welded to the tank in a position to suit the type of sender float. This will usually be on top of the tank or on one side. Cut a hole slightly larger than the inside diameter of the collar. Some bending of the float arm may be required to make sure that the float does not settle on the bottom of the tank, giving a false reading. Bend the arm until the float is around 5mm from the bottom of the tank.

Cut a hole in the required position for the filler tube, slightly smaller than the tube itself, and seam weld the tube in position.

The outlet tube should be fitted in the front face of the tank. Drill a hole of the correct size for the tube you are using, around 10mm above the bottom to allow any sediment to settle below the level of the outlet and not be drawn into the fuel system. Insert the tube and weld fully to the tank. Finally, the other end-plate should be seam welded in position.

If your car features a fuel-injected engine then the tank requires two additional fixtures. The outlet pipe should be omitted and a swirl pot made and fitted as Fig. 7.6, with a suitable hole being made in the bottom of the main tank to fit the size of the pot. The outlet pipe is then connected near the bottom of the swirl pot. The swirl pot ensures that the injection pump is not starved of fuel, even during extreme handling manoeuvres. A fuel return pipe is also required, for returning unused fuel back to the tank. Drill a hole of suitable size near the top of the tank and fully weld a pipe in this position.

The tank can now be pressure-tested by fitting the sender unit and seal, temporarily sealing the filler hole and using the outlet pipe with a suitable adapter to slightly pressurise the tank. On no account use an air line or similar high-pressure line. By dribbling a 50/50 mixture of water and washing-up liquid over the welded seams, any leaks will be seen as bubbles.

Minor leaks can be dealt with by using a proprietary petrol tank sealer. Larger leaks should be ground out and re-welded, provided that the tank has NEVER been used to hold petrol or other inflammable liquid. Petrol fumes are very volatile and any attempt to weld a tank that has been used will, in all probability, lead to an explosion.

The tank is fitted by using two 3 x 25mm steel strips fixed by rivnuts or bolts and locking nuts to plate CP8. These plates should be bent around

all. The alternative – a piece of dowel, used as a gauge through the filler hole – is considerably cheaper, provided that 'out of sight, out of mind' doesn't lead you to run out!

The construction of the tank is quite straightforward, but it goes without saying that the welding has to be excellent. If you don't feel confident, take the tank to an experienced welder. Start by welding the long seam on the top of the tank. Next, push the tank end at the opposite end from the filler hole into position and seam weld.

The baffle needs to be positioned roughly in the centre and tack welded in position, making sure that it doesn't foul the sender unit or filler neck. It's not necessary to fully weld the baffle

▼ **Fig. 7.5** Fuel tank in position.

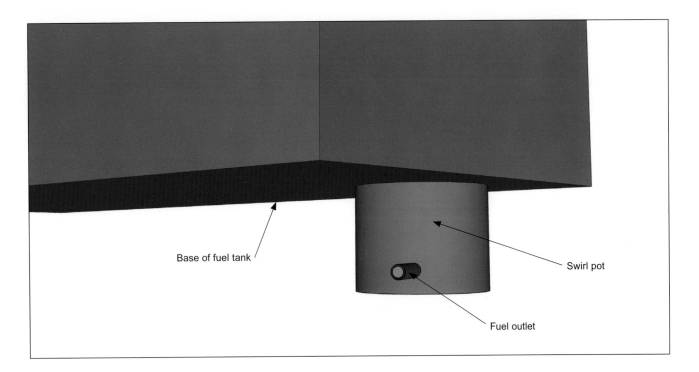

Base of fuel tank

Swirl pot

Fuel outlet

the outside of the tank. 30mm by 1mm rubber strip is used as an insulator under the strip, and on the mating surface on the top of the CP8 plates. If you intend to leave the top of the luggage area open, the filler can be attached directly to the top of the tank, most people however join the filler on the tank to a filler set into the back panel of the car, via flexible petrol-resistant hose and worm-drive clips.

The fuel lines should be run through the transmission tunnel, clipped to the chassis with P clips at 100mm centres, well away from the propshaft or any other moving parts. The lines themselves can be plastic (as used on production cars) copper, rubber or the braided type. The last named are very expensive. I favour copper pipes of the kind used for micro-bore central heating systems – they are very durable and look nicer than plastic or rubber pipes. Whichever pipe you use, it must be suitable for petrol. Rubber pipes will have this printed on the outside. If the pipes you use are rigid, then you must use a short length of flexible rubber pipe to join the pipe to the tank at one end and the engine at the other. It's a good idea to fit a fuel filter between the petrol pump and the carburettor. If you're using fuel injection, then you'll need a second pipe, fixed as before, from the injection system to return unused fuel to the tank.

▲ **Fig. 7.6** A typical swirl-pot installation.

◀ **Fig. 7.7** Fuel pipe clipped to perforated strip tacked into the transmission tunnel. The strip is 25 x 3mm with holes every 50mm for easy fixing of pipes and wiring loom with P-clips and rivets. It's easier to drill these holes in the strip and then fix to the chassis

8 MAKE AND FIT BODY PANELS

The body panels for the Roadster are quite simple to make and fit, the side panels, rear panel and bonnet are made of 1.2mm half-hard aluminium sheet and the nosecone and wings are glassfibre items. The scuttle (the panel over the dashboard) can be made of steel, aluminium or glassfibre.

Aluminium for the panels can be obtained cheaply by cutting from either caravan sides or the sides of Luton-type box vans. If you intend to obtain your aluminium in this way, I would recommend the use of either air or electric sheet-metal cutters. It's virtually impossible to successfully cut this sort and size of panel using Gilbow-type shears or tin snips, both from the point of view of giving yourself carpal tunnel syndrome and preventing distortion. Take at least two helpers to support the sheet while you cut, but make sure everyone is wearing thick gloves, as the edges will be very sharp. When you've liberated your aluminium, you have the problem of transporting it. One way is to loosely roll the panel along the shorter axis and secure with rope or tape. Salvaged aluminium will usually be painted on one side, and you should make sure this is the side that faces inwards when you come to make your panels. If, however, you intend to have the panels visible from inside the car, you should remove the paint carefully with paint stripper, and use a Scotchbrite pad to give a brushed appearance.

SIDE PANELS

Fig. 8.1 shows the layout of the main side panels. The panels are similar on both sides of the car, with the exception of the bend A–A, and the bends at the top and bottom of the panel, which obviously bend in opposite directions for each side.

The safest method for constructing these panels is to make a full-sized cardboard template of the panel and try it on the chassis, making adjustments until you're satisfied with the fit. Transfer the template to your aluminium, mark out and cut to the outline using snips. Depending on the configuration of your exhaust, you may need to cut a hole in the side panel for the exhaust to pass through. This hole will need to be trimmed so that it doesn't present a sharp edge at SVA time. It's not possible to use the usual push-on edging in this situation, as the heat from the exhaust pipe would melt it. The solution is to make an aluminium escutcheon plate from 3mm aluminium with the edges rounded over, and bolt or rivet it to the panel.

The exposed edges of the panels around the front suspension, steering rack and shock absorber should be trimmed with push-on edging for the SVA test. Note that you will need to remove the wishbones to fit the panels.

The bend A–A should be made before the panel is fitted, by clamping wood to either side of the sheet and carefully bending by hand and then knocking the bend over with another length of wood, as shown in Fig. 8.2. The other bends can be made on the chassis by clamping a length of wood on the outside of the chassis rail with the sheet trapped in between. The bend can then be made by pushing over by hand and then knocking the flange over with another piece of wood and a mallet. Making the bends in this way ensures that they fit. If you make the bends off the car, you run the risk of them being in the wrong position. If they are slightly too far apart,

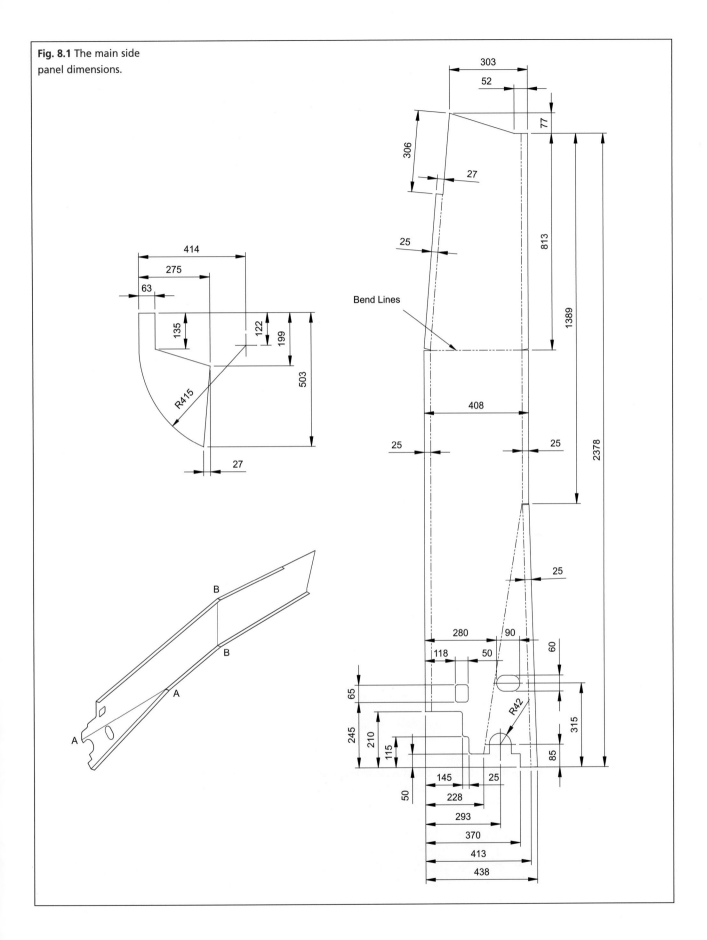

Fig. 8.1 The main side panel dimensions.

you will have a gap to fill, and if they're too close together, the panel won't fit onto the chassis and you'll have to make a new panel.

The side panels have a slight bend along the line B–B when the panel is flush against the chassis. Don't make a bend here. The panel will find its own curve when finally fitted. Offer the panel up to the chassis to ensure a good fit, with the rear of the panel flush with the back edge of rail SB1. When all is well, remove the panel and run a bead of sealant over all the rails which the panel touches. I used Polyurethane sealant/adhesive to secure the panels. This gives a very secure fixing and is difficult to remove without damage to the panel, so only use this on panels which you know you'll never have to remove for maintenance. A slightly cheaper alternative is silicone 'bath sealant', but don't use the stuff that has a 'vinegary' smell – it's corrosive and will damage the chassis and the panel eventually. Clamp the panels in position using wood or cloth spacers to prevent the clamps damaging the aluminium, and drill and fix the panels top and bottom with 3mm rivets to tubes TR1, TR2, TR3, TR4, BR3, BR4, BR5 and BR6 at 50mm spacings. Similarly fix the bent over sections at the front to rails BR1 and BR2.

Next, cut templates to make the rear wing infill panels as shown in Fig. 8.1. Because we had the facilities, we welded a strip of aluminium to the top of this panel over chassis strip SS1, but this can be covered using rounded aluminium edge trim. Stick the panel to plate CP11 and SB1, and rivet where shown – see Fig. 8.3. Try to make the joint between the side panel and the rear wing infill panel as tidy as possible, as the joint will be partially seen, particularly if you don't paint the car.

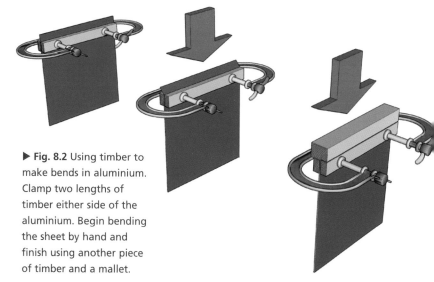

▶ **Fig. 8.2** Using timber to make bends in aluminium. Clamp two lengths of timber either side of the aluminium. Begin bending the sheet by hand and finish using another piece of timber and a mallet.

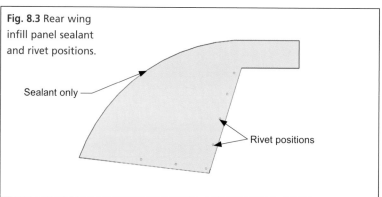

Fig. 8.3 Rear wing infill panel sealant and rivet positions.

Sealant only

Rivet positions

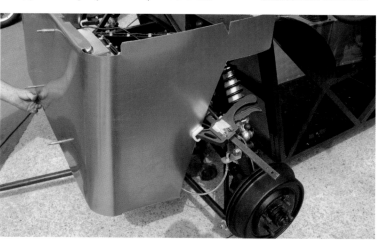

▼ **Fig. 8.4** The rear aluminium panel partially fitted to the chassis. Note the four Cleco fasteners used to locate the panel. These are fitted into holes in rails RP3 and are used for rivets when the Cleco fasteners are removed.

BACK PANEL

The back panel of the car is made in a similar way to the side panels, in that you should make a card template and trial fit to the chassis until a perfect fit is obtained. The template should be made allowing 25mm oversize top and bottom. Cut the template larger than you think you need, the angle is quite deceiving at the sides. When you're confident that the panel is correct, transfer to the aluminium and cut it out.

The bottom 25mm should be bent first using the method shown above for the side panels, and a series of V-cuts made where you need to form the curve at the bottom outside corners. Drill four holes through the back panel into rails RP3 (two per rail). Temporarily fit the panel using self-tapping screws, or Cleco fasteners if you have them. These holes should be filled with rivets when the panel is finally fitted. Carefully bend by hand the panels around the curves of tubes RP1 and RP2 and fix with 3mm rivets at 50mm spacings to the underside of RP1. Fixing the panel to RP2 requires a different method. The panel is bent over RP2 using a panel hammer or panel-beater's slapper as shown in Figs. 8.5 and 8.6. Support the outside of the

◀ **Fig. 8.5** Bending the top of the rear panel over, using a panel hammer and a length of timber.

◀ **Fig. 8.6** Bending over the corners of the rear panel using a panel beater's 'slapper' and a length of timber.

▼ **Fig. 8.7** A length of steel pipe clamped to two trestles for initial forming of the bonnet curves.

panel and knock the aluminium over and around the tube. Take your time and bend a little at a time until the aluminium forms a perfect curve over the tube. Finally fix the panel with rivets on the inside of rail RP2.

BONNET

To make the bonnet, follow the same procedure as for the other panels. You'll need to fit the scuttle and the nose cone. Make a template from card. Lay the card over the area – the card should naturally form the single curves of the bonnet. Carefully trim to size, allowing an extra 25mm overlap at each side, and mark the centre of each curve. When you're satisfied, transfer the pattern to 1.2mm half hard aluminium sheet and cut out. It's quite possible to make the bonnet without any special equipment. Fig. 8.7 shows a length of pipe secured at either end.

The aluminium should be carefully bent over the tube, starting at the centre of the bends. Bend a little at a time and keep trying the bonnet on the car. Eventually, when the fit is good, place the bonnet on the car, reach underneath and mark along the chassis rails on the inside. Remove the

▶ **Fig. 8.8** This gas bottle was exactly the right curve for our bonnet!

bonnet and re-mark the lines approximately 2mm further up the sides of the bonnet. This is to allow the catches to pull the bonnet down securely. Bend the marked out area inwards at 90° and remove 25mm at either end of the bent over section to clear the scuttle and nosecone. Secure the bonnet with SVA-friendly rubber catches.

▼ **Fig. 8.9** The driver's side bulkhead and footwell cover.

FRONT BULKHEAD/PEDAL COVER PANELS

This area is covered by two panels split at the centre.

The panels need to be made as shown in Figs. 8.9 and 8.10. A 40mm strip of aluminium is riveted to the panel on the driver's side to cover

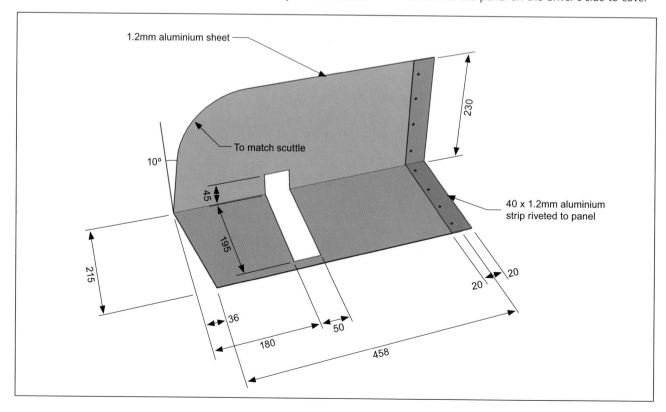

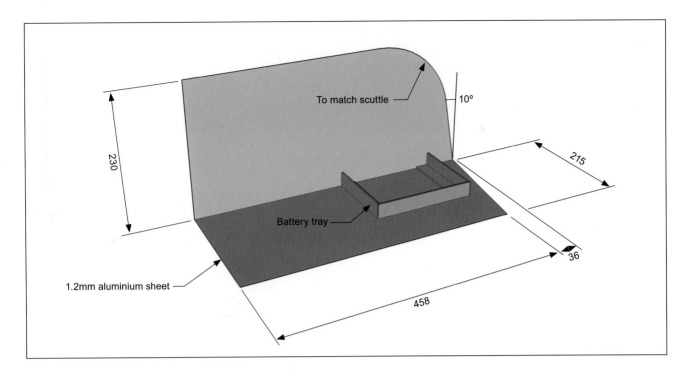

To match scuttle

10°

230

215

Battery tray

36

1.2mm aluminium sheet

458

the joint between the panels. Because we had the facilities, we made the driver's side-panel slightly bigger and put a stepped edge in the panel to do the same job.

The steering column cover is made as shown in Fig. 8.11, and is riveted to the panel, although we omitted the tabs and welded the cover

over the hole. On the passenger side we fitted a battery locating tray. This is made from 25 x 25mm aluminium angle. Measure the outside dimensions of the battery and mark the angle, removing the material from the insides of the bends with a hacksaw – see Fig. 8.12.

Bend the tray into shape and secure with

▲ **Fig. 8.10** The passenger's side bulkhead and footwell cover. Note the position of the battery tray.

◀ **Fig. 8.11** The dimensions of the steering column cover.

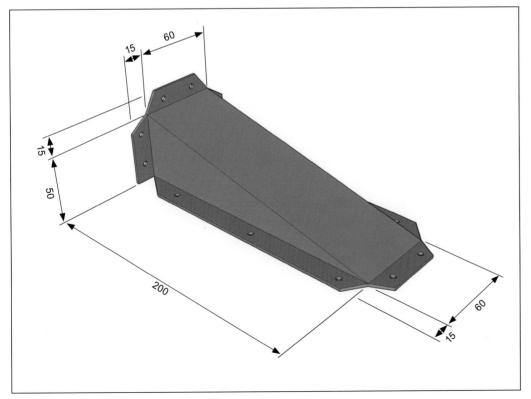

15

60

15

50

200

60

15

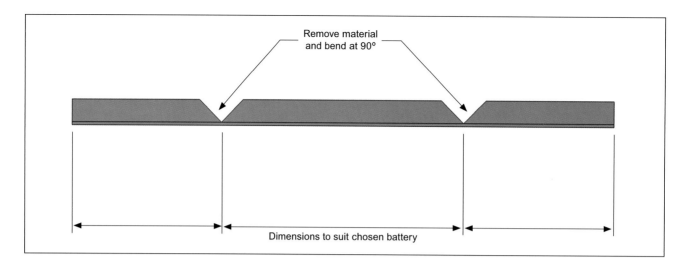

Remove material
and bend at 90°

Dimensions to suit chosen battery

▲ **Fig. 8.12**
Aluminium angle for
the battery tray.

rivets. 6mm steel threaded rod is secured
through the base of the nearside bulkhead panel
either side of the tray with locking nuts, and
another piece of 25 x 25mm aluminium is placed
across the top of the battery to secure it, making
sure that it's placed well away from the battery
terminals, to prevent short circuits. If you have an
aluminium bonnet, ensure that you have a cover
over the positive terminal of the battery.

BEHIND- SEAT PANEL AND
TRANSMISSION TUNNEL

Fig. 8.14 shows the dimensions for the panels,
made from 1.2mm aluminium. Some local
trimming may be required.

The transmission tunnel sides can be cut and
fitted using sealant and rivets, in the same way
as the side panels.

The seat back panel will need bending slightly

▶ **Fig. 8.13** The cover
required for the
forward top of the
transmission tunnel.

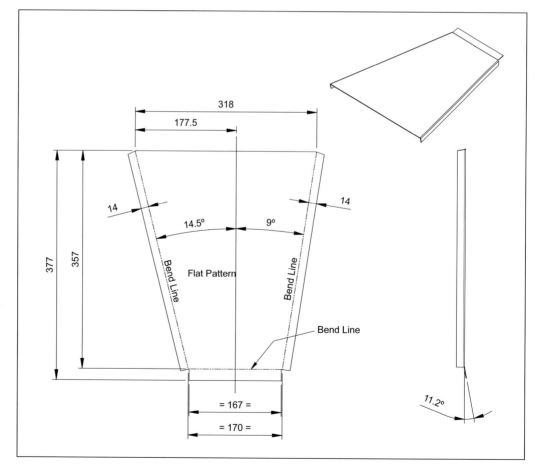

318

177.5

14

14

14.5°

9°

Bend Line

Bend Line

Flat Pattern

377

357

Bend Line

= 167 =

= 170 =

11.2°

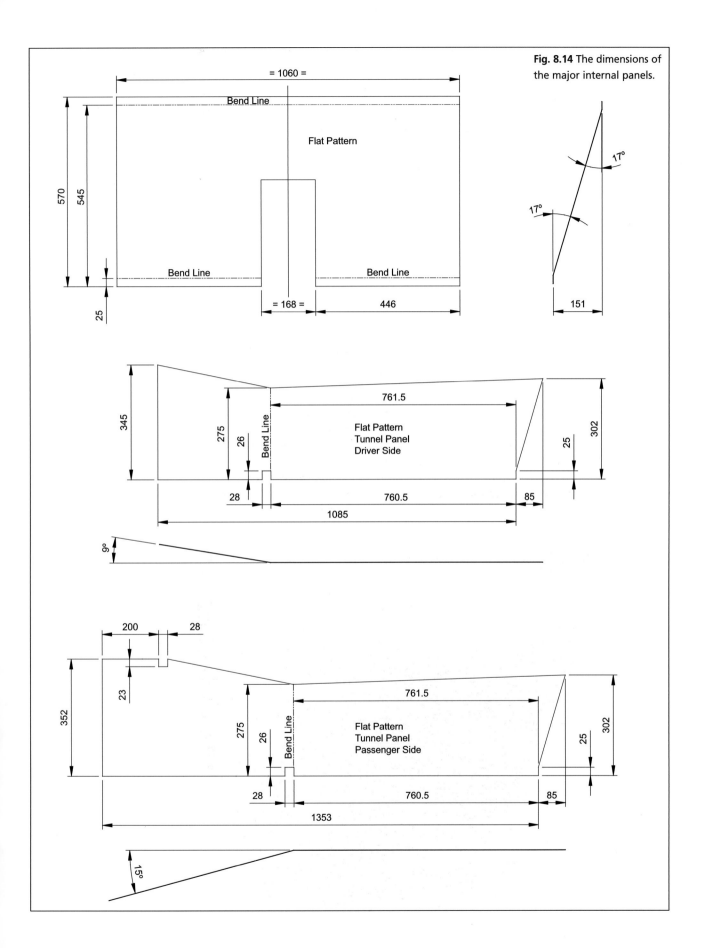

Fig. 8.14 The dimensions of the major internal panels.

= 1060 =

Bend Line

Flat Pattern

570

545

Bend Line

Bend Line

25

= 168 =

446

17°

17°

151

345

275

26

Bend Line

761.5

Flat Pattern
Tunnel Panel
Driver Side

25

302

28

760.5

85

1085

9°

200

28

352

23

275

26

Bend Line

761.5

Flat Pattern
Tunnel Panel
Passenger Side

25

302

28

760.5

85

1353

15°

at the top and bottom (see Fig. 8.14) to fit snugly against rails BR12 and SB2.

The front tunnel top (Fig. 8.13) should be cut and placed in position, with the tab on one side bent over. Scribe underneath to mark the location of the remaining bend, and remove and make the bend. Secure with sealant and rivets.

TRANSMISSION TUNNEL TOP

The top of the transmission tunnel needs to be removable to allow for maintenance of the propshaft or handbrake. Again, the best way to make this panel is to use a card template. Cut a piece of card of the correct length and cut out appropriate holes for the handbrake and gearlever, ensuring free movement in all positions – see Fig. 8.15.

Hold the card down to the tunnel and from underneath mark with a pencil down both sides of the tunnel. Mark a line 15mm out from this line and cut the card to size on the outer line. Mark the outline and the holes for the handbrake and gear lever onto some 1mm aluminium sheet and cut out carefully. Bend one of the 15mm edges over by placing the panel in place on the tunnel with a piece of timber on top, and

tapping the edge over with a mallet or panel hammer. Repeat for the other edge and fix to the tunnel using rivnuts and domed socket-head bolts or domed self-tapping screws. You may need to fill the holes in the top of dome head bolts with silicon sealant as they present a sharp edge for the SVA. No, really.

SCUTTLE PANEL

Glassfibre scuttles can be purchased from MK Engineering, or they can be constructed as follows. Cut another piece of 25 x 25mm box section identical to tube TR9 and two pieces as shown in Fig. 8.16. Clamp these pieces to the top of TR9 and to the top of rails TR1 and TR2 lined up with the front of the new upper 'TR9' tube. Tack weld these pieces together. Bend some 25 x 3mm steel strip to the profile as required for your dashboard shape. Tack this to the rear of the frame at the required 20° angle. This piece should also angle in at around 10°, and the corner radius is approximately 80mm. Make another two hoops of 25 x 3mm, similar to the rear dashboard hoop but vertical, and tack weld them together one inside the other as shown in Fig. 8.17.

▶ **Fig. 8.15** The main transmission tunnel top.

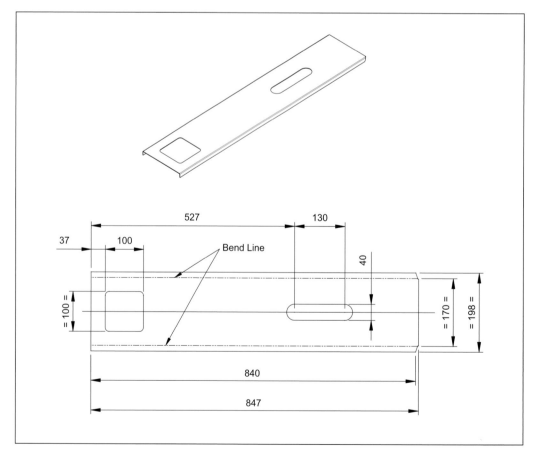

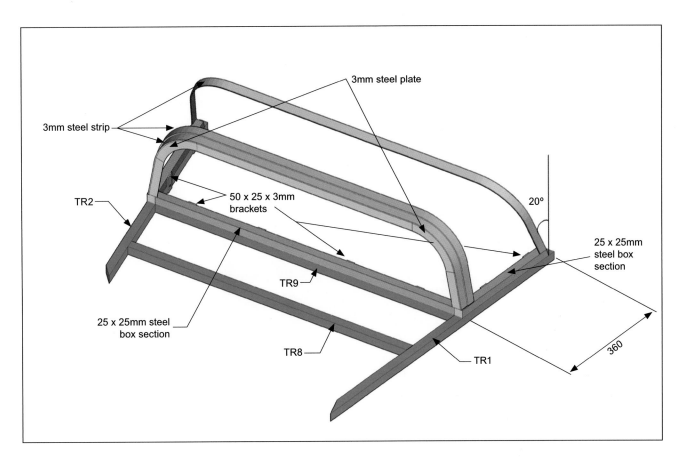

3mm steel plate

3mm steel strip

TR2

50 x 25 x 3mm
brackets

20°

25 x 25mm
steel box
section

TR9

25 x 25mm steel
box section

360

TR8

TR1

This forms the rear bonnet support flange. Tack the assembly, vertically lined up with the front of the frame. Tack 25 x 3mm strip to the front hoop and shape some 3mm plate to fill in the curved sections. This strip is used to fix the bulkhead panels.

You now have a choice. The scuttle can be covered in either aluminium or steel. Again, a template should be made, with a 20mm overlap at the sides to bend under the 25 x 25mm box section. Tack weld (steel) or use sealant and rivets (aluminium) to secure the skin.

To secure the scuttle to the chassis, weld 50 x 25 x 3mm portions of steel strip to the scuttle overlapping the chassis tubes, four on Tube TR9 and two each on tubes TR1/TR2. Drill through these tags and fit, using rivnuts and bolts, to the chassis top rails.

▲ **Fig. 8.16** Dimensions of the fabricated scuttle.

◀ **Fig. 8.17** Detail of the front nearside corner of the scuttle.

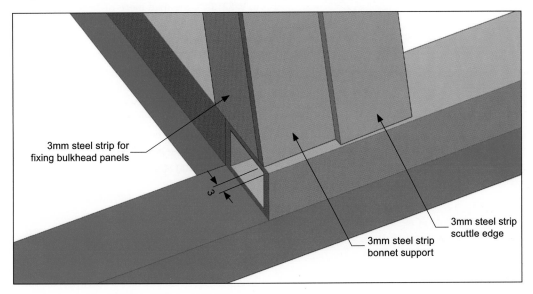

3mm steel strip for
fixing bulkhead panels

3

3mm steel strip
bonnet support

3mm steel strip
scuttle edge

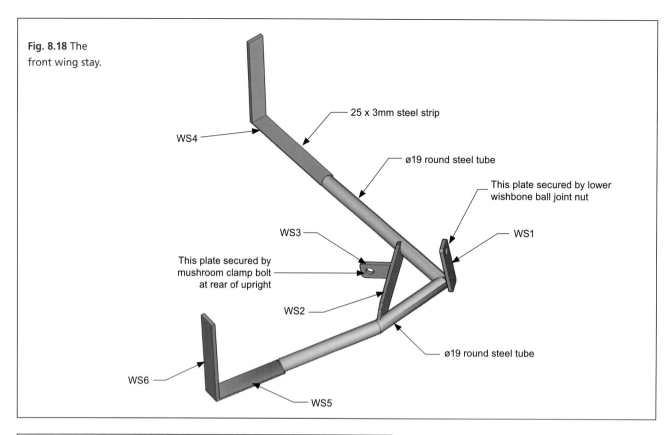

Fig. 8.18 The front wing stay.

WS4

25 x 3mm steel strip

ø19 round steel tube

This plate secured by lower wishbone ball joint nut

WS3

WS1

This plate secured by mushroom clamp bolt at rear of upright

WS2

ø19 round steel tube

WS6

WS5

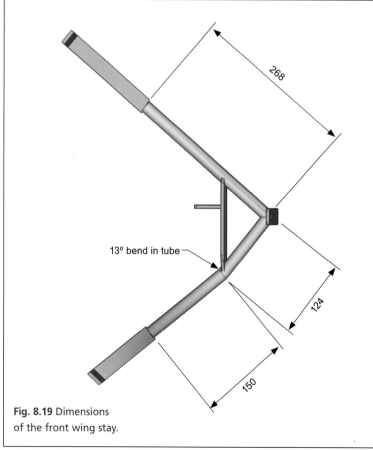

268

13° bend in tube

124

150

Fig. 8.19 Dimensions of the front wing stay.

FRONT WING STAYS

The front wing stays appear to be complex, but a little careful construction makes the job straightforward. Cut plates WS1 to WS5. Fix plate WS1 under the nut on the bottom balljoint and tack WS2 and WS3 together as shown. Fix the WS2/WS3 assembly at the rear of the upright (NOT in the middle of the clamp joint), to the clamp bolt that clamps the mushroom insert. Cut the round 19mm steel tube and tack to the WS1 plate and to WS2. Tack the third piece of 19mm round tube to WS2 and the lower portion of 19mm tube at the correct angle. Plates WS4 and WS5 slot into the ends of the 19mm round tubes, tack these together. Carefully fit the wheel and check the support for clearance. The horizontal parts of plates WS4 and WS5 should be approximately 15mm from the tyre tread. As the assembly is only tacked it should be quite easy to pull and push it into place. Make any adjustments necessary, remove the wing stay and fully weld.

GLASSFIBRE NOSE, WINGS & SCUTTLE

The Roadster's glassfibre panels are available from MK Engineering. Also, shop-soiled or damaged panels are sometimes available from manufacturers of similar kit cars, but the following guide will help if you want to make these panels yourself.

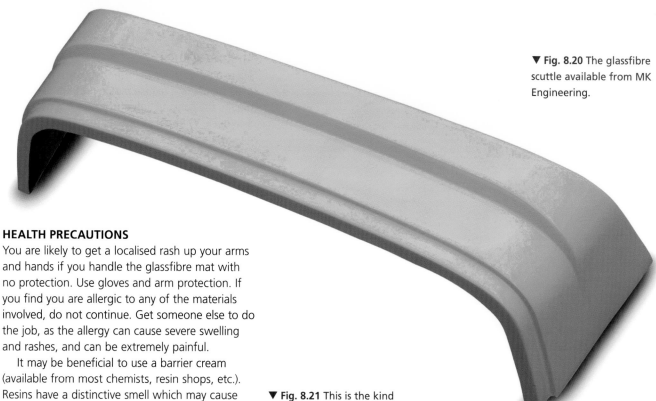

▼ Fig. 8.20 The glassfibre scuttle available from MK Engineering.

HEALTH PRECAUTIONS

You are likely to get a localised rash up your arms and hands if you handle the glassfibre mat with no protection. Use gloves and arm protection. If you find you are allergic to any of the materials involved, do not continue. Get someone else to do the job, as the allergy can cause severe swelling and rashes, and can be extremely painful.

It may be beneficial to use a barrier cream (available from most chemists, resin shops, etc.). Resins have a distinctive smell which may cause irritation. Always give yourself good ventilation when doing the job, since the heavy vapour given off (styrene) can cause headaches, and even unconsciousness if you are exposed to it for too long. If you ever feel drowsiness coming on, get out immediately into the fresh air. The warning signs for resins are an itchy nose and running eyes.

If any hardener gets on your skin, wash it off immediately as it will bleach your skin, and if it gets in your eyes, wash them for at least 10 minutes. If resins get on your skin, wipe them off immediately with a cloth dampened with acetone, then wash in warm soapy water and finally rub a moisturising cream over the area. If any resin is swallowed, drink quantities of water and induce vomiting – and seek medical aid immediately.

If any hardener spills on the ground or clothing, wash it away with plenty of water. In the case of resin spillage, cover with earth or sand and, when soaked in, dispose of safely. Wipe the residue off the ground with acetone.

▼ Fig. 8.21 This is the kind of protective equipment that professional glassfibre operatives use.

SAFETY DURING WORK

Fire is a major hazard. All resins, hardeners and acetone are extremely inflammable. All have low flash points, i.e. temperatures at which they may ignite. For resin it is 25–30°C. So do not use naked lights, and do not smoke while doing a job or even when you've finished, because the styrene vapour given off during curing is highly volatile. Fire can also be started by throwing away your unused liquid resin in the dustbin, because

the heat of reaction when it is setting is enough to set alight any paper. Always place the tin in a safe place and wait until it has 'gone off' and is stone cold before you dispose of it. If a fire starts, a CO_2 or dry powder extinguisher will cover all eventualities. Always keep an extinguisher handy. Water will not work on resins.

When working with GRP, use your common sense. Treat all chemicals with the respect they deserve and, if you're allergic, STOP.

▲ **Fig. 8.22** This buck for a front wheelarch is made from wood skimmed with filler, sanded, painted and polished.

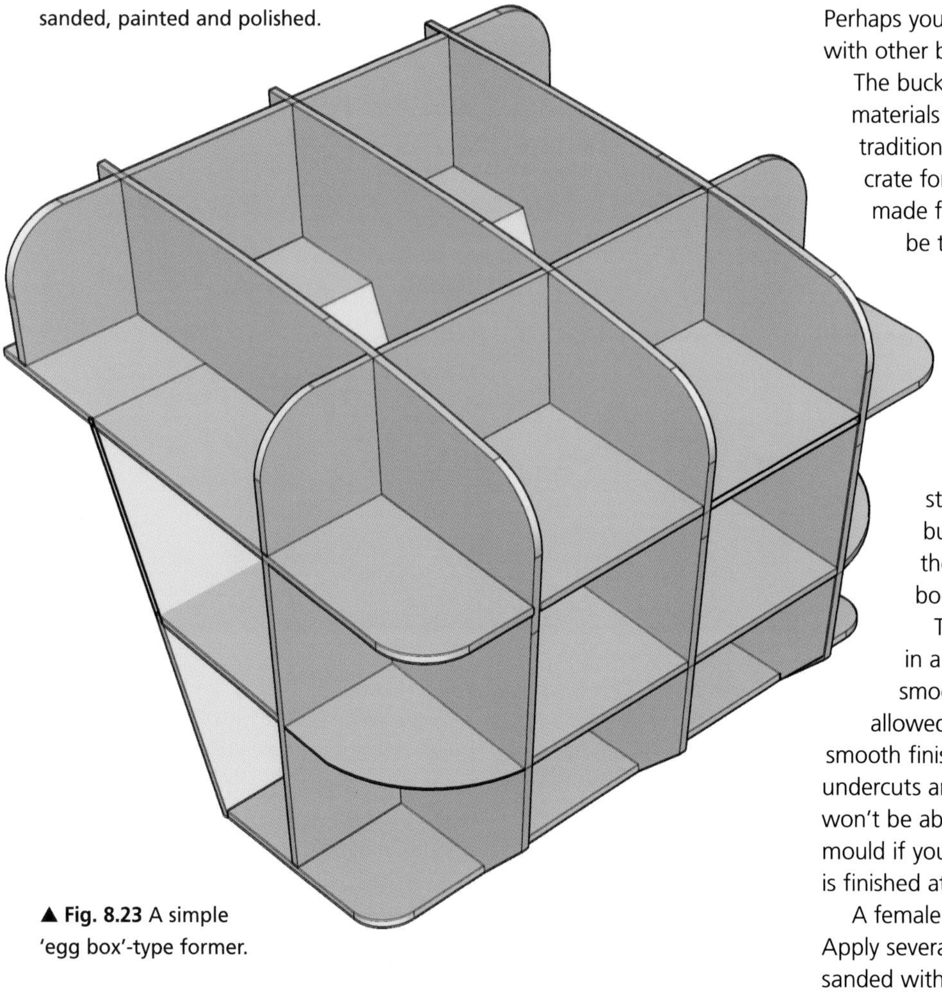

▲ **Fig. 8.23** A simple 'egg box'-type former.

MAKING A BUCK

There are two ways to form the items – using a male mould or a female mould. Both methods require the construction of a pattern, known as a buck. With a male mould the item is made directly on to the buck and the outside must be finished with car body filler. A buck for a female mould is finished on the surface to a standard that is required for the final moulding, usually painted and polished. The buck is then covered in gelcoat and glassfibre to form the mould. Once removed, polished and reinforced this mould is then used to form the final piece.

The buck for a male mould needs to be made slightly smaller than the item to be produced, as the glassfibre is laid directly on the buck and you need to allow for its thickness.

The buck for production of a female mould should be an exact replica of the part to be produced. If more than one item is required, then the additional work in making a female mould is rewarded by the ability to produce several mouldings from the same mould. Perhaps you could share the cost and effort with other builders.

The buck itself can be made from any materials that you have lying around. The traditional method is to make a wooden egg crate former (as in Fig. 8.23). This can be made from any sheet wood and need not be too precise; a basically correct shape is all that is required. The former should be slightly smaller than the finished item. The next stage is to cover the former with hexagonal chicken wire, fixed with staples, and then to cover this with sackcloth, again stapled on. An alternative is to use builder's blue insulation foam to make the former, covered in plaster or car body filler and finished as below.

The whole former is then covered in a 5–10mm layer of plaster, carefully smoothed as much as possible and allowed to dry. Sand the plaster to a smooth finish. Ensure that no return angles or undercuts are included in your design – you won't be able to remove the item from the mould if you do. With a male mould your buck is finished at this stage.

A female buck requires further finishing. Apply several coats of primer/filler. This is then sanded with progressively finer grades of wet

and dry paper until the surface is perfect, usually this will require the buck to be painted and polished.

At this stage the buck should be polished using mould release wax. Take great care to cover all areas that will come into contact with the glassfibre, and polish at least five times to ensure that the buck will release from the mould.

MATERIALS REQUIRED
■ Glassfibre mat
Strands of silicon (glass) chopped and laid down in varying densities and bonded together in sheets. 300gm is ideal for our use as it bends easily around corners.

■ Surface tissue
A very fine mat, looking like tissue. This is used to form a better surface finish, either on the inside of items made in a female mould, or to provide a better surface for finishing when using a male mould.

■ Resin
This is the other half of the GRP (glass reinforced plastic) composite and is clear polyester resin. Resin and fillers have a shelf life of around nine months. In other words, they may 'go off' after this time.

■ Gelcoat resin
Used in moulds, it is a thixotropic polyester resin, much thicker than the ordinary lay-up resin to help it stay in place on vertical surfaces.

■ Hardener
When you buy your resin you will automatically be given hardener, either in paste or liquid form. It is actually methyethyl ketone peroxide (MEK or MEKP for short).

■ Acetone or cellulose thinners
For brush or roller cleaning.

■ Brushes
Cheap paint brushes.

■ Car bodyfiller
Filler is chalk dust in resin and, when mixed with hardener, forms a spreadable paste which can be used to form a smooth surface to items made using a male mould.

▼ Fig. 8.25 Applying coloured gelcoat to a mould for a self-coloured moulding.

TOOLS

You'll also need a Stanley knife, stout scissors, plenty of tins or plastic containers and sticks to mix up the resin (NEVER use a glass container, as the heat of reaction between resin and hardener when it goes off will shatter the glass). You'll also need plenty of sandpapers in varying grades. A usual selection is P40 and P80 for rubbing down filler or plaster, and 360 and 600 wet-and-dry for final finishing prior to painting. It's probably worth purchasing a rubber block for sanding as it makes the job much easier.

MAKING THE MOULD

Male mould – The item is formed by putting two layers of 300gm glassfibre mat over the buck. Mix the resin according to the attached instructions and cut the mat into shape. Don't try to cover complex shapes in one piece; cut overlapping sections. Paint the entire buck with a coat of resin and then fully wet out a piece of mat and position on the buck. Stipple the surface to remove any trapped air and ensure that you don't get any puddles of resin or dry areas. Cover the whole buck, ensuring that the mat and resin

▶ **Fig. 8.26** The first layer of glassfibre mat is applied.

▼ **Fig. 8.27** Trimming a moulding using an air-powered abrasive cut-off wheel.

overlap the edge of the buck for trimming. Repeat with the second layer and add surface tissue if you have it – this gives a better surface for the filler.

Either trim the moulding to size with a Stanley knife when the moulding is 'green', i.e. set but not fully hardened, or wait until it's fully cured and trim with a metal cutting blade in a jigsaw. When the moulding is fully cured it can be skimmed with car body filler and finished using finer and finer grades of wet-and-dry until the surface is perfect, the item must then be painted.

Female mould – Once the surface of the buck is smooth, prepare it by polishing with mould release wax, at least five coats, and buff out. Mix up gelcoat resin and cover the buck. Special mould making gel is available, but ordinary gel is quite acceptable. Choose a dark colour – green and grey seem to be the best. When the gelcoat is tacky to the touch, paint the buck with ordinary resin, wet

out sections of mat and apply two layers, as with the male mould method. Add reinforcement in the form of wood glassed onto the outside of what has become your female mould. This has the smooth surface on the inside, this of course means that when we make a moulding from the mould the smooth surface is on the outside, where we want it.

Remove the female mould from the buck and wash it with soapy water and allow to dry thoroughly. Prepare the mould with the mould release wax as before. It might be a good idea to use some PVA release agent, which is painted on after the wax, at least for the first moulding.

The moulding itself is made in a similar way to the mould, this time using a coloured gelcoat in your preferred colour as the first coat. Two layers of mat are added and fully wetted out, ensuring there are no puddles of resin or dry spots.

From the mould itself we move on to the next stage where the moulding is released from the mould. If, for any reason, the moulding has not fully cured (i.e. it is still green), or has stuck fast because the release agent failed to release and too much force is applied, stress lines and cracks will appear and will show up as white lines. Then, if left unchecked, they immediately show through the paint that is applied subsequently. The remedy here is to make sure all the release agent is evenly applied – especially into any awkward corners – and that the moulding has fully cured before attempting to release it. It may also be that the mould design itself has been constructed in the wrong way to allow an easy release from the moulding, i.e. too sharp a radius on corners, overhanging angles, double curvatures, etc. If necessary a re-design must be done to prevent inherent cracks in the moulding. With a crack-free moulding released, in-built stresses may eventually appear as a crack, especially on hard butt edges where not enough thickness has been

applied. Support the moulding in the correct shape for at least two weeks.

Fitting the rear lights, for example, on newly painted wings must be done with care. Drill the rivet or screw hole oversize. If using 3mm rivets, use a 3.5mm drill. DO NOT force in a rivet or screw, because as soon as you tighten up – bang – a star crack will appear through the paint around the fixing. If possible, always use a washer behind the rivet or screw to spread the load. With badges, use double sided adhesive tape, if possible, to save using screws or rivets.

Make sure wheel arches are well protected by anti-stone-chip paint (3M supply a good one) or a good flexible underbody seal, so stones flung up by the wheel do not star crack the GRP from underneath.

FLY SCREEN AND WINDSCREEN

The prototype car has neither a full windscreen nor a fly screen. If you present your car for the SVA with no screen in place or a fly screen that your vision is normally above, your car won't be tested on anything connected with screens, ie, glass, screen wipers or washers. A fly screen can be made of Perspex or acrylic sheet and, as I mentioned, your normal line of vision must be above the top of the screen.

A full windscreen must be made of laminated safety glass and must be kite marked by the glass manufacturer – not the supplier.

◀ **Fig. 8.28** Yellow gelcoat applied to a scuttle mould.

▲ **Fig. 8.29** A finished moulding released from the mould.

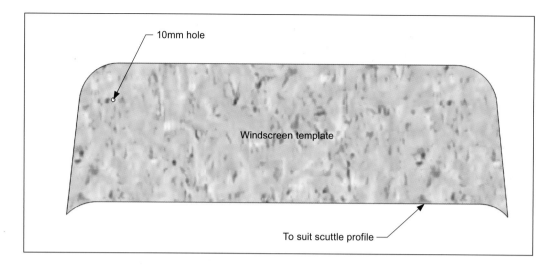

10mm hole

Windscreen template

To suit scuttle profile

For a full windscreen you must construct a
frame from aluminium channel. Some of the kit
car suppliers sell channel for this purpose, or you
can use extruded shower enclosure channel. The
channel should be annealed to aid bending. This
can be done by carefully heating with a blow torch
the section of the channel that you wish to bend,
and at intervals dragging a piece of timber over
the surface. When the timber leaves a burnt mark
it is heated sufficiently. Allow the channel to cool.

To bend the channel to shape, cut out a pattern
of the screen from plywood, MDF or chipboard
which is the same thickness as the inside of the
aluminium channel (Fig. 8.30). Mark the position
of the origin to the top curve of the screen and
drill a 10mm hole. If you intend to make more than
one screen you can reinforce the hole with plates,
countersink screwed to either side of the pattern
with the 10mm hole drilled in the same place.
I think for a one off this shouldn't be necessary.

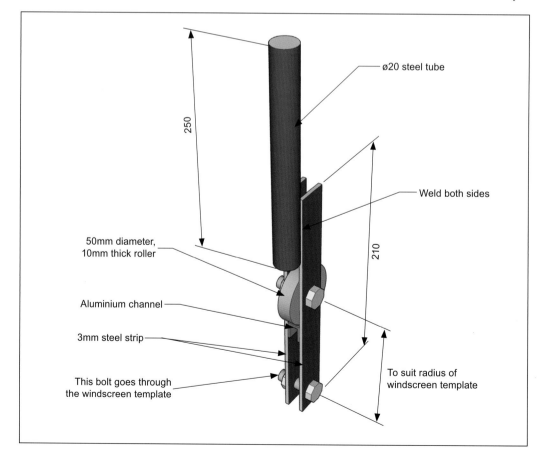

ø20 steel tube

Weld both sides

250

210

50mm diameter,
10mm thick roller

Aluminium channel

3mm steel strip

This bolt goes through
the windscreen template

To suit radius of
windscreen template

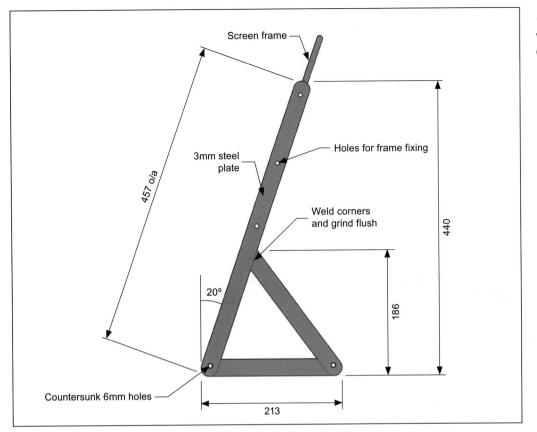

Screen frame

457 o/a

3mm steel
plate

Holes for frame fixing

Weld corners
and grind flush

440

186

20°

Countersunk 6mm holes

213

You will have to construct a simple tool to bend
the channel, as shown in Fig. 8.31.

Anneal the corners and fix the tool in place. Try
to make the bend in one smooth movement. The
result should be a kink-free bend. The bottom of
the screen can be made by hand. Again, anneal
the channel and push into shape on the template.
To hold the screen in place cut supports as shown
in Fig. 8.32.

Cut the supports from 25 x 3mm steel plate
and weld together. Bend the supports to fit the
scuttle and the screen frame. The supports can
be painted, or chromed if funds allow. Fasten the
frame to the support using countersunk bolts
from inside the frame. Ensure that these bolts
are flush, as any protrusion may crack the glass.
Use decorative dome-head nuts on the outside of
the support. The glass is held in the frame using
rubber channel available from trimming suppliers.
First, secure the bottom rail of the frame to the
scuttle with countersunk self-tapping screws and
place the rubber channel into the aluminium
channel. Carefully put the glass into the main part
of the frame with the rubber channel, and drop
the frame and glass into the bottom rail attached
to the car. Support the frame and glass in place
and mark the positions of holes in the supports

onto the scuttle. Remove the frame and drill the
holes through the scuttle. Next, fix the supports
and frame with countersunk socket-head bolts
from the outside – using a large washer or a
plate on the inside of the scuttle to spread the
load – and fix with locking nuts. A little silicone
sealant in the rubber channel should ensure a
watertight fit.

If you have fitted a full windscreen you'll need
to source a windscreen wiper and washer system.
A suitable wiper system is fitted to the Rover
Mini range (and many other BMC products).
Essentially, it's a motor with a spiral drive inside
a tube, which operates on wheelboxes attached
to the spindles and wiper arms. The set-up is too
wide for the Roadster, but the outer tubes can be
shortened to suit and the ends re-flared, bringing
the wheelboxes into the correct position. You'll
need to make a bracket to hold the motor, and
to drill the scuttle for the spindles.

The washer system from the donor car can
be fitted. This comprises the bottle and motor
assembly, and the jets. Fix the jets to the scuttle
and the bottle in the engine bay. Make sure that
the tubes that connect the bottle and the jets are
well attached – they'll be subjected to a blockage
test at SVA time.

9 BRAKING SYSTEM

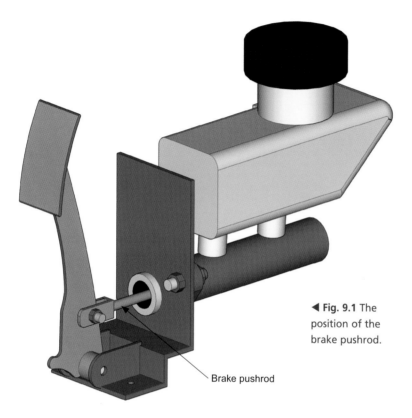

◀ **Fig. 9.1** The position of the brake pushrod.

Brake pushrod

The Roadster's braking system is taken from the donor Sierra. Two different systems were fitted to the donor cars, either disc front and drum rear, or an all-disc set-up. Each system requires a slightly different rear upright (see Chapter 5).

MASTER CYLINDER

The master cylinder is mounted on the pedal box, and the push-rod needs to be made as shown in Fig. 9.2. The push-rod can be fitted to the pedal using either a bolt and locking nut or a clevis pin, with either a circlip or a split pin to secure. If you use a nut and bolt, don't over-tighten it, as you need to ensure free movement of the pedal. Adjust the push-rod length to eliminate all but a slight amount of free play between the pedal and the master cylinder.

▶ **Fig. 9.2** The brake pushrod.

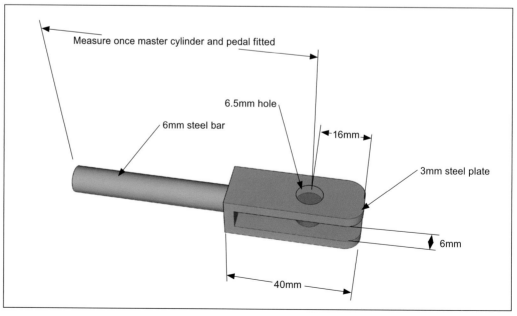

Measure once master cylinder and pedal fitted

6.5mm hole

6mm steel bar

16mm

3mm steel plate

6mm

40mm

BRAKE PIPES

Fit the new flexible brake pipes to the front callipers and the rear wheel cylinders. The front flexible pipes fit to plates CP23 on tubes U1 and U2, and the rears to plates CP23 on RS14.

Measure and cut to length the two rigid copper pipes for the front brakes. The pipes need to have a male fitting at the master cylinder end and a female fitting at the wheel end, for connection to the flexible pipes. If you're using the donor parts, these fittings will be standard metric M10. Alternative master cylinders or flexible pipes may have different threads.

You will need to hire or borrow a brake pipe flaring tool. Follow carefully the instructions that come with the tool, remembering that male ends have a single flare and female a double flare. Incidentally, don't forget to put the fittings on before you flare both ends! An alternative is to measure the lengths of pipes you need, specify the end-fittings required, and get your brake pipes made up at your local motor factor or spares shop. Secure the pipes, at around 250mm centres in the engine bay, with either plastic or rubber-lined metal P-clips, and tighten the fittings into the master cylinder and the front flexible pipes. Ensure that all brake pipes are secured well away from any moving parts.

The pipe to the rear brakes needs to be made in two or three parts depending on whether you are using drums or discs.

The brake pressure switch, which illuminates the brake lights, should be fixed close to the master cylinder on a bracket attached to the

chassis. A suitable switch is fitted to the Volvo and Rover Mini range. If you use the Mini switch, note that some switches have imperial end-sockets and that you should use matching fittings. Make a pipe to link the rear brake output of the master cylinder to the brake pressure switch.

The pipe that links the brake pressure switch and the rear T-piece should be one piece if you have drum-brakes at the rear, and it should be a two-piece item for disc-braked rear wheels.

▲ **Fig. 9.3** The brake pressure-switch for the rear brake lights.

◄ **Fig. 9.4** The brake master cylinder fitted.

▶ **Fig. 9.5** The rear brake T-piece and brake pipes.

The difference arises from the need to fit a brake-pressure proportioning valve in the brake line of a disc-brake set-up. This reduces the pressure to the rear brakes to prevent them from locking before the front brakes. Were they to do so it would probably cause the car to spin. It may be that, on testing the car, you need to add the valve later to a drum-braked car. My car didn't need it.

The valve salvaged from the Sierra can be used, but note the angle that the valve sits in on the donor car. The valve must be fitted at that same angle. An alternative valve can be found on the Fiat Uno range of cars. Attach the proportioning

valve in a convenient location and make a pipe to connect the brake-pressure switch to the proportioning valve, and then run a pipe to the rear T-piece.

On a drum-braked set-up, simply run a pipe from the pressure switch to the rear T-piece.

Brake pipes running through the transmission tunnel should be secured every 100mm, and the rear T-piece should be fitted to the chassis at the rear. Run rigid copper pipes from the T-piece to the rear flexible pipes at the CP23 brackets on RS14. Secure the pipes at 250mm centres in the rear chassis area.

HANDBRAKE

The handbrake system from the donor car can be adapted to suit the Roadster. The handbrake lever is attached to chassis plates CP12 and CP13 with 8mm bolts and locking nuts.

The handbrake cable needs to be shortened. Cut the nipple end from the cable on the nearside, and remove the two outer sheaths and the saddle connector, noting the order of the parts. Cut 60mm from the wheel ends of each outer sheath. Fit the cable into its correct location on the offside wheel hub, thread the cable through the sheath and push the stop on the sheath into the offside hole in chassis plate CP14. Ensure that the sheath is fixed well away

▼ **Fig. 9.6** The handbrake bolted in position on the transmission tunnel. Note that the link bar is retained to connect the handbrake lever to the yoke on the handbrake cable.

from any moving parts. Push the cable through the saddle connector and fasten the connector to the handbrake lever, using the clevis pin and a new split pin.

The cable should now be pushed through the nearside hole in chassis plate CP14 and threaded into the other sheath, with the adjuster pushed into the hole in CP14. Run the cable and sheath to the nearside wheel, ensuring the adjuster is wound fully off. You will now be able to see how much the cable needs to be shortened by placing it into position on the handbrake actuation lever on the brake backplate assembly. Mark the position, allowing for a new nipple to be fitted. The new nipple can be of the type which is a collar with locking grub screws, or a soldered item. Whichever you use, the plastic covering of the inner cable should be removed in the area of the nipple to ensure a good, solid fixing.

When the nipple is fitted, adjust the cable using the adjuster at chassis plate CP14 by winding it along the outer sheath to remove any slack from the cable. The lever should pull up around three clicks of the adjuster.

▲ **Fig. 9.7** The rear offside brake backplate and wheel cylinder.

◀ **Fig. 9.8** Chassis plate CP14, which holds the ends of the handbrake cable outers.

10 ELECTRICS

On such a simple car the electric set-up need not be complicated. The donor car loom can be used with wires, and indeed whole sections, removed.

When you strip the donor it's a good idea to re-attach electrical components to the wiring loom wherever possible, or label the wires clearly and permanently. One way to label them is to wrap the wire with masking tape and write on the tape. The disadvantage, though, is that the tape might become dirty or lost during the time you take to build the car. However, placing the ends into plastic freezer bags will help to preserve the tape.

Lay out the loom on a flat surface (the chassis building board is ideal) and place the components in the position they will be on the finished car, starting with the positions of the exterior lights. Add the other components, as many as possible in their correct positions.

The next task is to unpick all the loom tape. This is a messy and time-consuming job, and care must be taken not to cut the wires or to mix them up. Use small pieces of insulating tape or small tie-wraps to temporarily hold the wires into the same groups as when the loom was wrapped.

Next, identify components and connections that won't be required on your car. I'm thinking here of things like heated rear windows, door courtesy light switches (and the lamps), electric windows, sunroofs, etc.

If you aren't planning to fit them to your car, you can also remove the wiring to the heater, wiper motor, washers and stereo. Trace each wire back to the fuse box, or the junction with a wire that is required, and remove the unwanted wire.

When this process is complete you should be left with only the wires that you need. Some of them will be much too long. Shorten these wires, but take account of the route the wires will have to take in the finished car. If in doubt, wait until the loom is fitted to the car before you shorten them. If a wire needs extending, use wire of the same colour where possible. Wires that enter a loom in one colour and emerge in another can be a nightmare!

It may be possible to use a fuse box with fewer fuses, which takes up less space. The fuse box must be fitted in an easily accessible place for the changing of fuses. I placed mine on the bulkhead panel.

▼ Fig. 10.1 Wiring in the scuttle area. Some of the junctions in the wires have yet to be made properly.

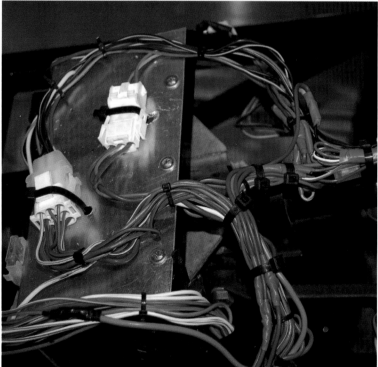

If the items have a plug which fits the component, leave at least 100mm of wire on the plug to enable you to join the wires. Opinion is divided on whether electrical connections should be soldered or crimped. Most professionals use crimped connections because they are quicker to make. This is fine if you have good-quality connectors and, more important, a top-quality crimping tool. The commonly available 'market quality' crimping tools don't make a sufficiently strong or secure connection. For this reason I'd recommend that you solder your connections. It's easier for the amateur to make good connections, provided that you make sure the solder has penetrated the fixing and the wire. Invest in a good-quality electric soldering iron, and slip on a sheath of heat-shrink material before you make the joint. Use a heat gun to shrink the sheath when the joint is complete. This makes for a very neat connection.

When you're satisfied that the loom is complete, rewrap it. The correct way to do this is to use non-adhesive loom tape. This looks like black insulating tape but has no adhesive on it. The tape is secured using insulating tape at one end, and then it is wrapped around the loom to the other end and again secured with insulating tape.

▲ **Fig. 10.2** A crimping tool set, complete with fittings. *(Draper Tools)*

▲ **Fig. 10.3** Heat-shrink covering is a neat way to finish wiring joints. *(Draper Tools)*

▶ **Fig. 10.4** A good quality electrical multi-meter is invaluable when working on the electrical system. *(Draper Tools)*

MK Engineering will sell you a purpose-made loom if the above seems too daunting.

The loom can then be fixed to the car. The SVA test demands that the wiring is securely fixed and not near any moving parts. Using P-clips riveted to the chassis, route the loom down the transmission tunnel, across the dashboard area and into the engine bay. Fix the P-clips at a maximum of 100mm apart in the transmission tunnel and 250mm apart in other areas. To prevent wires becoming frayed from rubbing on metal panel edges use rubber wiring grommets where wires pass through panels.

The simplest choice for switches and instruments is to use those that came with the donor car, as the wiring will plug straight into the steering column switches and instrument cluster.

If you decide to use other instruments or switches, be aware of the SVA requirements regarding internal projections. The bezels on these instruments are often not radiused for the SVA test. Make sure that sender units or capillaries are matched to the instrument, otherwise false readings may occur.

EXTERIOR LIGHTS
The Roadster requires the following:

- Two headlights and side lights which show a white light at the front.
- Two rear position lights showing a red light.
- Two front and two rear indicators which show an amber light.
- Two side repeater indicators which show an amber light.
- Two rear brake lights.
- A white rear number plate light.
- A minimum of one rear high-intensity fog light to the offside or on the centreline of the vehicle.

The fog light must have an audible or visible tell-tale when it is illuminated. This is achieved by having an illuminated switch or a light which comes on when the fog light is on. The fog light must not work when the sidelights and/or headlights are not illuminated.

Boy racers might note that the SVA test specifically excludes any blue lights on the vehicle!

11 INTERIOR

The interior of this type of car can be as simple or as complex as you like. Whilst the stripped-out race-car look is very popular (not to mention cheap), some builders are prepared to spend thousands of pounds on professionally trimmed interiors.

The interior might consist of just the dashboard and some simple car seating adapted for use. Rubber mats will suffice for floor covering, and the donor car's handbrake and gearlever gaiters can be reused.

DASHBOARD

Suitable dashboard materials include exterior-grade plywood or MDF (usually covered with vinyl), or aluminium, or textured plastic left uncovered. Adding a layer of thin foam under a vinyl covering gives a 'luxury' padded look and may be helpful in recessing fixtures like instruments.

The construction of a dashboard is a relatively simple job, but you need to take the requirements of the SVA test into account.

The dashboard must have a radiused edge to the bottom of at least 19mm, unless covered with a soft material, in which case the radius must be a minimum of 5mm. An exempt area exists behind the steering wheel and for a band of 127mm outside of the size of the rim. No, I don't know why it's 127mm either!

It's a good idea to get most of your switches in this area if at all possible. Outside this area all fittings must have a minimum radius of 5mm. This rules out the old-fashioned toggle switch, and care must be taken with second-hand instruments as the bezels often fail the test. Recessing them into a padded dashboard, or a recessed area of the dash, solves this problem.

The dashboard is one area where you can show your creativity. Once you've decided which instruments, switches, etc., you wish to use, make a card template of your dashboard and tape it in place on the front of your scuttle. Your aim is to place all the instruments where they can easily be seen from the driver's

▼ **Fig. 11.1** A simple dashboard under construction. Note the radiused lower edge. This is the one used in the prototype car.

seat. I tend to think that less is more with a dashboard. It's easy to get carried away and end up with something that looks like a Jumbo-jet flight deck. A recent development is the 'Bright Six' module (see Fig. 11.3). This useful item takes the place of separate lights for indicators, oil, ignition, brake failure and main-beam warning lights, and is very simple to wire.

Many people on a budget will re-use the instrument cluster from the donor Sierra, with the added advantage that the donor loom will plug straight back into the cluster. The cluster will need to be modified, with the 'wedge'-shaped Perspex and plastic part removed, and replaced by a flat piece of Perspex, see Fig. 11.2.

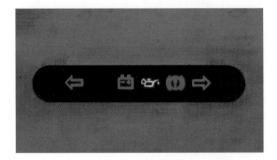

BULKHEAD PANELS

The panels to enclose the bulkheads should be made in two pieces, as shown in Chapter 8, from 1.2mm-thick aluminium. Bend the sheet to the dimensions shown, leaving the vertical leg oversize, and cut out the hole for the steering column. Place the panels in position and mark the curve of the scuttle on the back. Cut carefully to the correct profile.

▲ **Fig. 11.2** This neat installation of the donor car's instrument cluster is fixed in the centre of the dashboard.

◀ **Fig. 11.3** The 'Bright Six' module. This is neat and very easy to install.

◀ **Fig. 11.4** The battery fitted in place with aluminium angle and 6mm threaded steel bar.

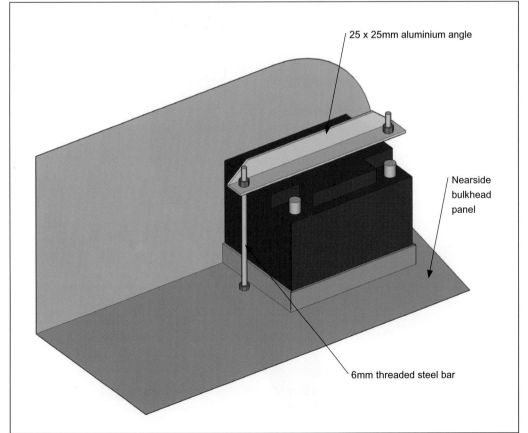

25 x 25mm aluminium angle

Nearside bulkhead panel

6mm threaded steel bar

The joint between the two pieces can be made as shown in Chapter 8, with a piece of aluminium riveted to the driver's side panel to cover the gap, or a step or 'joddle' can be made if you have the facilities. Cut the steering column cover and rivet to the driver's side panel. We had access to a TIG welder, so we welded it without the tags.

The panels should be fixed in place with rivnuts or self-tapping screws. Don't use any sealant on the driver's side panel as it needs to be removable to service the pedal box, etc. You can stick some domestic draught excluder around the mating surfaces of the panel to form a removable seal.

A battery tray should be added to the nearside bulkhead panel as detailed in Chapter 8. Rivet the angle to the panel and drill a 6mm hole either side of the battery tray. When the battery is fitted you will use these holes to fix a length of 6mm steel threaded bar from beneath on to another piece of angle which secures the battery. Use a large washer on the underside and seal the holes with a little sealant.

▼ **Fig. 11.5** A section through a typical cockpit side panel.

INTERIOR TRIM PANELS

The transmission tunnel sides and the forward upper part of the tunnel will need to be panelled in aluminium (see Chapter 8 for diagrams). Cut a card template, mark onto 1.2mm aluminium sheet, cut out and attach with silicon sealant and rivets, or self-tapping screws and brass cup washers if you decide to trim them as detailed below.

Side trim panels can be constructed from aluminium, thin ply or MDF, or textured plastic. Aluminium interior panels, either polished or brushed using a Scotchbright pad, can be made using card templates and fixed using bathroom sealant (to reduce drumming) and self-tapping screws with brass cup washers or rivets, as can textured plastic panels. Textured plastic is polyurethane sheet with a leather-grain finish, available from plastics stockholders.

You can also cover aluminium, ply or MDF panels with vinyl attached with contact adhesive. The vinyl should be folded over the edges of the panels by approximately 20mm, the overlaps should be glued with contact adhesive and can be reinforced with staples on wooden panels,

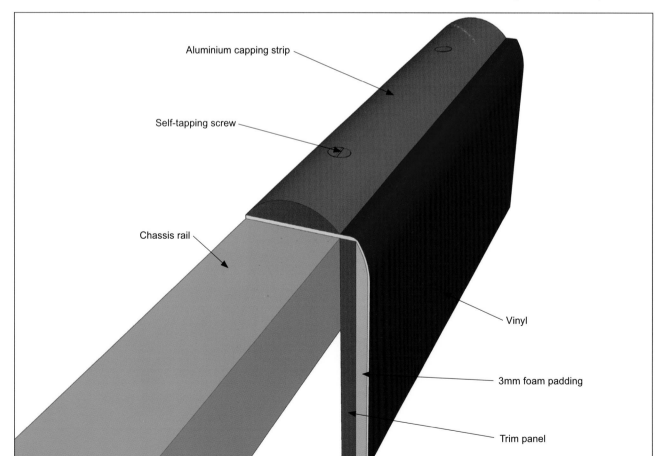

Aluminium capping strip

Self-tapping screw

Chassis rail

Vinyl

3mm foam padding

Trim panel

but make sure they are not so long as to come out of the face side of the panel. If curves are required, nick the overlap around the curve to allow the material to lie flat. Again, a layer of thin foam can be added if required.

Vinyl covered panels should be attached using sealant and self-tapping screws and brass cup washers. The cockpit edges should be covered with aluminium capping strips and, with a little thought, this capping strip can be used to secure the vinyl at the top, obviating the need for screw fixings and making for a neater job (see Fig. 11.5).

It's a good idea to make two panels to enclose the area under the dashboard. This means that these areas, which may have sharp edges, are not tested at the SVA.

FLOOR COVERINGS

Open cars are usually used in dry weather but, with typical unpredictability, that sunny afternoon can soon turn into a downpour. If your car has carpets it can take a long time to dry out, which is why I'd recommend rubber matting, either fixed or removable. It's worth noting that most people drill a couple of holes in the floor just after the first time they get caught in a downpour – the car can fill up with water, believe me!

If you do decide to use carpet, be sure it's designed for automotive use. Nothing looks more unsightly that a sports car with orange swirl-pattern Axminster carpets.

SEATS

The cheapest way to make seats is to follow the practice of special builders of the past and adapt the rear seat from a saloon car. If you can find a seat with a plywood back you can cut the back rest to size with a jig saw, and fold the seat covering around the edges and secure with contact adhesive and staples. If the seat you obtain doesn't have a plywood back, then you will need to make one in the correct shape to fit the seat back area of the car, and fold, glue and staple the edges.

The seat bases can be made in the same way. Fix seat back and bases securely to the car using nuts and bolts.

Small hatchback cars have seats which may be suitable for the Roadster. Take your tape measure and go to the breakers. The Mazda MX-5 has some very usable seats, as does the Suzuki Swift, particularly the GTi. If using seats from a production car, be wary of the height of the seat

▶ **Fig. 11.6** The fabricated seat assembled.

with runners. The base of the seat may be too high for the correct dimension to the harness mountings to be obtained for the SVA test. As a guide, a 136 x 53mm-high distance piece is placed on the seat, the mountings must be at least 450mm above the front uppermost corner of this piece.

I've included illustrations (Figs. 11.6 and 11.7) for a folded metal seat, which can be made in steel or aluminium. Weld the joints in a steel version, or add 15mm to the joining surfaces and rivet if using aluminium. The steel version is obviously heavier than the aluminium. Make a base pad from foam, possibly from a discarded sofa, and cover with vinyl or cloth. This could be the ideal opportunity to get your other half involved. He or she might be a dab hand with the sewing machine! Another pad is made for the back of the seat, and the edges should be covered with flexible edging for the SVA test.

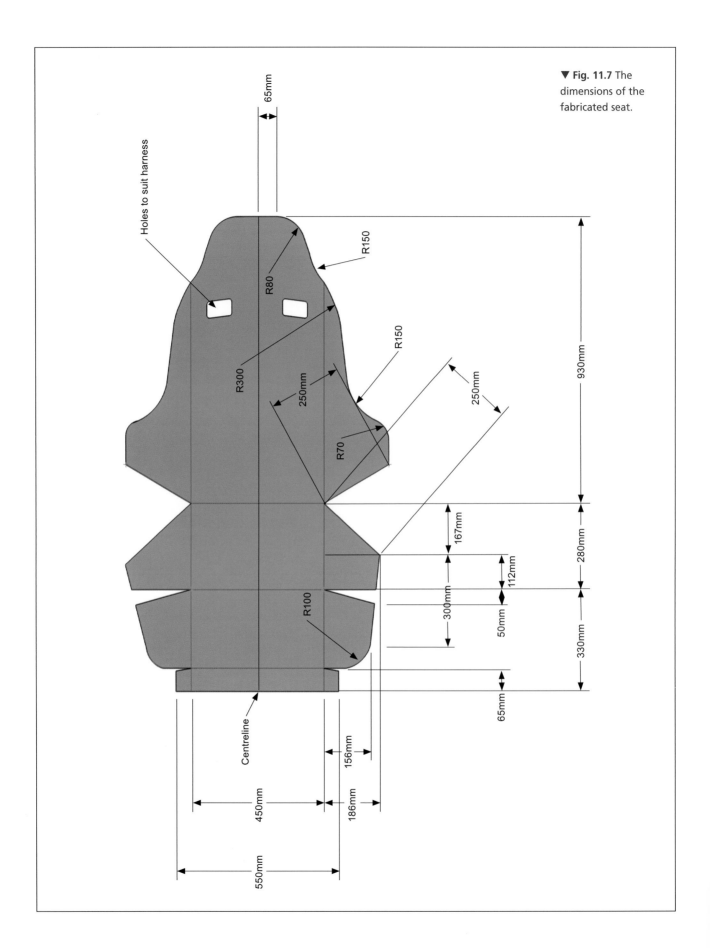

Holes to suit harness

65mm

R150

R80

R300

R150

250mm

250mm

R70

930mm

167mm

280mm

112mm

300mm

50mm

R100

330mm

65mm

Centreline

156mm

450mm

186mm

550mm

▼ **Fig. 11.7** The dimensions of the fabricated seat.

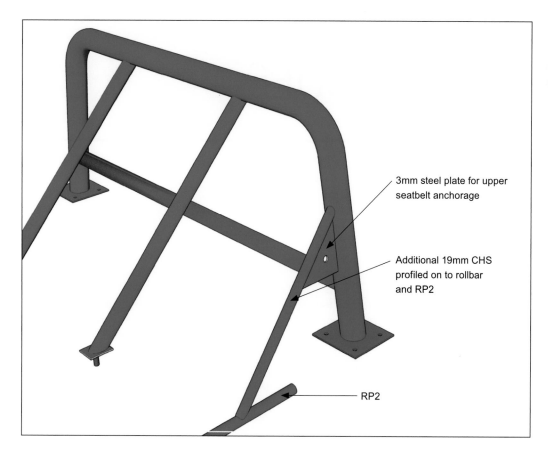

◀ **Fig. 11.8** Modifications required to fit inertia reel seat belt upper mountings.

3mm steel plate for upper seatbelt anchorage

Additional 19mm CHS profiled on to rollbar and RP2

RP2

SEAT BELTS

In the build of this car we have used four-point harnesses. Most people prefer this method of restraint for a sports car. The mountings are detailed in the chassis section. Note that the attachment points on the roll bar may need to be covered if the bolts have a radius which is too sharp for the SVA.

If you wish to use the donor's inertia reel seat belts, the bottom mounts, as detailed, are suitable, but a new upper mount will have to be fabricated on the roll bar (see Fig. 11.8).

GAITERS

As mentioned before, the donor car's handbrake and gear lever gaiters can be reused, or new ones can be made from vinyl. If you're going for the latter, it's a nice touch to make trim rings from 3mm aluminium as shown in Fig. 11.9. Cut the rings using a jig saw and file and sand to shape using progressively finer grades of sandpaper, rounding over the outside edges. Drill and countersink for the fixing screws, then either paint or polish and fit to the tunnel top.

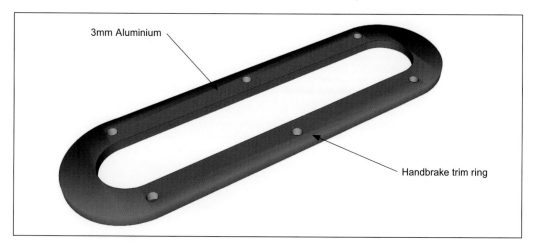

3mm Aluminium

Handbrake trim ring

◀ **Fig. 11.9** Aluminium trim-rings are a tidy way to finish the edges of the gaiters.

12 LEGAL ISSUES

Before you can drive your car legally on the road it must be inspected by a DVLA-appointed engineer to ensure it complies with the Single Vehicle Approval scheme (SVA).

If you were to build your car from all new parts, a current registration number would be issued. This may also apply if you used mainly new components with one or more components that are certified reconditioned to an 'as new' condition.

As we're building to a budget, it's likely that we will use parts from a single donor car or a number of different sources. You may be awarded the donor registration if the major components of your car can be proved to have come from a single car. This is decided on a points system and the magic number is 8, with points given for suspension, steering, etc. Read the leaflet and, if you think your car is eligible, tell the Driver and Vehicle Licensing Agency

▶ **Fig. 12.1** Further details of the SVA test can be found on the VOSA website. *(VOSA)*

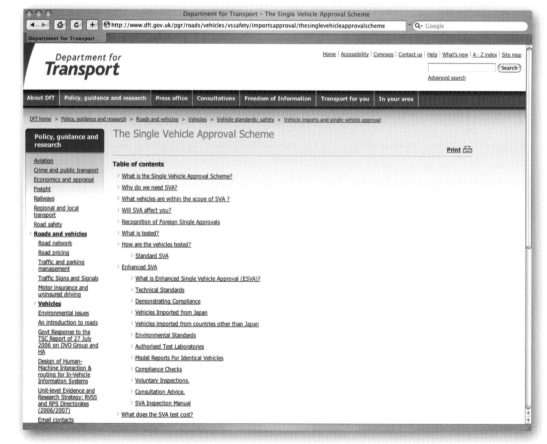

▲ Fig. 12.2 You'll need a trailer or a car transporter to take your car to the SVA test.

(DVLA) when you first apply, via their nearest Vehicle Registration Office (VRO). Their leaflet INF 26 explains the procedure. A full list of VROs is available on the internet at http://www.dvla.gov.uk/local/lo_map.htm

If neither of the above types of registration apply, you will be issued with a 'Q' plate. This indicates a vehicle of indeterminate age. These plates are non-transferable.

Whatever registration you eventually end up with, the procedure is the same. You must apply to the VRO for a chassis number, and the car will be inspected to ensure that the number is permanently marked on the chassis – a riveted plate is not acceptable. The best way to comply with this registration is to use a metal letter punch set to mark a chassis rail. The number must be on the offside of the vehicle. The regulations say that the number should be marked 'in such a way that it cannot be obliterated or deteriorate'.

After the DVLA inspection, it's time to book an SVA test at one of the 24 centres around the country. The locations can be found at http://www.vosa.gov.uk/vosa/carlgvowners/importing andbuildingvehicles/findingansvateststation.htm

There's usually a waiting list at these centres, which varies with the centre. It's probably best to call the station you intend to use and ask how long their waiting time is. This will enable you, ideally, to finish the car just before your SVA test. A few days before the SVA test you should take the car for an MoT test. The car will be tested on the chassis number. The MoT testing station computer may not have a make category to input for your car. At the moment they are using a reference from a similar kit car, but this bug is being worked on by the Vehicle Operator and Standards Agency (VOSA) and might be sorted by the time you take your test. This appointment will also give you a chance to obtain a letter confirming that the chassis number is permanently attached to the chassis. Rectify any faults, if necessary, and remember to take the MoT certificate to the SVA test.

Many people thought that the inception of the SVA test would be the end of 'special' building and a large chunk of the kit car industry. This proved not to be the case, as ways were found to overcome any problems. In fact, what the test has done is to greatly improve the standard of completed cars. The best way to ensure that your car passes the test is to purchase the SVA tester's manual from the vehicle inspectorate. Copies can be ordered, in writing, from VOSA, PO Box 12, Swansea, SA1 1BP. The cost at the time of writing was £30 including postage.

Most of the preparation for the test should focus on the common failure points. These are projections and insecure items.

THE SECTIONS OF THE SVA

The inspection relates to the construction of the vehicle and not the condition. For example, quite bizarrely, completely bald tyres wouldn't necessarily fail if they were the correct type and rating! The test is limited to parts that can be seen without dismantling other than carpet and trim.

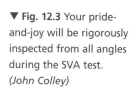

▼ **Fig. 12.3** Your pride-and-joy will be rigorously inspected from all angles during the SVA test. *(John Colley)*

Before the test, the tester will check that the vehicle is testable, ie, it is clean, easily accessible and has a Vehicle Identification Number (VIN) permanently stamped on the chassis.

It's a good idea to take all the documentation and build photos that you have with you to the test, to show things like seat-belt mountings are properly constructed,

and a description for the tester of the car's construction is also useful.

The driver must be present to operate controls, etc. You may be asked about your amateur status. To gain certain exemptions, you must not have a business constructing motor vehicles, and at least a substantial part of the car must have been constructed by an individual for personal use.

■ SECTION 1
ANTI-THEFT DEVICE

Two anti-theft devices must be fitted. This will generally be the ignition lock and one other. Most people go for a battery cut-off switch concealed in the car, or an immobiliser. If you use an immobiliser, take the documentation that comes with it – you may be asked to prove it complies with the regulations.

Whatever device is used, it mustn't operate on the braking system or be a mechanical device which operates on a driving system of the car (e.g. steering) if it is possible to start the car with the device in place. This rules out steering-wheel locks or handbrake/gearlever locks. It must not be possible to engage any mechanical device whilst the engine is running, and the action of any device must be distinct from stopping the engine.

■ SECTION 2
DEFROSTING/DEMISTING

For our purposes, this one's a bit like an ashtray on a motorbike. In an open car, demisting isn't usually a problem. However, if your car has a full windscreen, you will nevertheless have to provide some method of demisting the screen. A wind deflector that your line of vision is normally over the top of does not require demisting. The decision is down to the tester, based on a horizontal plane from the manual. You may decide to fit a heater behind the dashboard with demister vents on the top of the scuttle. Popular ones include those from Rover Minis and Volkswagen Polos because of their size. This decision needs to be taken at an early stage because you will need to fabricate mounts, etc., and leave sufficient space to get the heater in. This could affect the firewall/ bulkhead. Electrically-heated screens are available, at a price, as are small electric fan heaters which are fixed beneath the scuttle. If you don't fit a windscreen at the time of the test, you won't have to worry about this requirement.

■ SECTION 3
WINDSCREEN WASHERS AND WIPERS

As with the demisting requirements, no screen equals nothing to test. If you have wipers they must automatically clear an area sufficient for the driver's view, and they must operate at a minimum of 45 sweeps per minute. The wiper must park, automatically, beyond the outer edge of the swept area or out of the driver's normal vision, and be capable of being lifted for screen cleaning. Washers must have a tank with a minimum capacity of 1 litre and provide sufficient liquid to clear the screen. Washer jets must pass a blockage test.

▲ **Fig. 12.4** On the prototype Roadster the harness mountings are located on the roll bar. *(John Colley)*

▼ **Fig. 12.5** The prototype car was built with minimal interior fittings – the minimum required to pass the SVA test. *(John Colley)*

■ SECTION 4
SEATS AND ANCHORAGES

Seats must be attached to a load bearing part of the vehicle and must lock in all normal positions. Seats fastened only to an aluminium floor would probably fail on this point.

■ SECTION 5
SEAT BELTS

In this book we describe the fitting of harnesses in place of seat belts, so many of the SVA requirements don't apply. If you wish to use inertia reel seat belts, then you will have to ensure that the top anchorage is fitted high enough up on the roll bar, and that space is left for the reel mechanism when choosing seats.

Seat belts must be fitted to all seating positions. Anchorages for all belts must be sufficient in number for the belt fitted, and the anchorage, fixing and surround must be strong enough. All belts must be permanently marked with an acceptable approval marking.

■ SECTION 6
INTERIOR FITTINGS

We don't have many, but make sure that nothing in the interior is sharp or could cause injury. The bottom of the dashboard should be radiused to 19mm, or be padded. Any dials or switches should have a minimum radius of 2.5mm or be recessed into the dash, if beyond a zone centred on the steering wheel and extending 127mm beyond it. The steering wheel itself should have no holes or slots and should have a padded centre, if possible.

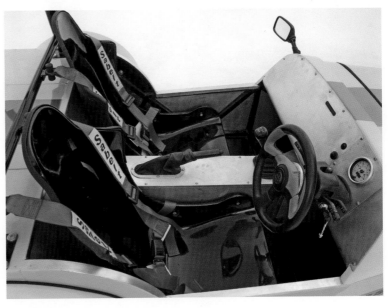

■ SECTION 7
RADIO SUPPRESSION
This isn't for your radio (why would you want one!) but for radio emissions from the vehicle. Suppressed plug leads should be used, mainly because you can't buy any other type anymore!

■ SECTION 8
GLAZING
Just the windscreen usually. The glass must be kite-marked by the manufacturer, not the supplier, to prove that it is safety glass with an approved BS standard. Glass must be secure and give a clear view to the driver.

■ SECTION 9
LIGHTING
The test is similar to the MoT test for lighting – white lights to the front and red to the rear, apart from indicators. All lights must be working, and the fog light must have a tell-tale light that shows when it is on, and a visible or audible warning must be fitted for the indicators. The tester will check that the lights are visible from certain angles around the car. The SVA manual has a drawing showing the statutory light positions. A common failure is the front indicators not being far enough apart. The outside edges of the front indicator lenses have to be 400mm, or less, from the outside of the car (outer edge of the front wings).

▼ **Fig. 12.6** A wide range of aftermarket light units is available. Motorcycle rear indicator lights work well at the front of the Roadster. *(John Colley)*

■ SECTION 10
MIRRORS
This section causes quite a few failures. Two mirrors are required, one on the offside and a central rear view mirror. They must be 'E' marked and be adjustable from the driver's seat. They must also be vibration free and hinge inward on impact. The common failure point is that the mirrors used do not comply with the radius rules on projections, any radius on the mirror, stem or base must be over 2.5mm to comply. Motorcycle mirrors are often used.

■ SECTION 11
TYRES
There are rules regarding the mixing of crossply and radial tyres, which are superfluous. You'd have to contact a specialist to buy crossply tyres these days. The tyres must be of the correct size for the wheel and have the correct speed rating for the stated maximum design speed of the car. The tyres must be 'E' marked and have the following information permanently moulded into the tyre: Nominal size, load capacity, speed capacity and construction type.

■ SECTION 12
DOORS LATCHES AND HINGES
Not too much in this section applies to the Roadster. Any boot cover must be capable of being secured when closed, and the bonnet catches and any boot lock must pass the exterior projections test in Section 13.

■ SECTION 13
EXTERIOR PROJECTIONS
This section is very complicated, but it can be summarised by saying that the car must not have anything that may 'catch on or increase the risk of injury' to anyone who might come into contact with it. The regulations are concerned with projections between the 'floor line' and any fittings up to 2 metres above it. The floor line is determined using a 30°-angled cone, wherever the cone touches the car is the floor line.

The Roadster has a particular problem in that the front suspension is exposed. The various nut heads and bolts can be made to comply by using plastic or rubber covers, but they must appear to the tester to be 'permanent'. In the past it was permitted to use foam pipe lagging, tie-wrapped on, but this isn't acceptable now. You can use split heater hose, fixed with tie-wraps for any area that might be tested. Ensure that the 'buckles' of the tie-wraps are placed at the rear of the component, so that the tie-wrap itself doesn't present a sharp edge. It's a good idea to use a piece of large heater hose to cover the lower portion of the front coil-over shock absorber to 'hide' the collar and the adjustment knob.

Any hard projections in the testable zone (mirrors, for example) must have a minimum radius of 2.5mm. One common failure point to watch is the radius of any grille fitted to the nose cone. There are many more regulations, and I recommend reading the SVA manual to get the full picture.

■ SECTION 14
STEERING
The steering wheel should have spokes with edges of a 2.5 mm minimum radius and have no slots or holes.

The steering column should be of the collapsible type, having two or more offset sections to prevent the column being pushed into the driver in the case of a collision – the manual contains diagrams. The donor Sierra column or the alternative Nova column comply, provided no modification has taken place to the collapsible section.

The steering column mounting and upper bearing must be strong enough to resist movement of the column in an accident, so that the collapsible section works properly.

■ SECTION 15
GENERAL VEHICLE DESIGN AND CONSTRUCTION
The purpose of the test is to ensure that any motor vehicle tested is roadworthy. The car will be very carefully looked over to ensure that it is safe for the occupants and other road users. The structure, the chassis, the steering and the suspension will be inspected to ensure that the components are adequate for their function in all conditions and that they are mounted properly, including the inspection of welding and fasteners. The steering will be checked for fouling of any other component. Sometimes a stop needs to be fitted to ensure that the wheels do not contact the brake flexible pipes on full lock. The foot pedals must be fitted with a non-slip surface. The standard rubber pads from the donor car comply, but the 'go faster' aluminium type may not. Fuel tank caps must be sealed and secure and the fuel lines, tank and connections will be inspected for security and leakage, and that movement of the vehicle will not cause any contact with the components.

▲ Fig. 12.7 The steering wheel must be carefully chosen, bearing in mind SVA requirements. *(John Colley)*

The electrical system is also checked in the same manner. From a practical point of view this means that all fuel lines, wiring or brake pipes must be securely clipped to the chassis at about every 100mm in the transmission tunnel and 250mm elsewhere. If in doubt, put another clip in! The insulation and capacity of the electrical system are also inspected.

■ SECTION 16
BRAKES
The brakes must function on all four wheels and be operated by the driver without removing his hands from the steering wheel. The brake system must be of the dual-circuit type to ensure that the failure of one brake pipe does not mean that you have no brakes. The handbrake must act on two wheels on the same axle, be capable of being applied from the driver's seat and be restrained in the on position. The whole of the braking system will be inspected for security and adequacy of the components for their application.

▲ **Fig. 12.8** Passing the SVA test is the first, and greatest, hurdle on the way to putting your car on the road. *(John Colley)*

▼ **Fig. 12.9** Older engines, such as the Pinto, will not need a catalytic converter, although you may be asked for documentation to prove the age of the donor car. *(John Colley)*

Each brake must be adjustable individually, and the front brakes must adjust automatically. Correctly working disc brakes of the type used on the Roadster are self-adjusting. The fluid reservoir must be transparent with a clearly visible minimum marking, or have a tell-tale light for low fluid level. A way of testing the bulb in the light should be incorporated. Wiring in the handbrake light to the same circuit does this. The light will illuminate when the handbrake is applied. It may be necessary to remove the reservoir cap to prove that the sensor works.

The car will be brake tested as with an MoT test, either on rollers or, as sometimes happens because of the low ground clearance, on a test drive using a decelerometer.

■ **SECTION 17**
NOISE
The car must have an exhaust system complete with silencer. Side exhausts must meet the external projection requirements of Section 13. The noise level of the car is tested with a decibel meter at 45° to the outlet at a distance of 0.5 metres in a horizontal plane. The limit at the time of writing was 101dba.

■ **SECTION 18**
EMISSIONS
The test is dependent on the age of the engine. Newer engines will require a catalytic converter. If you have it, some documentation about the build date of the engine may be useful. The log book of the donor car may be accepted, or the information might be available through the manufacturer of the engine. The limits are similar to the MoT test.

■ **SECTION 19**
SPEEDOMETER
A working speedometer must be fitted, and illuminated at night. If the speedometer is from the donor vehicle, along with the same drivetrain and wheel-tyre combination, then the speedometer should be accurate. Any changes will require the speedometer to be recalibrated. Speedometers cannot under-read but may over-read by 10%.

DESIGN WEIGHTS

Also a frequent cause of failure. The maximum permitted axle weights and the maximum gross weight are entered onto the form before the test. Guidance on suitable weights may be obtained from other builders or the club. However, the tester may allow you to alter the form to comply with the weights he's measured. As a guide, my car was rated at 450kg front axle and 450kg rear axle, for a total of 900kg. Note that this is the design weight not the actual weight. At the SVA my car weighed just under 750kg with the driver.

AFTER THE SVA TEST

When the test is over you'll either be given a sheet listing the failure points or a Minister's Approval Certificate (MAC). If the car fails, you'll have to make the necessary adjustments or repairs and have the car re-tested, unless the failure points are easily (and quickly) remedied at the testing station. The tester might allow you some time to rectify the problems and have another look. They aren't obliged to, so it pays to be civil to the testers. With this in mind, take along tools and spares that you think you might need. We had a steering column with a broken steering column lock which we didn't know about. The tester allowed us to change it for a spare we had in the van while he 'went for a cup of tea'. The spanners were flying, I can tell you!

Once the test is passed, the next step is to send the MAC along with your insurance details, a form for vehicle registration and a chassis number certificate plus a cheque for the road fund duty, to the VRO that issued your chassis number. If you want a new registration or the donor registration, then you'll have to include bills and receipts to prove your claim. They will issue you with a tax disc and a registration number, and the log book (registration document) will be issued by the DVLA in two to three weeks. Have number plates made up – you'll need the log book and another form of identification to get them done – fix them to the car in the appropriate position and that's it, you've done it!

THE IVA IS COMING

At some point during 2009 or 2010 the SVA test will be replaced by the IVA test.

IVA (which stands for Individual Vehicle Approval) is a new standard which will be used to bring the UK in line with the rest of Europe, via the Recast Framework Directive 2007/46EC.

Broadly speaking the IVA will be very similar to the current SVA test, with a few additions. Some of the main differences are listed below:

- Switches and driver information systems will need to be labelled for easy identification.
- A horn must be fitted and working (it's quite surprising that this wasn't a requirement before!)
- The chassis (VIN) number must be stamped on the chassis *and* a plate.
- There will be a check that head restraints or high-back seats are fitted.
- The tester will ensure that sufficient space has been left for a rear number plate of a standard size.
- A working reverse gear or similar device must be fitted.

I don't think the IVA will be much more difficult to pass than the SVA test, as well-prepared cars should have all the necessary items already fitted.

For up-to-date information consult the Roadster forum at: http://www.haynes.co.uk/forums/index.php

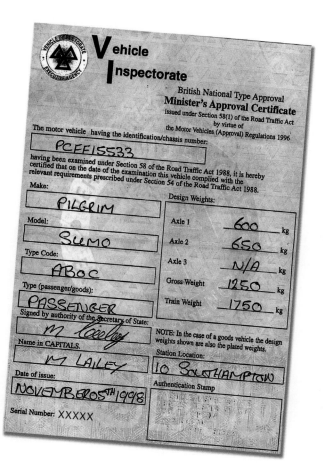

▼ Fig. 12.10 A Minister's Approval Certificate (MAC). (Kit Car *Magazine*)

13 WHAT'S NEXT?

With the car built and ready for the road, what uses can we put it to? In this chapter we'll investigate some of the alternatives available to enhance your enjoyment of your new Roadster. Personally, I love just cruising around on a summer evening, sometimes with my wife, sometimes in convoy with other owners. The cars attract attention wherever we go – people seem to be interested in how the cars are built and how fast they are!

▼ **Fig. 13.1** An LCC gathering at one of the major kit car shows.

THE LOCOST CAR CLUB

The Locost Car Club (LCC) is one of the largest specialist car clubs in the UK, with 800 members from all over the country and abroad, including Australia, America and Scandinavia.

The LCC will welcome new members building Roadsters, and the help and support available is invaluable. The club organises 20 or so local meetings throughout the UK each month, where members can meet, discuss their

builds and have a general chin-wag. The club
has a presence at all the major kit car shows
in the country and an annual gathering at the
Stoneleigh kit car show at the beginning of May.
There's also an annual pilgrimage to the 24-Hour
race at Le Mans in France.

The club is very friendly and informal, with
most members agreeing to have their contact
details passed to other members in their area so
they can help new builders. We've had quite a
few 'engine fitting parties' and the like. Quite a
lot of us who have completed cars still have the
itch to build things, and are more than willing
to help out.

Information on joining the club is available
from The Locost Car Club, c/o 31 Campion Drive,
Swinton, Rotherham S64 8QZ. Or see the Club
website at www.locostcarclub.co.uk.

TOURING

One of the great pleasures in owning this
type of car is in touring, especially abroad. As
I mentioned before, we take an annual trip to
La Sarthe for the Le Mans 24-Hour race. The
interest the cars attract is amazing. The French in
particular are fascinated. It's virtually impossible
to register any kind of special or kit car in France.

These days we take a 'support vehicle' with
us (usually some sort of people carrier) to carry
all the tents and luggage. After all, any fool
can be uncomfortable, but in the past we've
done the trip in three Locosts with six people.
Obviously this calls for a little creative packing.
If you're travelling alone, most of the stuff will
fit into the passenger seat and footwell. When
you're carrying a passenger it's possible to take
everything you need – on the rear of the car.
The tent goes on first, followed by a large holdall
each, all held on with strategically placed elastic
bungee straps. Your sleeping bag becomes extra
thigh support when you put it in front of your
seat. Keep travel documents and cash in a small
bag in the cockpit, there's nothing worse than
arriving at a ferry and realising that your passport
is at the bottom of your carefully packed holdall!

If possible, take a spare gallon of fuel in one
of the cars and a tow rope in one of the others,
along with an emergency triangle and spare
bulb kit. If you have room, a few spares can be
carried. I'd suggest a clutch and accelerator cable,
fuses and relays, a length of electrical wire and
some tools to fit them.

If you've never travelled in the country you're
visiting, find out the country's rules of the road.

▲ **Fig. 13.3** You can get close to the action at Le Mans. Here, mechanics prepare the 2006 Lister Storm.

Wherever you go, stick to the speed limits – not many countries have as many speed cameras as there are in the UK, but what they do have are policemen with guns. Worth thinking about, eh?

TRACK DAYS

The explosion in the track day scene is in part due to the proliferation of speed cameras, nose-to-tail traffic and the ever present roadworks on our roads. If you have a passion for driving rather than seeing the car as 'transport', then track days are for you. On a track day you can drive as fast as you like, explore the handling of your car and, in the process, become a better driver.

No special licence is required for track days, but you'll need a helmet – some organisers insist on a full face helmet, particularly in open cars. Arrive early for the day so that you don't miss the driver briefing. This talk is usually given by the organisers, it covers the rules of the day regarding safety, track times (some events are run in sessions for different types of car), passing etiquette, any special track conditions and the meanings of the various flags used by the marshals. Listen carefully and take heed. Anyone

breaking the rules will be 'black flagged', i.e. removed from the track. This might be for a telling off or, in serious cases, you may be asked to leave. One thing that is not allowed is racing. This may sound strange, but all forms of racing or time-keeping are forbidden. You may not block a faster car or try to overtake irresponsibly. You will be told at the driver briefing what to do if a faster car approaches from behind – usually which side the faster car should pass. It's good practice to raise your hand on that side to indicate to the other driver that you have seen him and are letting him past. It's worth noting that your road insurance probably won't cover you for track day use, so you should extend your cover or take out a specific track day policy.

The organisers arrange medical cover and marshalling, and usually there are catering facilities and toilets. Many organisers provide qualified instructors for hire to clients at a reasonable cost. I would suggest, if you can afford it, that you take advantage of this service at your first track day – you'll learn more in that session than in many hours of circulating on your own.

Preparing for a track day begins with routine maintenance of the car. You don't want to spend time in the paddock bleeding brakes or topping up the oil when you should be out enjoying yourself. Check all fluids and tyre pressures before you get to the track. Many drivers will stiffen the suspension prior to a track day, and some even fit stiffer springs or a front anti-roll bar. If you are going to use your car for track days regularly it's probably a good idea to upgrade the braking system. Repeated heavy braking can cause a disconcerting condition called brake fade when using standard brake components, leaving you with decreasing braking efficiency.

Only when you're satisfied that the suspension and brakes are in order should you consider increasing the power of the engine. Believe it or not, good brakes will improve your lap times more than a slight increase in power. It may be worth considering an external electrical cut-off switch (with the appropriate sticker) and a fire extinguisher if you do a lot of track work. Remember that any modifications you make to your car for a track day may adversely affect it's on-road performance.

When the time comes to enter the track, you will be held at the entrance either by a red light or a marshal. You'll be released when a gap in the traffic appears. At least for the first few laps, try to stay in this gap, don't try to catch cars in front, and do let faster cars past. This will allow you some space to get used to the track conditions and provide some breathing room should you make a mistake on cold tyres.

Driving techniques are outside the limits of this book, but a vast array of information is available on the internet and in print on the theory of going fast. Study before you go so that you've got the basics, but there's no substitute for getting out there and doing it. Remember that you are not racing – aggressive or bullying driving will be dealt with very severely. The pride and satisfaction in driving a lap well is immense, but doing it all safely is more important. Look out for and respond to any flags or signals given by the marshals and be ready to stop or leave the circuit if an incident occurs.

When you feel like a break, or the session ends, approach the exit and slow down with the appropriate indicator flashing. Make sure you're going slowly enough to deal with any bends in your path, as exits often curve away from the track for safety reasons. After your well-earned cuppa, check the fluid levels and tyre pressures, and do a visual check of the suspension before you return to the track.

▼ Fig. 13.4 Track days put the fun back into driving, and also improve your driving. *(Tony Sissons, Fullframe Photography)*

SPRINTS AND HILLCLIMBS

The next stage up the ladder would be to compete in sprints or hillclimbs. The basic difference between a sprint and a hillclimb is that sprints are on flat courses (usually racing circuits, but occasionally public roads), and hillclimbs are up hills. You're not competing directly against other people but against the clock. Each competitor has two attempts to drive the course alone, the winner being the competitor with the fastest time.

Because there are no other competitors on the course at the same time there is no chance of hitting anyone else, but because sprints and, in particular, hillclimbs are held on ordinary roads there are no run off areas or Armco barriers. The potential for hitting something solid like a tree is greatly increased.

It's a real joy to walk around the paddock at one of these events. The sheer diversity of cars is astounding. You'll find everything from a standard 850cc Mini to an ex-Formula One car. Many types of vehicle compete, in classes based on engine capacity.

The days usually consist of morning practice sessions, usually one or two, followed by timed runs, usually two. You will need an approved helmet, fireproof clothing and a fire extinguisher; and your car will be scrutinised prior to the race. You'll also need an MSA 'speed' licence. See Appendix 2 for contact details for the MSA, the Hillclimb and Sprint Association and the British Motor Sprint Association.

▲ **Fig. 13.5** The prototype Roadster in action on the track. *(Lee Parsons)*

▼ **Fig. 13.6** Hillclimbs and sprints are held throughout the country. *(Tony Sissons, Fullframe Photography)*

AUTOTESTING

If you've ever seen those car stunt shows where cars are slid into impossibly small spaces or turned around in the length of the car, then you've witnessed the skills involved in autotesting. The aim, as ever, is to get through the course in the quickest time. The courses are usually flat tarmac – anything from airport taxiways to supermarket car parks. The course is set out using traffic cones, painted lines or markers to form any combination of slaloms, tight turns, confined spaces and anything else the devious organisers can think of to test the manoeuvrability of the car, both forwards and in reverse! Any mistakes, such as striking a cone or crossing a line, incur a time penalty added to your total time at the end. The winner is decided by aggregate over a number of tests during the day. You'll need an MSA speed licence for this as well.

Autotesting is very hard on a car. The constant accelerating, braking, twisting and turning puts great strain on the tyres, suspension, gearbox, engine and brakes. The handbrake is particularly hard worked as it's used almost constantly during cornering.

Autotesting is immensely popular because it's inexpensive and great fun. Some would say it's the epitome of car control.

CIRCUIT RACING

The Roadster will be eligible for many classes, depending on the engine fitted, in the 750 Motor Club racing series.

The Locost has it's own 750MC racing series – one of the most successful series they run. Full grids and close racing make it a great spectacle. Again, it's an inexpensive way to get into the sport. The 750MC intend to run a series for Haynes Roadsters when the specifications are finalised.

You'll need to organise an MSA Class B licence and complete an ARDS (Association of Racing Drivers Schools) course. These courses are run at most of the motor racing circuits. You'll also have to have a medical with your local GP, and when this is done you must return the forms to the MSA along with the appropriate fee.

The personal equipment required includes flame-resistant overalls, gloves, balaclava, socks and underwear. An MSA-approved helmet is also required.

Car preparation is a vast subject and reference should be made to the MSA Blue Book and any supplementary race series information. In short the car needs to meet the regulations on the following:

- **Full roll cage of the correct specification**
- **Fuel tank caps, vents and security**
- **Rear warning lights**
- **Fire extinguisher**
- **Seat harnesses**
- **Head restraint**
- **Electrical cut-off switch**
- **Oil catch tank**
- **Front and rear towing eyes**
- **Exhaust noise and security**
- **Tyre type and condition**

If you intend to race your car, it's a good idea to go along and talk to other competitors in the series you'll race in. They might not let you into any trade secrets, but you'll see how things are done.

▲ **Fig. 13.7** The 750 Motor Club organises grass roots racing in many categories. This is their popular Locost race series. *(Tony Sissons, Fullframe Photography)*

THE EXPERTS

HOOD AND SIDE SCREEN CONSTRUCTION

BY DEREK MANDERS

Derek designed and made a hood and sidescreens for his Locost, but the principles involved apply equally to the Haynes Roadster.

▼ Fig. 14.1 Derek and his car at the Stoneleigh kit car show.

The best modification I've made to my car has to be the side screens and hood. The side screens alone have completely transformed it, and in the years since fitting them I've not driven the car without them on. They make for a much more civilised ride, especially on days when the weather is a bit windy.

Having a hood meant that I would need a windscreen demister or even a full heating system, but as the car was built without a heater in mind, there was nowhere to fit one. So I moved the battery and relocated the fusebox to create a suitable area under the bonnet in front of the scuttle immediately above the transmission tunnel. Even so, the only way I could think of getting a heater to fit in the space available was to make one, so I did, using the original matrix and motor from my Mk II Escort donor car – a bit crude but it works a treat.

If you are about to start to build a car of your own I would strongly recommend that you give very serious thought to fitting a heater at the planning stage of your project. If you are building a car for UK use with a full windscreen, you will have to have a demister of some sort anyway, for the SVA test.

Whilst I was building my original Locost car, my friend and colleague Alan Horton was doing the same, and so we tackled the design of a hood and side screens together, basing the final style on the conventional Caterham type.

Fortunately, when both of us built our cars (make note of these points, it may well save you some extra work at a later date) we mounted the rear wings well down the side of the car, leaving a good lip between the top of the

wings and the top of the curved rear wing support. This is needed for the hood-retaining fasteners and for the side screens to butt up to. We also reinforced the top of the windscreen channel with an aluminium insert, which was needed for hood-retaining fastener screws. My original screen support brackets were neither strong enough nor big enough to support the hinges for the side screens, so new ones had to be made. For this I used 3mm thick stainless steel sheet.

▲ **Fig. 14.2** Hood frame, with string stretched over it to show clearance of roll bar. Also, the forward and rearward kinks in the frame uprights are clearly visible.

▼ **Fig. 14.3** Aluminium frame material showing insert strip and Tenax fastener from the end.

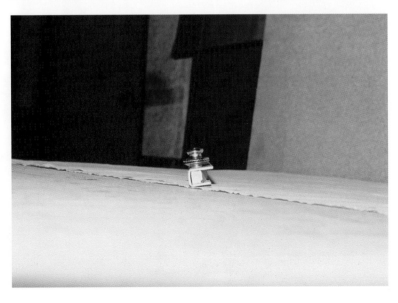

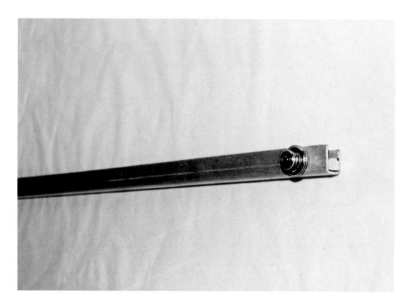

straight edge from the top of the screen to
the top of the roll bar, which had already been
positioned to give me the required headroom.
One thing to watch is that, where the top of
the side screen is to meet the hood, it should be
on the vertical and not on the curvature of the
side of the hood. Also make sure that the height
of the rear of them is sufficient to give you
headroom for easy access. Not that access with a
hood on is very easy at the best of times!

As I liked the elbow bulges in the Caterham
side screens, and felt I needed the extra elbow
room, I made some bulges out of 20 gauge
aluminium and riveted these to the frames,
smoothing out the lips and joints with filler.
Because this made the screens heavier, I used
an extra hinge bracket on the top hinge, with a
removable stainless steel pin passing through all
three brackets (hinges used are Caterham).

Just as I was finishing the side screen frames,
a work colleague pointed me in the direction of a
local man who specialised in making hoods and
canopies for boats ranging from little tenders
to ocean-going racing yachts. Not the sort
of business you'd immediately associate with
rural Lincolnshire, but I thought if he can make
waterproof canopies for such a variety of boats,

I was fortunate in having been given a pair of
old Lotus 7 side screens – the type with lift-up
flaps to enable the driver to use hand signals.
These were offered up to the car and found
to be too short. So a new pair of frames were
fabricated out of mild steel strip and sheet,
similar to the Lotus screens but a bit bigger to
suit my needs. To ensure that I got the right
angle and position for the top edge, I put a

◀ **Fig. 14.6** Side screen showing filler to smooth out joint and rivets, etc. Also painted before being covered.

▼ **Fig. 14.7** Side screen fitted to the car showing flap tucked inside screen support. Note flap at the back which eliminates draught coming in at the back edge – it's also useful as something to grab hold of when opening the side screen. Also clearly shown is the position of the zip which enables the window to be opened.

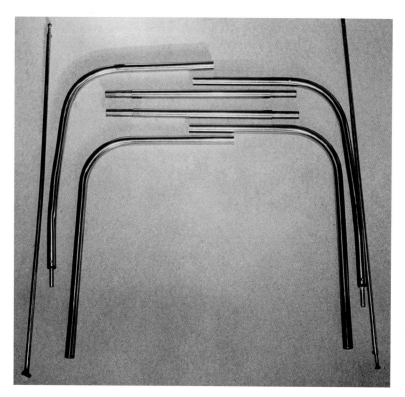

▼ **Fig. 14.9** Above, the
spigot (bottom) end of
one of the front hood-
frame loops. Below, the
inverted U on the end
of the long screen-to-
front-loop support.

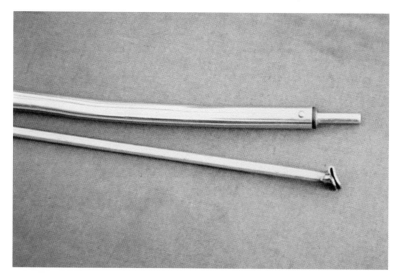

then a car hood should be child's play to him.
So contact was made and a deal struck (a very
good deal I might add). He would make a hood
to suit the frame that I would make myself, and
he would cover the side screen frames that I had
already made.

To enable me to see out if the side windows
suffered from condensation with the hood on,
he would fit a single zip along the top and down
the back edge of the window. This would allow
the back top corner of the window to be bent
down, offering a clear view at road junctions,
etc. This has proved to be a very useful bit of

forethought, as condensation is quite a problem
in cool damp weather with the hood fitted.

Back to the hood frame. This was made,
out of 19mm stainless steel shower-rail tube. It
consists of two loops, one front and one rear,
each made in three pieces to enable easy storage
in the boot, and two long 8mm stainless steel
tubes to act as supports between the front loop
and the top of the windscreen frame. Whilst
making Alan's frame we both decided that we
ought to try to give some support to the top
of the screen frame when the hood is fitted, as
we felt that there would be pressure on it, and
therefore strain on the glass screen. This fear
proved to be well founded.

Another thing to be aware of is that the hood
shrinks when it is cold, so if it is made in the
summer or in a nice warm workshop and you
want to fit it to the car in the winter you may
well struggle to get the press studs on. Also
allow for shrinking when making it, because
when it does shrink it puts the windscreen under
considerable pressure. But do not make it too
loose-fitting because, especially in warm weather,
the buffeting from the wind will cause it to flap
about and vibrate in the frame loops.

The height of the front loops was decided by
the amount of headroom required, which the
roll bar had already been tailored for. So the
front hoop was bent to give enough clearance to
prevent the hood from chafing on the roll bar.

The two side pieces were bent individually,
and a piece of spacer tube was cut to an
appropriate length to separate them. To form
the spigot joint for this piece, I took two lengths
of the same tube and cut them lengthways,
then squeezed them up until they were a snug
fit inside the spacer tube. I then drilled a couple
of holes in each end of the spacer tube, pushed
the spigots halfway in and spot-welded them in
through the holes.

The front loop is mounted to the car by
having a short length of stainless steel 10mm
internal diameter tube welded in the appropriate
places to chassis sections D7 and D8. These
pieces of tube then pass through the top of
the curved rear wing support SS1, with the
aluminium cover strip having a 10mm hole in it
for the loop mounting spigot to pass through.

The ideal way to get these holes to line up is
to fit the cover strip to the completed car, drill
a pilot hole through the cover strip and the top
of the curved rear wing support, remove the
cover strip and open the hole out in the curved

support to the outside diameter of the tube to be used, then open the hole out in the cover strip to 10mm to accommodate the spigot.

When positioning the two side pieces of the loop, I made sure that they were on the same vertical line as the windscreen-mounting pillars, otherwise the side screens would need to be made with a bend in them to compensate. The spigots on the bottom of the frame loops were turned down out of stainless steel bar (ensuring an interference fit in the loop tube). These spigots were secured with the aid of a blind rivet.

As you will see from the photos, these loops are bent forward. This is because of a miscalculation in the positioning of the aforementioned locating tubes. Without the forward kink they were positioned too far back. The rear ones are also bent, but this time backwards, due to yet another miscalculation. Well they do say, "He who has never dropped one has never done nowt."

The back loop is made in a similar way to the front (in three pieces), but this time, to get the position and height of it, I used a piece of string which I pulled tightly from the top edge of the windscreen frame over the front loop, over the back loop, and down to the back edge of the boot. By moving the back loop about I could position it where I thought it looked best and where it would prevent the hood from chafing on the roll bar.

Once the position was decided on, suitable fixing points were made out of tube that the loop would fit into. These were attached with the aid of some small brackets to the inner edge of the boot top rail (RP2). The back loop then pushes into these two fixing points.

Now we move back to the front and to the supports for the screen frame to hood loop.

Two lengths of 8mm stainless steel tube were cut just long enough to fit between the screen frame top edge and the front hood frame loop. One end of these tubes (the loop end) has a 6mm bolt fastened in with the aid of Loctite, the other end has a thin piece of stainless steel welded onto it and bent over to form an inverted U-shape.

▼ **Fig. 14.10** View from the rear of the car showing that the vertical on the front hood loop matches the vertical on the screen frame.

▲ **Fig. 14.11** Back loop fixing point and rear window unzipped.

This inverted U fits into a small bracket which is bolted/screwed onto the top edge of the screen frame, just in board from where the top corner curve ends. The 6mm bolt on the other end passes through an appropriately drilled hole in the front frame loop.

There we have it; hood and side screen frames, made and ready for the hood.

▶ **Fig. 14.12** One of the brackets used to attach the long screen-frame to front-hood-frame loop to the screen frame. The cutaway is not necessary – this I did for the unsuccessful Mk1 version, and I didn't need to alter it for the current Mk2 version.

After a discussion with hoodmaker Chris Potts about the different types of fastener available, we decided to use Tenax ones. These are what he uses on boat canopies. They consist of a male stud which fastens to the car body or screen frame with a nut, just like a nut and bolt (they are also available with self-tapping threads), and a very neat spring-loaded press stud which is fastened to the hood. This just pushes onto the stud with the spring holding it firmly in place. To remove it you just pull the little knob on the top of the press stud which releases the spring and it's off. Quite brilliant, and very neat.

As I didn't make the hood myself, I'm unable to describe the manufacturing process, but I will try to give you some pointers to make life easier for you should you decide to make your own.

Starting with the side screens. They are covered in the same material as used for the hood, and it looks like the inner and outer skin have been cut out to the required shape before being sewn up separately, then sewn together trapping the metal frame, plastic window, and zip fastener between the two skins. Up the front edge (the edge to which the hinges are attached), along the top and down the back of the side screen (to where it meets the rear wing) there is a lip of about 30mm of double thickness material with a square

◀ **Fig. 14.13** Opening rear window of hood, also rear frame loop mounting point.

section cut out where the front edge and top edge meet, and a small 'V' cut in the outer edge of the top rear curve. This 'V' is to make it easier to tuck the soft lip of the screen frame into the pocket which is formed along the top inner edge of the hood, and to tuck the soft lip down the back edge inside the hood for a reasonably draughtproof seal.

The square section cut out at the front is again to enable the lip to be tucked under the pocket in the hood and – also to allow the side screen to be opened easily when the lip up the front edge is tucked behind the screen support to which the hinges are mounted. Tucking this lip inside the screen support is another weatherproofing feature.

▼ **Fig. 14.14** The inside of the nearside side-screen. The elastic and press-stud fasteners which hold them shut from the inside can be seen.

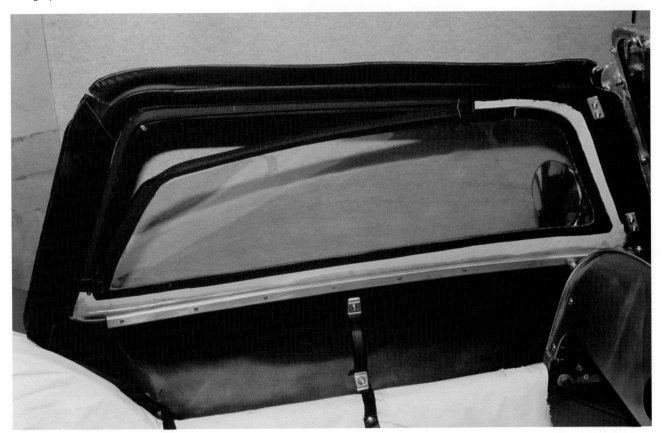

▶ **Fig. 14.15** Felt-lined rubber tube on top edge of screen, strip on top inside edge of screen aperture, and 8mm screen-to-front-loop support.

▼ **Fig. 14.16** Showing the weatherproof seal sewn on outside of rear window, along with the zip-fastener for the fold-down rear window.

As the lip on the back of the side screen is tucked inside the hood it leaves a forward-facing loose edge on the hood, just right for wind and rain to find its way in. To prevent this, a quite large flap which covers the opening is sewn to the outside of the side screen, thus eliminating the forward-facing loose edge. This flap is also useful to pull on when opening the side screen from the outside.

Now to the hood. The top and sides appear to be made of three separate pieces, with various tucks, cuts and stitches in the appropriate places to get the required shape. The front edge, with the Tenax fasteners that attach the hood to the top of the screen frame, is a separate unjointed piece of double thickness hood material which runs the full width of the hood and is cut to the shape of the screen frame. It has a length of felt-lined rubber tube sown along the seam which acts as a draught seal along the top of the screen on the top only. It does not go beyond the curve in the screen frame.

The bottom edges where the Tenax fasteners are fixed, for fastening the hood round the back of the boot/luggage area, are also double thickness, as are the edges of the rear corner windows.

The clear plastic rear window is sandwiched between two pieces of hood material to form a frame appropriate to the shape of the hole in the back of the hood but a bit bigger. This has a zip fastener running from the bottom of one side, over the top and down the other side of the frame. When the window is sewn into the hood (from the inside) the zip is just inside the inner edge of the hole in the back of the hood.

The bottom edge of the frame is attached along the bottom of the back of the hood, just above the rear Tenax fasteners.

To make a weatherproof seal round the side and top of the window, another piece of hood material is cut to the shape of the window and sown on the outside, round the top and sides of the rear window so that it overlaps the clear plastic by about 20mm.

A very important area to give a bit of thought to is round the edges of the side screen aperture. The top inside edge has a strip sown in to form a pocket that is long enough to reach from past the outer edge of the back of the aperture to the inside edge of the screen frame and behind the screen support bracket. This piece protrudes below

the bottom edge of the aperture by about 20mm. The soft, top edge of the side screen tucks in between these two pieces. On the outside, another piece of doubled-up hood material is cut to the same shape as the aperture, running from the very front to the bottom of the back edge. This is sewn along the bottom edge of the aperture so that it forms a V-shape, which acts as a gutter.

The fasteners for the side screens are nice and simple – a doubled-up piece of strong elastic fastened to the side screens, with a press stud on the other end which clips onto the inside of the car. Two are used on each screen, one in the back lower corner and one halfway along the bottom edge. Although these look feeble, they are quite capable of holding the side screens shut without the hood on at speed.

Originally the rearview/side mirrors were mounted on the windscreen support brackets. These had to be refitted onto the side screens because the side screens wouldn't open far enough and I couldn't see them because of the front edge of the side screens.

No problem now, and they don't suffer from vibration as I thought they might.

▲ **Fig. 14.17** Front edge of gutter round side screen and two Tenax fasteners which attach to studs on the front face of the screen frame.

WELDING PRACTICES
BY MARTIN KEENAN

EQUIPMENT

Welding using a MIG welder isn't too difficult. Most people find that – once they have overcome the initial anxiety (usually people are worried by the flashes and sparks) and become comfortable with the process – after a few hours tuition they become reasonably competent welders. Further practice will increase your experience and skill.

Obviously, the first requirement is welding equipment, and I'd recommend at least a 150amp welder. Welding sets with less power than this may not be powerful enough to produce welds of sufficient strength for the chassis. Pick a welder with a proper wire feed motor, like the one illustrated in Fig. 14.19.

You'll also need good safety equipment. A welding mask or helmet and sturdy gauntlets are essential, and all areas of skin should be fully covered. Failure to wear eye protection will lead to 'arc eye', a condition not unlike having grit rubbed into your eyeballs – ask anyone who's had it – it's not pleasant. Make sure all combustible material is removed from the area where you are going to weld, and keep a fire extinguisher close by.

Preparation is important when MIG welding. Any oil on new steel should be wiped off, and any surface rust must be removed. Grinding a slight angle on the pieces to be joined aids penetration. All the tubes and plates in our chassis will require the use of 0.8mm welding wire. Be sure to match your contact tube, torch liner, and drive rolls to the wire size you are using. Refer to the machine recommendations for the welding capacity of your set.

Hold the torch at an angle of 60° to 70° with the tip 5–10mm from the work piece. Keep the

▼ **Fig. 14.18** MIG welding is the easiest way to assemble the spaceframe chassis.

◀ **Fig. 14.19** A typical good quality MIG welding wire feed system.

torch liner as straight as possible when welding, to avoid poor wire feeding. Where possible use both hands to steady the gun and, for best control of your weld bead, keep the wire directed at the leading edge of the weld pool.

When welding out of position (vertical, horizontal, or overhead welding), keep the weld pool small for best weld bead control, and use the smallest wire diameter size you can.

It's important to clean the torch liner and drive rolls occasionally, and keep the gun nozzle clean of spatter. Replace the contact tip if blocked or feeding poorly. Don't try to clean the tips, it rarely works and the tips are not expensive. Keep the wire feeder hub tension and drive roll pressure just tight enough to feed wire, but don't overtighten. Also, to avoid picking up contaminants that may lead to poor welds, try to keep MIG wire in a clean, dry place when not welding.

Fig. 14.20 shows my 11-year-old daughter Clarice having some practice at fillet welding. She loves it and comes in to play with the welder whenever she can. If she can produce good, strong welds (and she can) I'm sure it's not beyond you!

◀ **Fig. 14.20** Clarice loves to practise her welding!

PAINTWORK
BY TONY SKELDING OF BODICRAFT

The whole topic of automotive paintwork and preparation can be divided up into three areas: preparation, paint application, and final polishing.

PREPARATION
This is the most important part of any good paint job. Good preparation will ensure better results when the last coats of paint are being applied.

First, we need to look at the types of materials we want to paint. The three most likely are mild steel, aluminium, and glassfibre.

■ MILD STEEL
For many of us, the most common use of mild steel will be for our chassis. The tube used will come with a film of oil applied to the surface to keep corrosion at bay. The oil must be completely removed before any paint can be applied to the surface. A cloth soaked with panel wipe, thinners or white spirit should be used to remove the oil. Then wipe off any remaining residue with a clean dry cloth. It's also a good idea to give the bare metal a light rub over with a fine abrasive – something like a 320-grit sanding pad. This will give the surface a good key for the paint to stick to.

It may be worth mentioning at this stage that a good addition to any painter's tool kit would be a random orbital sander or a DA (dual action) sander – either air-powered or electric. It can save a lot of time and effort. Air-powered DAs are generally the cheapest option, but you will need an air-compressor to run it. Machine Mart or Sealey are a good starting point, or try your local paint refinishing suppliers.

Back to the preparation of steelwork. Well, that's about it for chassis work, but if you have any mild steel panel work you may have to make some localised repairs to welding and grinding marks or small dents. Some dents can be knocked out with a hammer and dolly, but in many cases a layer of body filler is the only solution. U-pol make a good range of body fillers for all types of materials. You'll find them at any car spares shop, or your local refinishing suppliers.

▼ **Fig. 14.21** Tony in his Cosworth turbo-powered car.

As with the chassis, first remove any oil residues, then lightly sand with a 180-grit pad. Blow or brush off any dust and apply a thin layer (12mm max) of body filler to the damaged area. Remember to fill the whole area, plus about 50mm all round onto the good metal. Many people try to get away with just filling the damaged area, but this doesn't work. I know, I've learnt the hard way! Don't try to fill the dent in one go, either. Apply multiple layers to get a smooth, flat, and level finish. Remember, good preparation is vital.

Once the first layer has dried hard, sand it down with a reasonably rough pad (80-grit) to achieve the correct shape and level. You'll probably take too much off at some point, but it doesn't matter. Just mix up some more and have another go. When sanding, don't press too hard, and try to keep the sander/sanding block level. Don't be tempted to use the edge of the sanding disc in an effort to take more filler off quicker. All you will do is create ripples in the filler, and these can be difficult to remove on larger areas of filler. When sanding larger areas of body filler, a useful tip is to use a long flat block of wood (300–450mm) wrapped in sandpaper. This helps to eliminate the possibility of getting ripples in the filler. This will also give you a good idea what areas require more filler, i.e. the areas left untouched by the sanding block.

As you are rubbing the filler down, keep stopping to check the level and shape of the panel. Run your hand slowly over the whole area. Feel is a lot more accurate than sight. If it doesn't feel right it will not look right, especially with some dark colours or pale metallics. Try closing your eyes as you run your hand over the repair. This heightens your sense of feel. What can at first feel reasonably level can suddenly become a ploughed field! Remember to remove any traces of dust between each application of filler, as any trapped dust could stop each layer of filler bonding to the previous layer.

Once you're happy the repaired area is level and to the correct shape, then apply one last very fine layer of filler to remove any remaining deep scratches and pin holes. This last layer should be very gently sanded off with a 180-grit or finer grade pad.

Give the whole area one last dust off, then clean with panel wipe, and you're ready to apply a few coats of primer.

▲ Fig. 14.22 Hopefully you won't need this amount of filler! Small DIY tins are available from your local motor spares shop.

■ ALUMINIUM

Many of you will be making side panels, bonnets, etc. out of aluminium, and the good news is that the preparation method is very similar to mild steel. However, unlike mild steel there isn't a need for a protective layer of oil to be removed, but there sometimes maybe a polythene skin that needs to be peeled off.

If the surface of the aluminium is good, with no imperfections or dents, then simply sand down with a 320-grit pad to provide a good key for the paint to stick to. Aluminium is more malleable than mild steel, so minor dents take much less effort to knock out with a hammer and dolly. However, aluminium stretches much more easily than steel, so be careful not to work the surface too much, otherwise the dent could become bigger! My advice would be to lightly knock out any smaller dents and finish with body filler as previously described. I recommend the use of special body fillers for aluminium, such as U-pol D or Galv X. These have superior bonding properties and are formulated for use on alloys and specially-treated metals.

Larger dents can be more difficult to remove because the material will have been stretched much more, so more layers of filler will be required. An experienced panel beater would achieve a much better repair with a lot less body filler, but the skills and tools required are beyond the reach of most of us. Alternatively, fit a new panel. Once you are happy with any repairs you have completed, and the rest of the bare aluminium surface has been suitably keyed with a 320-grit pad, then give the surface a clean off with panel wipe. You are now ready for priming.

■ GLASSFIBRE

This will largely be wheelarches and nose cone. There can be a wide variation in the quality of glassfibre panels. A common problem is small air holes trapped in the gelcoat surface, or larger air pockets trapped between the gelcoat and the first layers of matting. This can often occur on or around corners or on sharp edges. Surface pinholes are easily dealt with by filling with body filler, but the larger air pockets under the surface of the gelcoat need to be located and filled with body filler. Should these air pockets not be removed, once your car is complete and you take it out on a warm sunny day, the air trapped under the gelcoat will expand and cause the paint to blister, thus ruining all your hard work. The best way to avoid this happening is to start by holding a light behind the panel to look for any potential problem areas in the form of thin gelcoat or matting. Circle the areas where you think there could be a problem, then place the panel in front of a heater to warm the surface. An oven is ideal for this, but you will find your panels do not fit in the kitchen cooker, which is probably a good thing! As the surface gets hot you will see the blisters appear. Be careful not to allow the panel to get too hot as the heat could cause it to warp. Scrape away the gelcoat to leave the hole and then fill back level with the surface. Some panels may have stress cracks in the gelcoat. These need to be ground back until the crack disappears. Use an angle grinder along the line of the crack and fill with bridging filler (a resin plus fibre base filler) to just below the surface, and finish with normal body filler. It may be necessary to reinforce the rear of the panel with resin and matting if the cracks are very deep.

Once all the holes and cracks have been dug out and repaired, lightly key the surface with 320-grit to remove the shine, and clean as before.

■ WOOD

If you are using plywood on your car (probably for your dashboard) and you are going to paint it, then all that is needed is to make sure the surface is suitably keyed and that the grain has been filled with stopper or fine body filler.

■ PRE-PAINTED PANELS

If some of you are using panels blagged from someone else or the side panels of old fridges and washers, etc., these may have already been painted before. Provided the existing paintwork is sound, then it is simply a case of rubbing down and painting. Use 800 to 1200 wet-and-dry paper if you intend applying your top coat directly to the existing surface. However, I would always advise the use of a suitable isolator, or primer, over existing paintwork unless you know exactly what type of paint was previously used.

Paintwork that is old and flaking should be sanded back to bare metal or stripped using a suitable paint stripper to avoid any future problems when over-painting. Any minor dents and scratches can be repaired as previously explained.

TYPES OF PAINT

There are two basic types of paint in use for finishing cars – solvent-based, and water-based. Water-based paints are a relatively new concept and are therefore only usable in larger bodyshops with the correct curing/drying equipment. All the paints suitable for small-scale or DIY use are solvent-based.

■ PRIMERS

Depending on the type of material to be painted, there are several different types of primer which can be used.

ETCH PRIMERS

These should be used as your primary coating on aluminium, bare steelwork, and glassfibre. In the bodywork trade it is more commonly known as two-pack etch primer, because it consists of a base primer and an etching activator, or active thinner. When the two components are mixed together the mixed paint has etching properties which help it to bite into the surface of the panel more effectively, thus reducing the possibility of future lifting or peeling problems. This type of paint normally comes supplied as a pack, which requires equal mixing ratios of 50% primer to 50% activator.

CELLULOSE-BASED PRIMERS

These types of primer are the best for the home/DIY user, as they are easy to mix (normally 50% paint to 50% thinners), reasonably quick drying, and generally available from all car spares shops and paint suppliers.

They have good high build characteristics for covering any minor scratches in the panel surface. However, cellulose paints can sometimes cause a reaction with some other paints, or when used over existing older paints, usually synthetic paints. So, if you are unsure, it's always a good idea to use a good quality isolator like U-pol Bar Coat prior to applying cellulose paints. If you are painting bare panels, though, you should be all right, but apply two to three coats of etch primer first as described.

SYNTHETIC PRIMERS

Only use synthetic primers if you intend to use synthetic top coats. These are generally cheaper paints. They give an excellent coverage and high build characteristics, due to the mixing quantities of 80–90% paint to 10–20% thinners. However, they can take ages to dry and it can be difficult to get a run-free finish. Within the bodywork trade, synthetic primers are generally regarded as a cheap paint mainly used by and for cheap bodgers! (sorry if that offends anyone).

TWO-PACK PRIMERS

These primers are the best to use. They are very stable and have the highest build qualities, but unfortunately they are recommended for professional use only, as they contain highly poisonous cyanide-based chemicals. A proper mask with its own external-air-fed supply is imperative, and it is very unlikely that a home/DIY painter will have such a facility. So, I would never advise the use of two-pack paints unless you have access to a fully-equipped spray booth.

OTHER PRIMERS

Zinc-based primers, red oxide, Hammerite, etc., are all good for certain uses. My only advice is to be careful when over-painting and when using over previous paints. A reaction can often occur between paint types. Always do a small test sample first.

MIXING PAINT

At this point it may be worth making yourself a paint mixing stick. We use a mixing stick to measure out the correct amount of paints and activators, thinners, additives, etc. You may be able to buy one from your local paint suppliers, but you can always use a steel ruler or make your own mixing stick. Simply cut a metal strip, and file or saw a series of marks, equal distances apart, along one edge. Then

do the same on the opposite edge, but make the spaces between each mark double the size. Different mixing sticks can be made to suit your own requirements for different types of paint. Remember to mix your paint in a container with parallel sides like a spare clean paint tin, otherwise your mixing stick will give an incorrect mix.

Once you have mixed your paint, it's always a good idea to pour it through a paint strainer into the spray gun pot to eliminate the chances of contamination from bits of dirt or dry paint that could have fallen in from around the rim of the paint tin. Alternatively, simply fit a paint filter to the pick up tube of your spray gun.

■ TOP COATS

There are various types of top-coat paint, but the main types are cellulose, synthetic and two-pack. As with the primers, two-pack top coats are not suitable for DIY use, due to the toxic chemicals they contain. Always make sure that the primers and top coat you're intending to use are compatible.

TYPES OF SPRAY GUN

There are generally two types of spray gun – gravity feed and suction feed. Gravity feed guns have the paint reservoir above the nozzle, allowing the paint to flow downwards through

▼ Fig. 14.23 Two types of suction-feed spray guns. The smaller gun is used for primer.

▲ **Fig. 14.24** An air-fed paint-spraying helmet. The regulator is worn on a belt around the waist and plugged into the airline.

the gun, whereas suction feed guns have the paint reservoir below the nozzle. These rely on a negative air pressure or vacuum effect at the nozzle to pull the paint up from within the reservoir when the trigger is pulled. Both types of gun give equally good results, so your choice of gun is more a case of what you feel comfortable with. Many paint sprayers find that they tend to learn with one type of gun and then stick with it from then on. For this reason I prefer to use a suction feed gun. The advantages for both guns are as follows:

■ SUCTION FEED
Paint reservoir below handle – not top heavy when full. Bigger paint reservoir, so bigger painting capacity between refills. Free standing when not in use.

■ GRAVITY FEED
Smaller amounts of paints can be mixed because every last drop can be used. Thicker consistency paint can be applied. Lightweight gun, so easier to control.

FINAL PREPERATION
So we've got our spray gun full of etch primer and we are ready to go. Well not quite.

First, make sure that anything that doesn't

want painting is masked up, and that everything else that is lying about in your garage is covered up. Some of these paints will settle on and stick to anything, which makes for a long and unnecessary job cleaning up later. Second, make sure you have sufficient ventilation to take away any paint fumes. And no naked flames, unless you want to find yourself painting on the moon! Third, good clean overalls, latex gloves and suitable respiratory equipment should be used. There are many types of face masks and respirators available. Speak to your local paint suppliers. They will advise you of what's best for the type of paint you are using.

SPRAY GUN SET-UP
We can't just plug into the airline and go blasting away at the first panel we come across. It's worth having a test panel of some type that we can use to set the gun up on. A large sheet of card or paper taped to the wall is as good as anything. On the back of the gun there are usually two thumbscrews. These are used to adjust the fan width and paint flow. Turn the top screw fully open to give the widest fan width available. Set the bottom thumbscrew to midway. This should allow a suitable level of paint to flow. On the front of the gun you will notice that the nozzle has two horns. Setting these horizontally this will give you a vertical fan. Turn the nozzle through 90° to give you a horizontal fan. Most guns usually work at a pressure between 40psi and 60psi. So, set your regulator somewhere within this region. If the pressure is too high, the paint will come out too fast, and within a few minutes you will be painting in a room full of thick fog! If the pressure is too low the paint will not atomise enough and will come out in droplets which are too big, giving a rough orange-peel effect. Incorrect paint viscosity can also cause orange peel, but we will assume the paint is mixed up correctly.

Now that your gun is set up with a vertical fan and ready for painting, the only thing to do is to plug into your air line and have a go on your test panel. Start from the top left corner and move steadily towards the right. Hold the gun square to the panel at a distance of approximately six inches while pulling the trigger fully in. You will notice that the gun will have a half trigger setting which will just allow air to flow through the gun but not paint. When you reach the end of each pass, either fully release the trigger or release to half trigger, otherwise when you move down to make your next pass you will get a build up of paint at either end of the panel. This will eventually cause runs which will need to be flatted out when dry. You will probably get some runs and some dry patches anyway, until you get used to the feel of the spray gun, and how much paint is being fed through the gun. It's now just a case of fiddling about with the gun set-up until you get a feel and finish that you are comfortable with. It may take a bit of practice, but once you get the hang of it, achieving a really top-quality finish will no longer be a dream for you. To achieve a good consistent level of primer, simply turn the nozzle through 90° for each alternative application of the paint. Now make vertical passes over the panel, starting again at the top left corner. As we are only at the primer stage, if you do get some runs, it's not a problem because they can be flatted out once dry, and some more primer added later if necessary.

SPRAYING PRIMER

First, apply two to three coats of etch primer, allowing each coat to dry, then apply three to four coats of cellulose primer, again allowing to dry between each coat. Finally, use a dark colour, mixed very thin, and apply one light coat over the primer. This will act as a guide coat when preparing for the top coat later.

FLATTING OFF

All panels, other than glassfibre (see note in box on right), should be left for about a week for the primer to dry before tackling the next stage.

Once the primer has been left long enough to dry, the next step is flatting off, and it's during this process that the purpose of your guide coat becomes evident as it will clearly show any areas that may need further remedial work. It's possible to dry flat the primer with the DA sander using a 320–400 pad, but you must be very careful not to go through the primer on the edges. This is a much faster method of flatting if time savings are important, or if you're experienced enough to not remove too much paint. Dry flatting is ideal for two-pack primers as they generally give a much higher build, resulting in a thicker layer of paint to sand down. However, for the home/DIY painter I would recommend wet flatting, using wet-and-dry paper. I find that 800-grit gives a suitably flat finish for two-pack top coats, and 1200-grit is better for cellulose based top coats. To achieve the best finish I would recommend the use of a rubber wet-flatting block to wrap the wet-and-dry around when flatting off.

Place the panel on a level surface, with an old cushion or a piece of foam under it, then start in one area gently rubbing the surface down with the block. Keep dipping the block into a bucket of clean water or, better still, use a trigger action sprayer directly onto the panel. This is so that we are always using clean water with no particles of dirt, or grit contamination that could be trapped under the wet-and-dry and scratch the paint surface. Also remember to keep both the panel surface and the block surface flooded with clean water to wash away any contaminants.

As you rub the surface you will see the dark guide coat disappear, leaving a clean unblemished surface below. Continue across the whole panel surface until the guide coat is removed. You may find that in some areas where a localised repair was made, a black circle around the repair will appear. The circle represents the edge of the bodyfiller used for the repair. By using the block we can see the areas that may require more attention, whereas, if we just used the wet-and-dry in our hand, it would follow the contours of the panel, thus not highlighting any sub-standard repairs. If the primer is thick enough you may be able to rub out the marks before going right through the primer, or you may have to apply more filler and primer to achieve a perfect surface. Any pin holes and minor scratches will simply require levelling up with a fine grade surface filler and then wet-flatting back once dry. Any areas where you have gone through the primer will need covering with more primer.

IMPORTANT NOTE

When painting glassfibre, be careful not to apply too much paint too quickly as the glassfibre surface may absorb the thinners in the paint. This can give a false impression that the paint is dry when actually the glassfibre has sponged up the thinners in the primer. Problems may not arise until much later when you over-paint with your top coat, and trap the thinners in the glassfibre – which can have the same effect as the small air pockets described above. Micro-blisters may appear in the paint surface as the thinners try to evaporate off whilst being trapped under the gloss top coat. For this reason, as a general rule, it is advised to leave the panel after priming for approximately a week per coat under normal drying conditions (three coats etch, plus four coats cellulose means seven weeks drying). This may seem like a long time, but it can be reduced by artificial heating methods. Your paint supplier should be able to give you the best advice depending on the type of paint you are using.

All the panels should be flatted off using the same procedure, which can be quite time consuming, but if the panels are separate (wings, nose cone, etc.) there's no reason why you can't paint some panels prior to preparing others. You will probably find it too much to prepare the whole car in one go, plus it makes sense to break the jobs down into smaller more manageable stages. Also, if you do have a problem at the painting stage it will only occur on one or two of the panels rather than the whole car.

Once the panels have been flatted off, and the guide coat has been fully removed, all that remains is to clean off any remaining dirt/dust from flatting. Use a suitable panel wipe as before, then remove any last specs of dust with a tac rag. Make sure any areas that don't need painting are masked up. You are now ready for painting.

If you are planning on using cellulose solid colour paint I would recommend a mixing ratio of approximately 50% paint to 50% thinners. The important thing to remember when using cellulose paints is that for every litre of mixed paint applied, half a litre will evaporate off. So a good few coats will be required to achieve a decent build of colour. Make sure you have enough paint for the whole job and some spare for any repairs later (5 litres minimum). Use the same application method as described for the primer stage, starting off with one light coat that binds to the primer surface. Leave it for a few minutes, then apply successive coats that give a smooth glossy finish. You will find that the cellulose paint dries fairly quickly, which can result in dry patches forming through over-spray. The secret of achieving a good quality finish with cellulose paint is maintaining a wet paint surface across the whole panel. This will gradually move down the panel as you apply the paint with each pass. It's fairly straightforward on smaller panels, but it can be more difficult on larger vehicles like transit van sides, where the over-spray line from one panel to the next creates a natural dry patch, because it is impossible to keep the whole surface wet whilst painting.

Again, you will probably get some runs or dry patches, but with a bit of practice you should be able to minimise any runs. Apply three to four coats as above, then leave to dry off (two to three days minimum). Lightly flat off using 1200-grit wet-and-dry, then apply three to four more coats. Allow to dry again, flat off, and then apply another three to four coats. You should now be getting to the stage where a really deep shine is starting to appear. Flat off again and apply three

to four last coats, but increase the mix for the last two coats to 60–70% thinners 30–40% paint. This will allow the surface to stay wet for longer, thus minimising any dry patches. However, you must be careful to avoid getting more runs because the paint is much thinner now. You should have applied between nine to twelve coats of gloss by this stage, which will give a really top-quality finish and a good thickness of paint which can be buffed and polished later once dry.

If you opt for a metallic finish, the process of paint application is slightly different, in that you will need to apply a metallic base coat first to colour the panels, then seal the paint surface with a clear lacquer. It can be a little more difficult to achieve a perfect finish with metallic paints, especially with pale metallics like silver, because of the way the light reflects off the surface of the paint. Some common problems associated with pale metallics are a striping effect in the paintwork or a patchy/blotchy effect. These can be caused by inconsistent application of both the base coat and the lacquer.

SPRAYING COLOUR-COAT

If you are planning on using a darker metallic colour, like deeper blues or reds, you should not encounter these problems. Once the panels have been fully prepared, clean and mask up, then apply three to four light coats of the metallic base, as described before. Leave to dry and lightly flat off. You don't need to apply really wet coats as any runs within the metallic base coat will have to be flatted out and over-painted again prior to the lacquer being applied. Apply another three to four coats of metallic, which should be enough to be sure the colour is no longer transparent. Leave the panel long enough for the metallic base to become touch dry, then apply four to five coats of clear lacquer. Use cellulose lacquer or one pack RFU (ready for use) lacquer. Depending on the paint manufacturer, some makes may not require thinners. Leave to dry as for solid colour top coats. There is no need to flat off and reapply clear lacquer. Again, be careful to minimise any runs, as these could disturb the metallic base coat finish which no amount of flatting will remove! If this happens, you will have to rub the panel down and re-apply the coloured base coat and the clear lacquer. The panels should now be left for about a week for the paint to fully dry before buffing and polishing.

If it's your intention to use synthetic paints, the mixing quantities are slightly different (normally 80% paint 20% thinners) depending on the paint manufacturer. The application procedure is also different as it's simply a case of applying one light coat followed by two thicker coats to achieve a glossy finish. However, it can take many weeks for synthetic paints to dry out, so making the process of removing any runs much more time consuming. The paint finish can also look a little 'plasticy', with a false glossy finish to it.

As mentioned before, two-pack paints and lacquers give the best results, but because of their poisonous nature these should only be used by professional painters. The technique of application is very similar to synthetic paints but with the advantage of drying/curing times being greatly reduced – to a few hours in some cases. A top-quality finish can be obtained with the minimum of effort, but this is only the case in experienced hands. Some paint manufacturers are now making isocyanate-free two-pack paints, but these are a bit of an unknown quantity for me. Your paint supplier should be able to advise you better.

POLISHING

So, once we have given the panels a good deep top coat and the paint has fully dried (leave for about a week) we can set about buffing and polishing the paintwork. You will probably notice that during the painting stage some dust particles will have settled on the paint surface, resulting in some minor imperfections in the paint. These, along with any minor runs and orange peel areas, now have to be flatted out. For the final flatting and polishing stages I would use a very fine grade (1500–2000-grit) wet-and-dry. The panels should be rubbed down just as in the preparation stage, but the utmost care must be taken not to catch any dirt between the paint surface and the wet-and-dry. At this stage I would say that it's imperative that you use a trigger sprayer for the water, and complete the flatting indoors in a room where there are no draughts. This will minimise the possibility of any airborne dust/dirt being collected on the panel. Dirt that gets caught under the wet-and-dry could potentially cause deep scratches in the paintwork which will be much more difficult to polish out later. It's not so important to use the rubbing block on the top coat, but better results can be achieved by using a small block of wood approximately an inch square for any dust particles and minor runs. That way you will not damage a larger surrounding area than necessary on the good paintwork. Use a circular motion with light pressure. Keep drying the surface at regular intervals. As you remove

the imperfections you will see a matt area appear, surrounded by the gloss of the good area. Keep going until the surface has become level. The same technique applies for minor runs, but be careful not to remove too much paint around the run. It's all too easy to get carried away and rub right through the top coat. I know, I've done it on many occasions! Orange peel areas can simply be flatted off by hand without the use of a rubbing block. Once all the minor imperfections have been removed, it's simply a case of buffing the surface back up to a high gloss finish. This involves using a good quality buffing compound like Farecla or Autoglym and a buffing machine. You may be able to hire a professional buffing machine. On the other hand, a number of retail outlets, such as Halfords, have reasonably-priced home/DIY paint buffers. Alternatively, you could adapt an electric drill for buffing, but be sure you use a variable speed drill, as you only require 1500–2000rpm free running speed for the best results. You can achieve the same results with patience and elbow grease (hand polishing). Several types of buffing pads are available from lambswool pads to thick sponge pads. I wouldn't recommend the use of lambswool pads as they quickly clog up with buffing compound and can easily burn the paint surface. Thick sponge pads are more forgiving, but a good deal of caution is required around any sharp edges/corners on the panels. Most buffing compounds will require the addition of a small amount of water to keep the paint surface cool and well lubricated.

Start by adding a small amount of compound to the centre of the buffing pad, and place it on the panel. Move the buffer around on the surface in a couple of small circles to spread out the buffing compound. Now press the trigger and move the machine slowly around the panel, covering a small area about 18 inches square. Keep adding small amounts of water to the surface. Don't spend too long in one area as you will cause a build-up of heat. You may have to leave that area to cool and come back to it later. You will gradually see the shine come back as you go over the surface with the buffer. It could take several applications of buffing compound before all the fine flatting marks disappear. Once you are happy with the finish, simply wipe off any remaining buffing compound then apply a good-quality wax to seal the surface of the paint. This will give it a long-lasting shine and help reduce oxidation of the top layer of paint.

And that's it, job done!

GLASSFIBRE MOULDING
BY PAUL WALKER

To make complex shapes in metal calls for a skill that few can claim to have, and for the majority of DIY car-builders the only practical solution is to use glass-reinforced plastic (GRP). It's a fairly long road to travel down, but if you're determined to do it all yourself it can be a rewarding experience. However, by its nature, glassfibre moulding lends itself to the manufacture of things in small to medium quantities, and to be realistic it doesn't warrant the effort for a one-off component, especially one of small value.

First, you will need a pattern. This will be made of wood and filler, and if you don't feel able to make it yourself, visit your local pattern-maker and provide him with all the drawings and measurements he'll need to produce one for you.

Once made, the pattern has to be prepared for making a mould from which you can form your finished product. Use a suitable sealer to prepare the surface of the pattern for the finish required – in this case, a high gloss. Then treat it with a release agent to prevent the mould from sticking to it.

Now apply the first of two coats of gelcoat to the treated surface, followed by several layers of glass mat and resin. How many layers depends on the thickness and size of your end-product. Put the pattern and mould away somewhere warm for a few days to finish curing. After that it's time to prise the mould off the pattern. Careful use of wedges, air, and (sometimes) water will probably be needed to coax it off in one piece and without damage. Time now to inspect the results of your handiwork and either give yourself a well-earned pat on the back, or go and drown your sorrows.

Assuming the new mould is all right, it must now be treated with a release agent just as you did with your pattern. After a suitable number of applications, apply the first layer of gelcoat in the colour of your choice. Once the gelcoat has cured, the required layers of glass mat are placed on top and saturated with catalysed resin. This must now be consolidated with a roller to remove any trapped air, and then be given a final dab down with a brush to lay down any protruding fibres. Once cured, about 24 hours later, your part can be removed from the mould and any excess trimmed away.

▼ **Fig. 14.25** Paul starts to apply the first layer of gelcoat to a new moulding.

HANDLING AND ROADHOLDING
BY RORY PERRETT

By handling I don't mean ultimate roadholding and the ability to go round corners as fast as possible. Handling is about the balance of the car, how it feels to drive. Good handling is a product of compromise, personal preference and what you want from your car.

If you want ultimate roadholding, fit a set of wide wheels and tyres, clamp everything down and eliminate as much suspension movement as possible. Fit high-rate springs and dampers and replace all those rubber bushes with something a lot harder. This is fine if you are going to go racing on the track (racers want to minimise movement and reduce the variable effects of changes in the suspension geometry as the car is pushed to its limit around a circuit). But it's not so good if you want to prevent your body, and more important that of your passenger, being pulverised to a mush on that summer's evening drive to the local hostelry.

Always try to keep in mind what you want the car for. Change one thing at a time and maximise the benefit from the change before moving on to the next thing.

In the best tradition, spending money is no guarantee of success, you could even end up with a car that is less to your liking than when you started. I'm sure they won't thank me for mentioning it, but if Mercedes can spend millions on their A Class and still get it wrong then there's hope for us all.

There's a considerable amount of nonsense talked about the handling and set-up of cars. For most of us, achieving the 'perfect' settings for camber, spring rates, etc., will not be an issue. Mild bump steer will not be noticed on our country drives, nor will the understeer which appears when trying to execute a left turn off a roundabout at 85mph. However, sensible changes can be made to improve your car and make it just that little bit more enjoyable for you to drive.

STATIC HANDLING

This might seem a strange idea. No one has problems with the handling of a stationary vehicle, but good handling starts with weight distribution. The total weight carried by the tyres will always equal the total weight of the car and contents. While changing the total weight of the car is not necessarily an option, and here you have

▲ Fig. 14.26 In the '70s, even F1 teams used glorified bathroom scales to set cornerweights! *(sutton-images.com)*

an advantage, you can affect the distribution of weight. However, and this is the first compromise, are you setting up for a full tank of fuel and two passengers or just the driver and half a tank?

Gauges for measuring the corner weights are available, although you might be able to get away with two bathroom scales and a suitable cross member. A car like the one this book is about, plus driver and half a tank of fuel, will typically weigh 500kg to 700kg in total, so you are going to need a range up to about 250kg to weigh each corner. Remember that if you are weighing each corner in turn you'll need to chock under the other wheels to keep the car level. Ideally you want to achieve 25% of the total weight on each wheel. Failing that, the corner weights should be equalised across each axle.

To achieve the required weight distribution, some items can be positioned favourably during the build. Consider fitting the fuel tank and battery on the passenger side to help balance the weight of the driver along with wiper motors, heater boxes, etc. For those who have splashed out on a set of shock absorbers with adjustable spring platforms, corner weights can be set by raising or lowering each spring seat. However, this approach should only be used for the final fine tuning to correct small differences, not for trying to compensate for a large imbalance. While remembering that keeping the ride height of the car as low as practical is an advantage, raise the spring platform to increase the weight on that wheel, lower it to reduce the weight. Don't be tempted to try to achieve an equal weight distribution across the wheels by having the shock absorber mounting brackets in different positions on each side.

DYNAMIC HANDLING

Once on the move, the way a car behaves results from a set of complex interactions between the various elements and components that connect the car to the road. These will change depending on the way in which the car is being driven and the road it is being driven on. How the car stops, goes and steers comes down to the performance of the four tyres at the point where they are in contact with the road. The effect of any changes that are made to the suspension system and components must be considered in the context of how they affect the way the tyres do their job.

The ability of a tyre to perform is related to the grip it can generate. If what we are asking of a tyre is less than the grip available then there is no problem. Demand more grip than is available from any, or all four, of the tyres and you have a problem. The grip available from a tyre is relative to the area of the tyre in contact with the road and the weight being carried by that tyre at the time. Of course, the road surface plays a big part as well but we generally have little or no control over that.

A characteristic of tyre performance is that the grip from a tyre increases as the load on it increases. This is why Formula 1 and other race cars have wings to create downforce to push the car into the ground and increase the load on the tyres – giving a total load greater than the weight of the car. However, this effect is not linear. Doubling the load does not double the grip; the increase in grip is less than doubled. Similarly, halving the load means that the tyre has more than half the grip. Good handling is not about the ultimate level of grip but about the balance between the grip provided by tyres on the same axle and the balance between the total grip provided at the front and back of the car. Spread the load more evenly around the four wheels, or between wheels on the same axle, and you will have more overall grip. Making changes to help even out the weight distribution, especially when cornering, will help improve handling.

The dynamic handling of the car comes down to the way in which the weight carried by each tyre changes as the car is driven, but remember that the total weight must stay the same at all times. (This is assuming that there are no aerodynamic devices or effects producing downforce or uplift and thereby altering the loadings on the tyres.)

The basic design of a car has a fundamental effect on the way weight is redistributed during cornering, etc., and this relates to the car's centre of gravity. As you go round a corner, weight is transferred to the outside wheels, and the amount transferred depends upon the height of the centre of gravity and the width of the track. Low and wide cars transfer less weight than tall narrow ones (back to the Mercedes A Class here). The car in this book, being more like a Formula 1 car than an A Class, has the advantage. This advantage can be increased by keeping the ride height as low as practical and by mounting the engine and gearbox, fuel tank and driver as low as possible in the chassis.

Once your car is finished, the options for altering the way weight is transferred, and thus the handling, are limited to component changes and adjustments within the suspension.

SUSPENSION GEOMETRY

Whilst fitting wider tyres will increase the area of tyre on the road, it could make the steering unacceptably heavy. Before you go for wider tyres, and probably wheels as well, it would be better to ensure that you have the maximum contact area from the tyres you have got.

When the car is not moving you will maximise the contact area by having the wheels vertical. However, you want maximum grip, not when the car is standing in the garage but when cornering. On road cars, the suspension is not solidly attached to the car. Rubber bushes are used to reduce the level of shocks, vibration and noise transmitted to the body and that inevitably leads to some movement of the components when subjected to a load.

When cornering, the forces/load on the outside wheels will have a tendency to make it 'lean' out at the top – this is called positive camber. Setting a negative camber (the wheel leaning in at the top) when the car is static will allow the wheel to move to the vertical (zero camber) when under dynamic load when cornering.

The movement of the suspension up and down will also affect the camber angle of the wheel. Here we see how complex the relationship between the various elements of the suspension can be. The spring rates affect the ultimate angle of body roll, the dampers affect the speed at which the angle is reached, which also depends on the centre of gravity and the weight transfer. The suspension geometry, the movement in the suspension and the static camber angle will affect the camber of the wheels during cornering as will the size of the tyre the speed of the car and the tightness of the corner. Change one of these and you can affect all the rest.

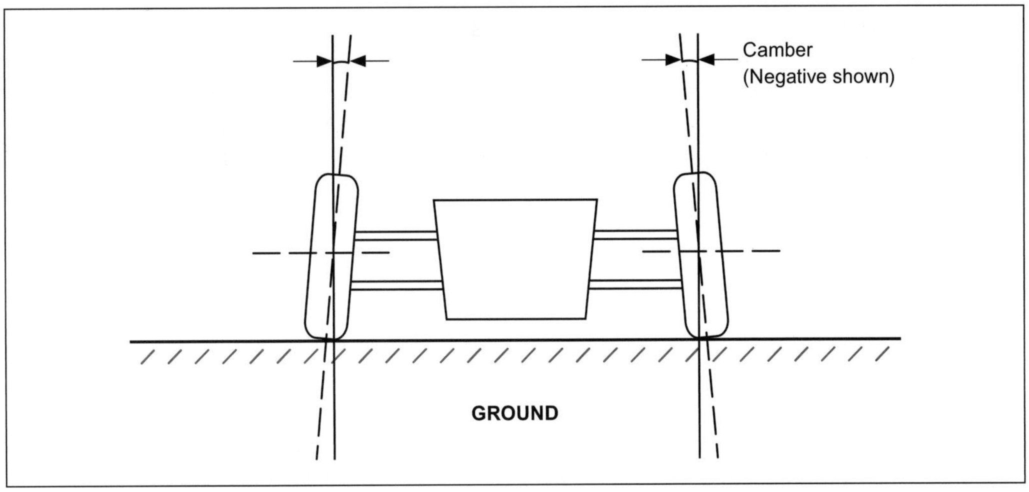

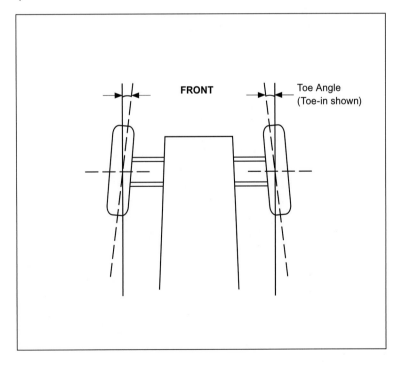

◀ **Fig. 14.27** Negative camber – the wheels are leaning in at the top.

Toe-in or toe-out is another adjustment like camber. A static setting of toe-in on the front wheels is set on RWD cars. Under driving conditions, movement in the suspension normally results in the front wheels moving towards zero toe-in. With its independent rear suspension, the rear suspension geometry of the car can also be adjusted, allowing toe and camber to be set.

SPRINGS

Changing the rates of the springs fitted to your car can also be used to alter the weight transfer when driving. Fitting a higher rate (stronger) spring to a wheel will increase the load carried by that wheel, and (of course) a lower-rated spring will reduce the weight carried. Higher spring rates will result in a harsher ride, which is why car manufacturers prefer softer springs with anti-roll bars.

ANTI-ROLL BARS (ANTI-SWAY BARS)

Anti-roll bars, front or rear, effectively connect the two wheels on one axle together and consequently they reduce the level of independence in an independent suspension set-up. They are designed to reduce body roll and the weight transfer to the outside wheel by moving the inside wheel in the same direction, ie, as the outside wheel moves closer to the body as the body rolls, the anti-roll bar causes the inside wheel to raise also, effectively levelling out the body and reducing weight transfer. Roll bars need to be matched to the rest of the suspension set-up, especially the springs, and big (stiff) is not always necessarily best. A car with soft springs and a stiff roll bar may corner well but is likely to experience significant pitching, with the nose diving under braking and the rear squatting under acceleration.

SHOCK ABSORBERS (DAMPERS)

Shock absorbers only affect the car when the piston inside the shock absorber is moving, which fortunately is most of the time. The advantage is that adjustable shock absorbers are available and are usually fairly quick and easy to adjust on the car. While the attitude of the car is changing, eg, as it enters and leaves a corner, the shock absorbers can be used to give the same effect as springs. Stiff dampers will reduce the rate at which the car reaches its roll angle and equilibrium. Until equilibrium is reached, the stiffer shock absorber will act like a higher spring rate. Adjustable shock absorbers allow you to alter the rate at which the roll angle and equilibrium are reached.

▼ **Fig. 14.28** Front wheel toe-in – the front edges of the wheels are angled inwards when viewed from above.

▶ **Fig. 14.29** Master-class 1 – Graham Hill demonstrates oversteer in his 1963 BRM F1 car. Note the angle of the front wheels as the car drifts past with its nose pointing towards the cameraman. *(LAT)*

▼ **Fig. 14.30** Master-class 2 – Jochen Rindt demonstrates understeer in his 1966 Cooper F1 car. Note the front wheels are pointing towards the cameraman as the driver tries to persuade the car to turn further into the corner. *(sutton-images.com)*

TYRE PRESSURES

Changing tyre pressures should be the last adjustments made. This is another of those fine-tuning touches rather than the route to achieving big changes in handling characteristics. The car in this book will typically run with tyre pressures around 18–20psi front and rear. If you have to alter these by more than the odd psi to get the handling you want, it would suggest that something elswhere needs sorting out or adjusting first.

OVERSTEER AND UNDERSTEER

Oversteer and understeer are much-used terms in the motoring press. A well-balanced car should be neutral and display neither, but manufacturers seem to consider that understeer is more desirable in the safety stakes than oversteer if neutrality under all conditions cannot be maintained.

Oversteer is where the car turns more than the driver expects from the amount the steering wheel has been turned. In terms of the tyres, it means that the front tyres are gripping more than the back. Under these conditions the car will tend to spin round – at least you won't be able to see what it is you are crashing into.

Understeer is the opposite; the car turns less than expected and feels like it wants to go straight on rather than round the corner. The front tyres have less grip than the back and will skid first, you go off the road forward and benefit from grandstand seats for the ensuing accident.

For good handling, a set-up which gives neutral handling under most conditions, tending to slight understeer when pushed, is considered the ideal. The following table might help you sort out a handling package that meets your needs.

Having made a component change, an adjustment may be required to the front wheel camber or toe to maximise the benefit. In general, wider tyres on the front will increase the forces on the suspension, requiring an increase in negative camber and toe in. Fitting uprated/harder springs/dampers or bushes will reduce suspension movement and mean a decrease in negative camber and toe in is possible.

Whatever you do, have fun experimenting to get the car just as you want it, but please no tyre smoking, brake squealing, massive oversteer power slides in Sainsbury's car park just to see if that +1° camber change has done the trick!

ADJUSTING HANDLING

To reduce oversteer (increase understeer)	To reduce understeer (increase oversteer)
Increase front spring rates	Decrease front spring rates
Decrease rear spring rates	Increase rear spring rates
Stiffen front damper	Soften front damper
Soften rear damper	Stiffen rear damper
Increase rear tyre width	Decrease rear tyre width
Decrease front tyre width	Increase front tyre width
Increase rear tyre pressure	Decrease rear tyre pressure
Decrease front tyre pressure	Increase front tyre pressure
More positive front wheel camber	More negative front wheel camber
More negative rear wheel camber	More positive rear wheel camber
Stiffer (thicker) front anti-roll bar	Softer (thinner) front anti-roll bar
Softer (thinner) rear anti-roll bar	Stiffer (thicker) rear anti-roll bar
More weight to the front	Less weight to the front
Less weight to the rear	More weight to the rear

RECOMMENDED STARTING POINTS FOR SET-UP

The optimum set-up for any individual car is dependant on a number of factors, such as the weight distribution (influenced by the weight of the engine used), the spring/damper units used, the tyres, etc, and, not least, the personal preference of the driver. The following set-up was used for the prototype Haynes Roadster, and should serve as a good starting point.

Rear camber	1 degree negative
Front camber	1 degree negative
Front toe angle	0–0.5 degrees toe-in
Tyre pressures	18–20psi front & rear

This appendix shows the cutting dimensions for all tubes, plates and jigs required during the building of the Haynes Roadster. The component codes, eg, U1 & U2, refer to the codes shown in the illustrations and text in the main chapters.

> **NOTE: Precise dimensions are provided for all components, but in practice allowance must be made for welded joints and distortion. It is advisable to cut tubes – and check and trim as necessary – as the chassis is built up, rather than cutting all tubes before work starts.**

All dimensions in mm
R   Radius
ø   Diameter
=x=   Dimension equal about centreline
(x)   Nominal check (resultant) dimension

UPRIGHT RAILS

Upright chassis rail U1 & U2
25 x 25 RHS

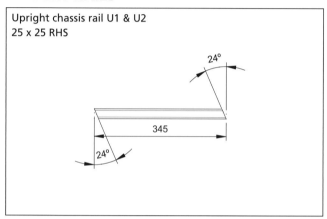

Upright chassis rail U3, U6, U7 & U8
25 x 25 RHS

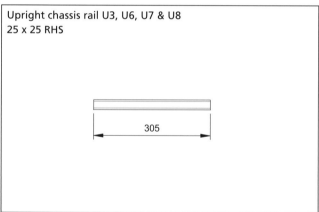

Upright chassis rail U4 & U5
25 x 25 RHS

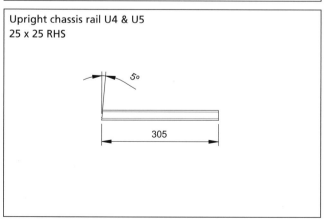

BOTTOM RAILS

Bottom chassis rail BR1 & BR2
25 x 25 RHS

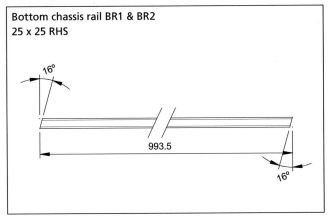

Bottom chassis rail BR3 & BR4
25 x 25 RHS

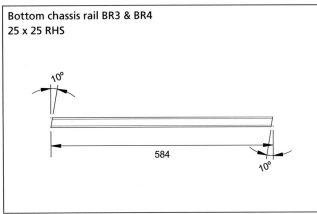

Bottom chassis rail BR5 & BR6
25 x 25 RHS

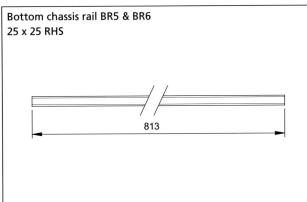

Bottom chassis rail BR7
25 x 25 RHS

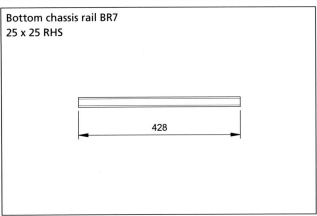

Bottom chassis rail BR8 & BR9
25 x 25 RHS

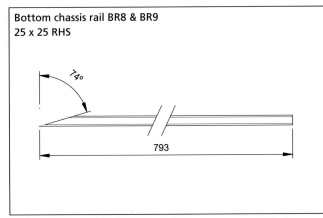

Bottom chassis rail BR10
25 x 25 RHS

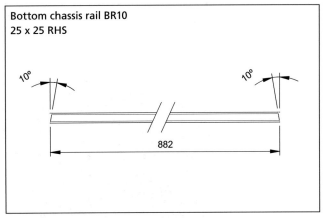

Bottom chassis rail BR11 & BR12
25 x 25 RHS

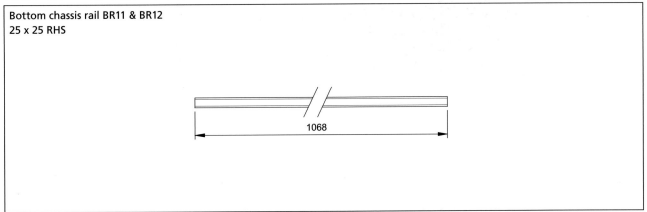

FRONT FRAME

Front frame rail FF2 as drawn
Front frame rail FF3 opp. hand
25 x 25 RHS

Note this is a true plan – the
overall length of FF2 and FF3
is 359.5mm

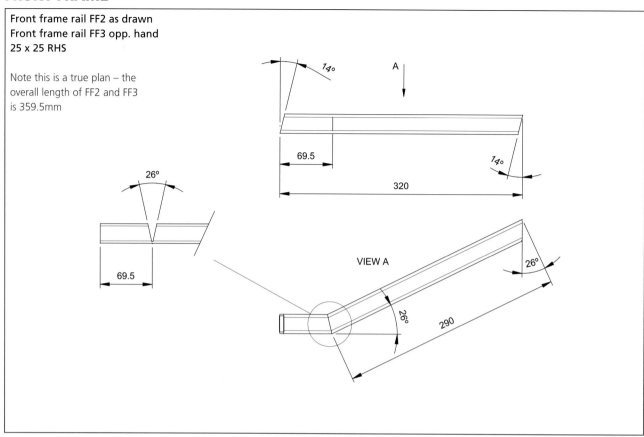

Front frame rail FF1
25 x 25 RHS

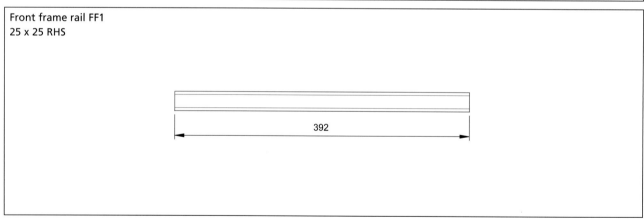

Front frame rail FF4
25 x 25 RHS

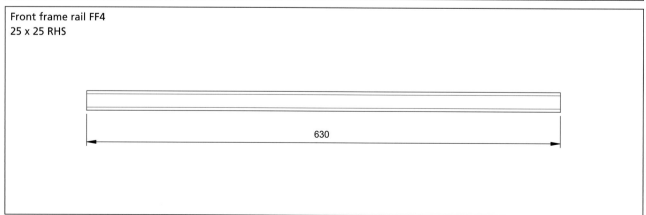

TOP CHASSIS RAILS

Top chassis rail TR1 & TR2
25 x 25 RHS

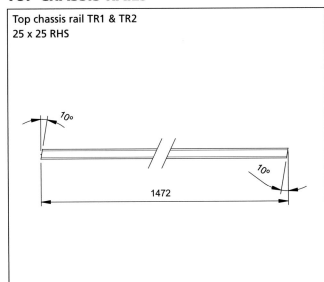

Top chassis rail TR3 & TR4
25 x 25 RHS

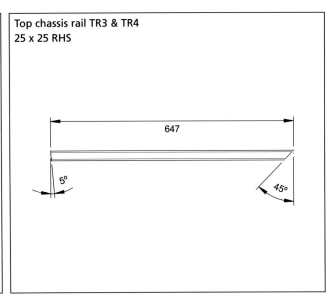

Top chassis rail TR5
25 x 25 RHS

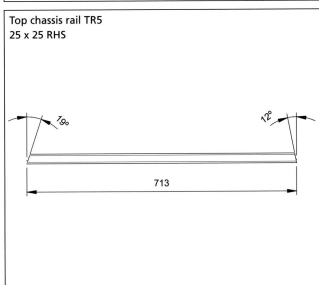

Top chassis rail TR6 & TR7
25 x 25 RHS

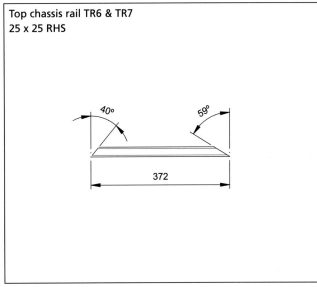

Top chassis rail TR8
25 x 25 RHS

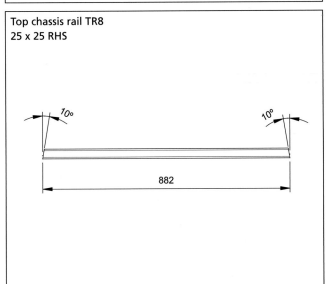

Top chassis rail TR9
25 x 25 RHS

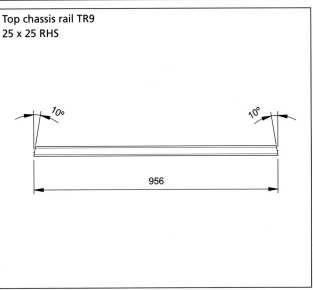

DIAGONAL CHASSIS RAILS

Diagonal chassis rail D1 as drawn
Diagonal chassis rail D2 as opp. hand
19 x 19 RHS

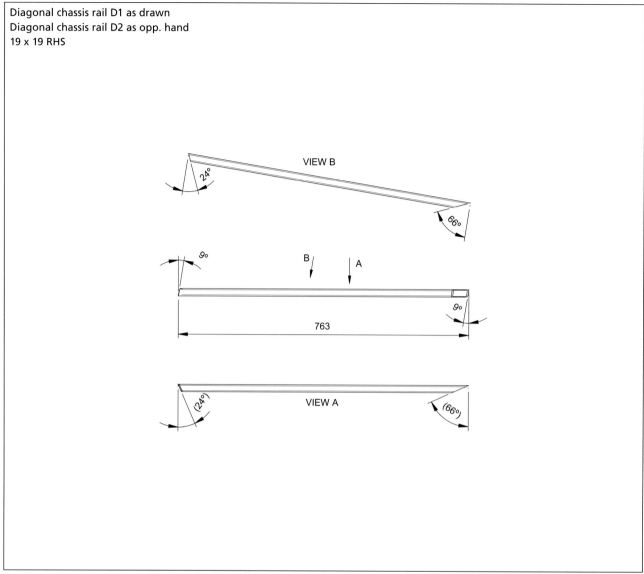

Diagonal chassis rail D3 & D4
19 x 19 RHS

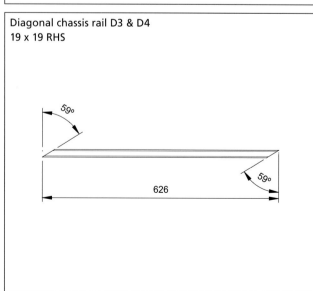

Diagonal chassis rail D5 & D6
25 x 25 RHS

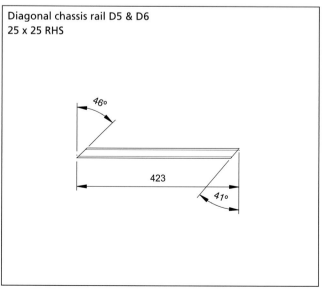

DIAGONAL CHASSIS RAILS CONTINUED

Diagonal chassis rail D7 & D8
25 x 25 RHS

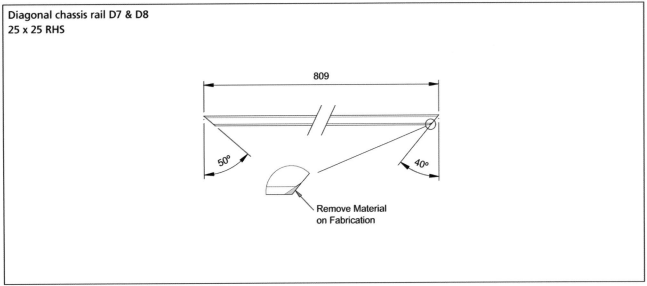

Remove Material
on Fabrication

Diagonal chassis rail D9 & D10
25 x 25 RHS

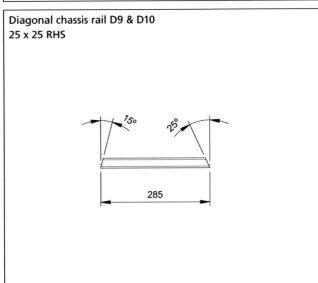

Diagonal chassis rail D11
19 x 19 RHS

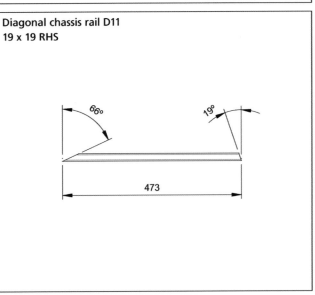

Diagonal chassis rail D12
19 x 19 RHS

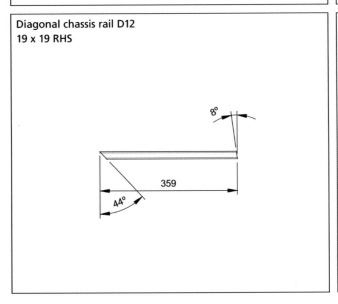

Diagonal chassis rail D13
19 x 19 RHS

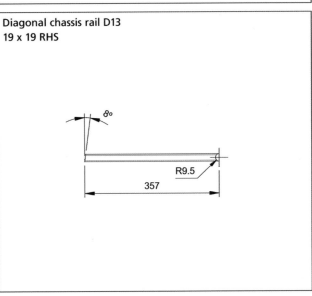

SEAT BACK RAILS

Seat back rail SB1
25 x 25 RHS

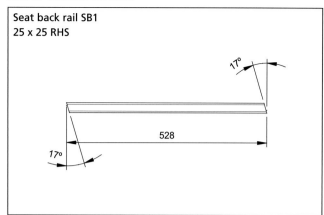

528

17°

17°

Seat back rail SB2
25 x 25 RHS

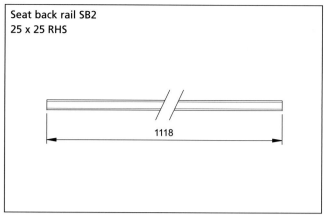

1118

Seat back rail SB3
25 x 25 RHS

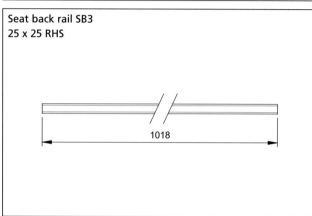

1018

Seat back rail SB4
25 x 25 RHS

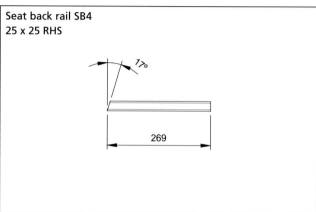

17°

269

Seat back rail SB5 & SB6
25 x 25 RHS

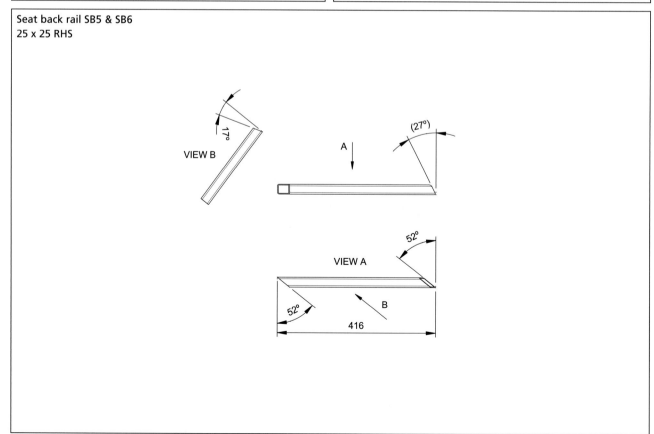

17°

VIEW B

A

(27°)

52°

VIEW A

52°

B

416

REAR SUSPENSION AREA

Rear suspension area rail RS1 as drawn
Rear suspension area rail RS2 opp. hand
25 x 25 RHS

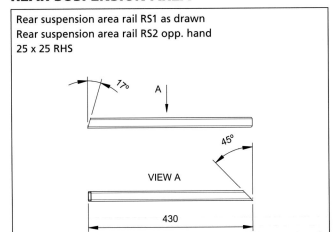

Rear suspension area rail RS3
25 x 25 RHS

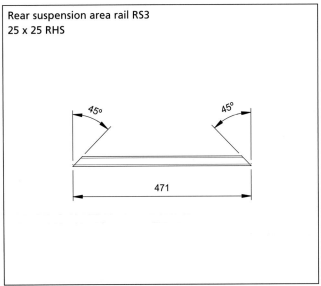

Rear suspension area rail RS4 & RS5
25 x 25 RHS

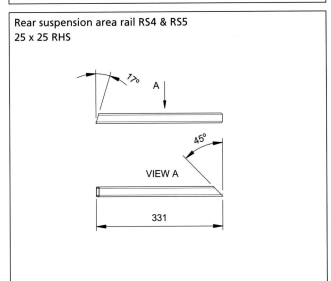

Rear suspension area rail RS6
25 x 25 RHS

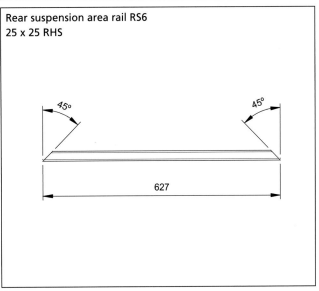

Rear suspension area rail RS7 & RS7a
25 x 25 RHS

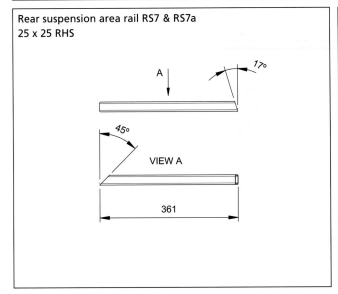

Rear suspension area rail RS8 & RS9
25 x 25 RHS

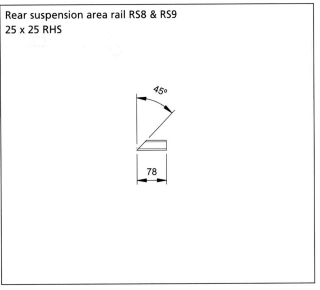

REAR SUSPENSION AREA CONTINUED

Rear suspension area rail RS11 & RS12
25 x 25 RHS

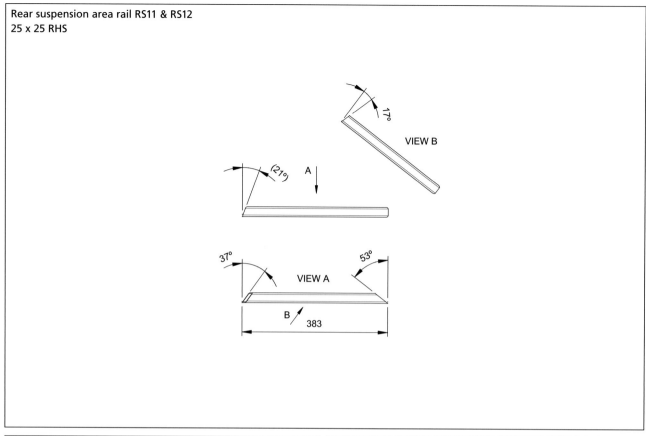

Rear suspension area rail RS10
25 x 25 RHS

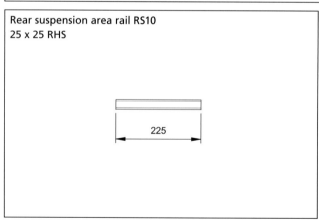

Rear suspension area rail RS13
25 x 25 RHS

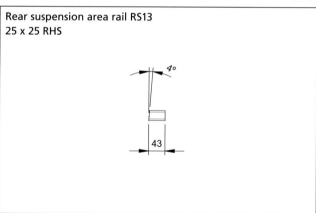

Rear suspension area rail RS14
25 x 25 RHS

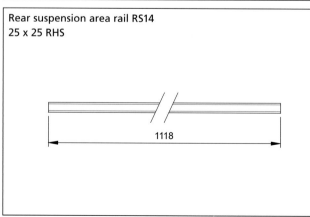

Rear suspension area rail RS15
19 x 19 RHS

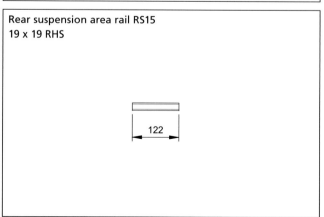

REAR PANEL

Rear panel tube RP1
19 Dia. Tube

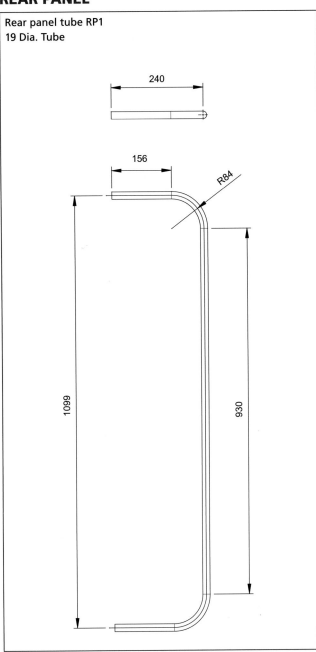

Rear panel tube RP2
19 Dia. Tube

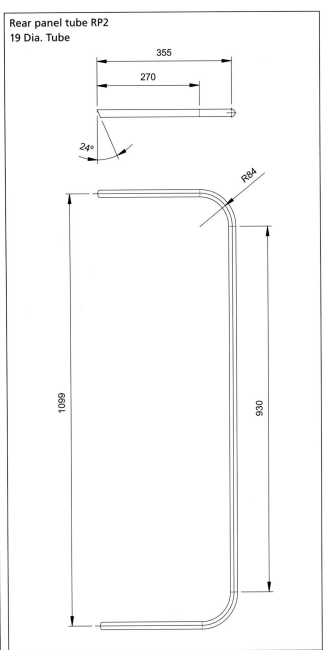

Rear panel tube RP3
19 x 19 RHS

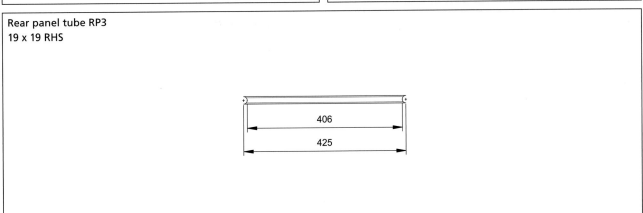

STEERING WHEEL SUPPORT FRAME

Steering wheel support frame SW1
19 x 19 RHS

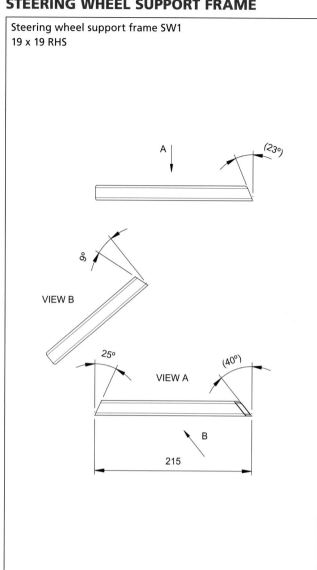

Steering wheel support frame SW3
19 x 19 RHS

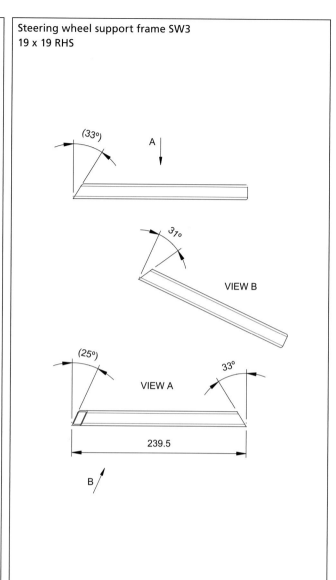

Steering wheel support frame SW2
19 x 19 RHS

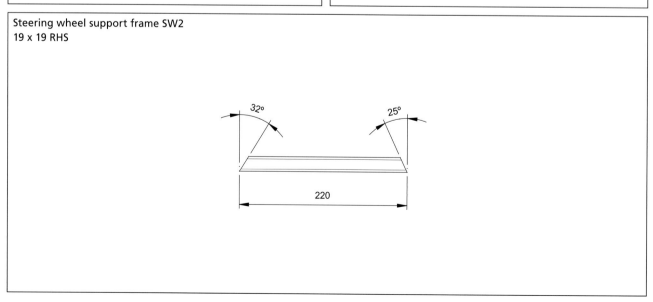

TRANSMISSION TUNNEL

Transmission tunnel rail TT1
19 x 19 RHS

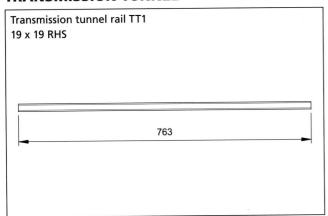

763

Transmission tunnel bottom rail TT2
19 x 19 RHS

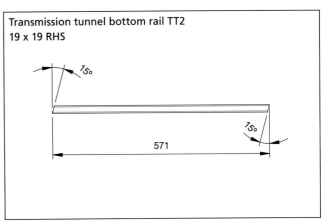

15°

15°

571

Transmission tunnel bottom rail TT3
19 x 19 RHS

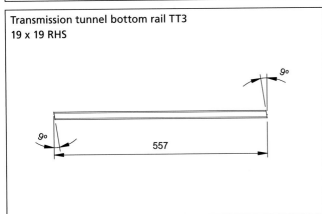

9°

9°

557

Transmission tunnel upright rail TT4
19 x 19 RHS

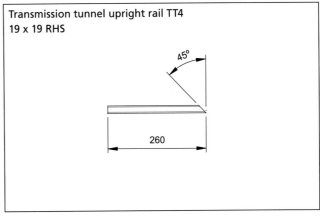

45°

260

Transmission tunnel top rail TT5
19 x 19 RHS

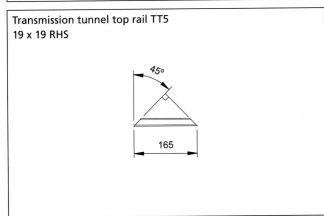

45°

165

Transmission tunnel upright rail TT6
19 x 19 RHS

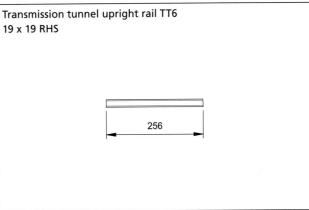

256

Transmission tunnel top rail TT7
19 x 19 RHS

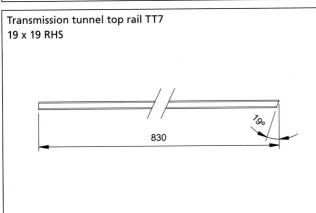

830

19°

Transmission tunnel rail TT8
19 x 19 RHS

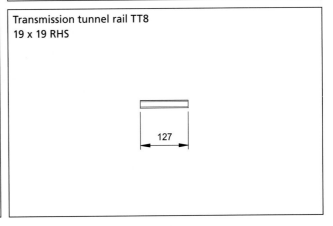

127

TRANSMISSION TUNNEL CONTINUED

Transmission tunnel top rail TT9
19 x 19 RHS

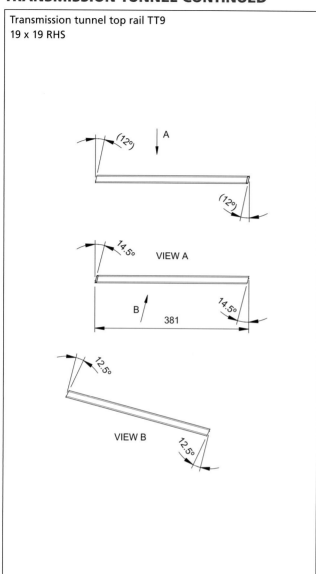

VIEW A

VIEW B

Transmission tunnel top rail TT11
19 x 19 RHS

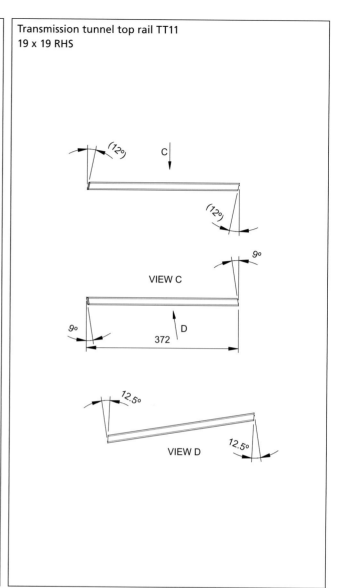

VIEW C

VIEW D

Transmission tunnel top rail TT10
19 x 19 RHS

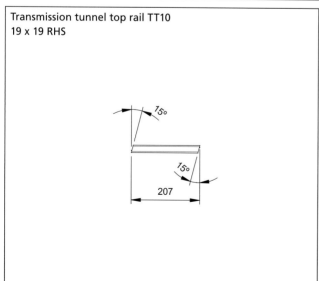

Transmission tunnel top rail TT12
19 x 19 RHS

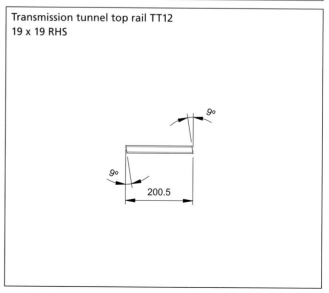

CHASSIS PLATES

Chassis plates CP1 x2
3 Plate

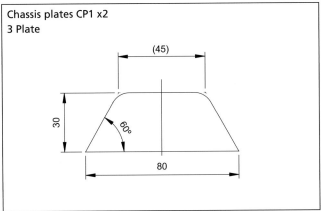

Chassis plates CP2 x2
3 Plate

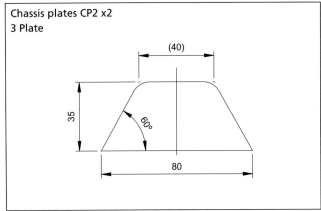

Roll bar attachment and upper damper bracket CP3
Roll bar attachment and upper damper bracket CP4
3 Plate

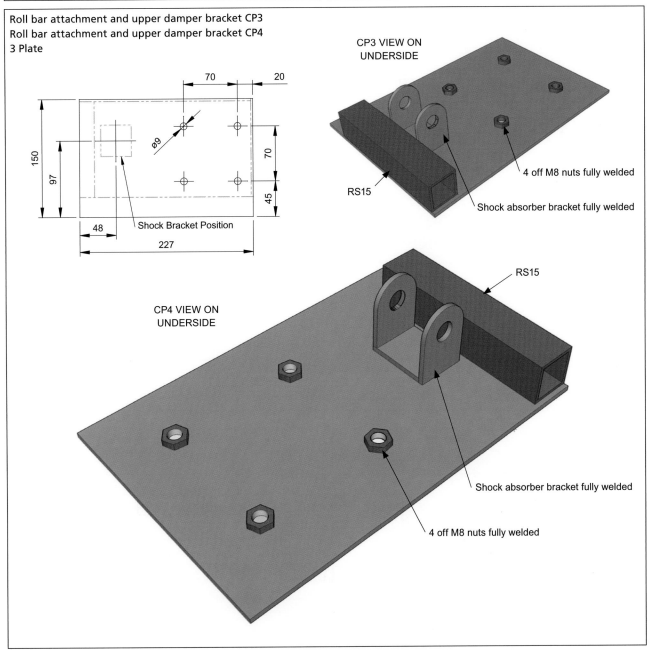

CP3 VIEW ON
UNDERSIDE

4 off M8 nuts fully welded

RS15

Shock absorber bracket fully welded

Shock Bracket Position

CP4 VIEW ON
UNDERSIDE

RS15

Shock absorber bracket fully welded

4 off M8 nuts fully welded

CHASSIS PLATES CONTINUED

Chassis plate CP5 x2
3 Plate

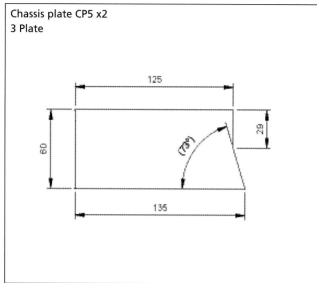

Chassis plate CP6 x2
3 Plate

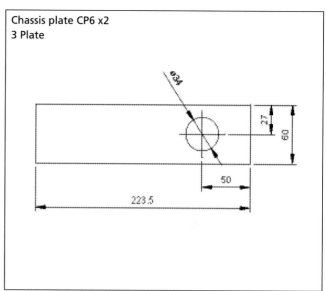

Chassis plate CP7 x2
3 Plate

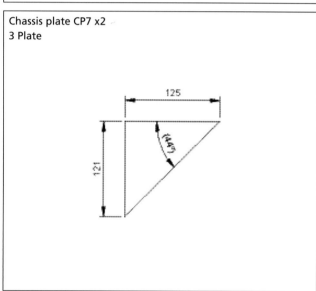

Chassis plate CP8 x2
3 Plate

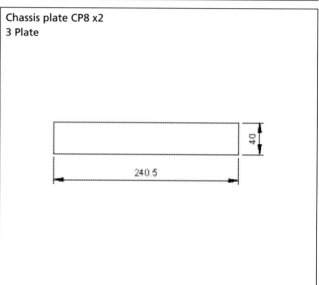

Chassis plate CP9 x2
3 Plate

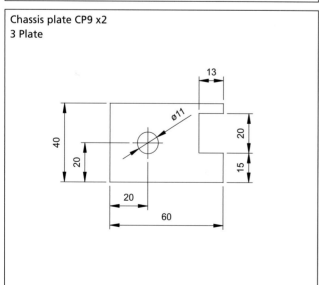

Chassis plate CP10 x2
5 Plate

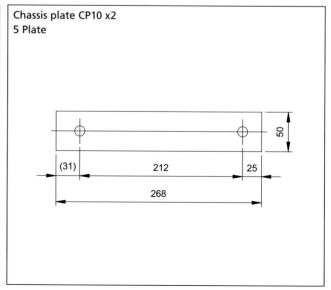

CHASSIS PLATES CONTINUED

Chassis side plate CP11 x2
1 Plate

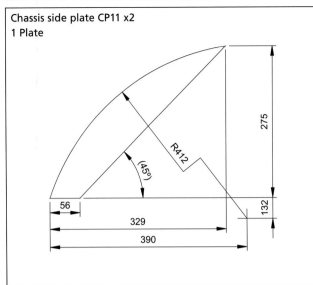

Chassis plate CP12
Chassis plate CP13
3 Plate

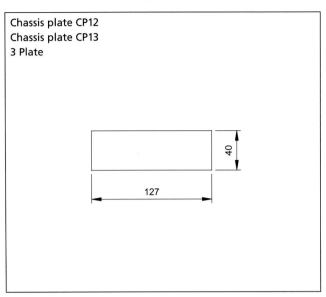

Chassis side plate CP14
3 Plate

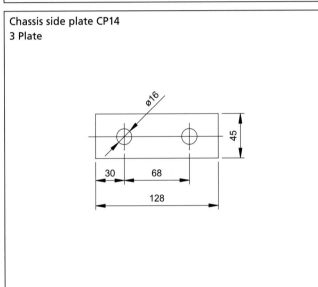

Chassis side plate CP15
3 Plate

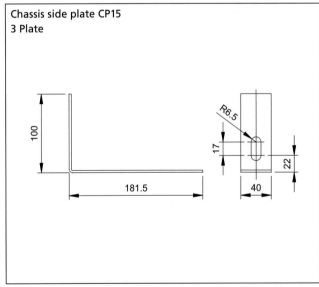

Chassis side plate CP18
3 Plate

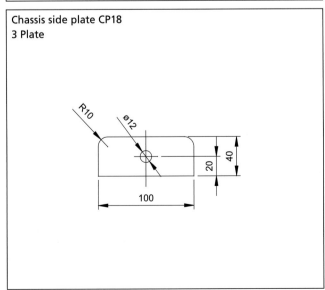

Steering rack support CP19
Steering rack support CP20
3 Plate

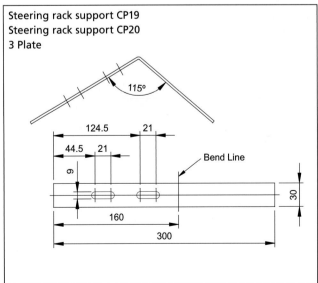

CHASSIS PLATES CONTINUED

Chassis plate CP16
1 Plate

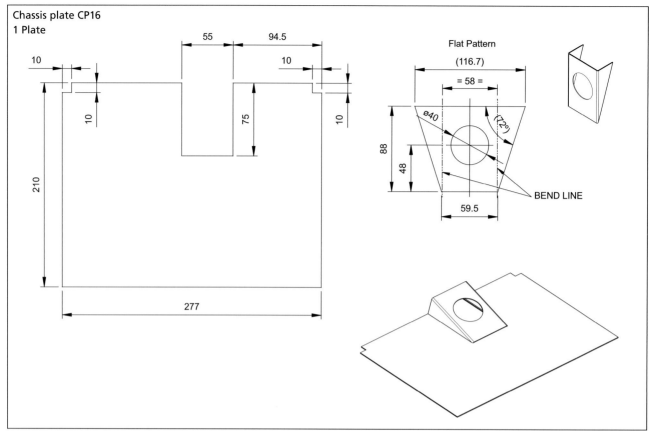

Flat Pattern
(116.7)
= 58 =
ø40
(72°)
BEND LINE

Chassis plate CP17
1 Plate

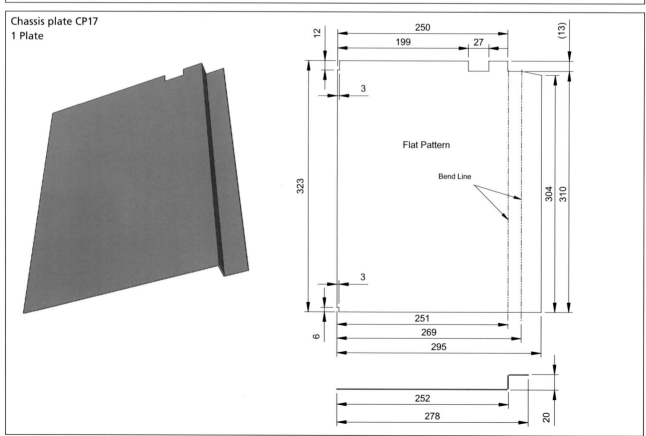

Flat Pattern

Bend Line

CHASSIS PLATES CONTINUED

Steering rack brace CP21
3 Plate

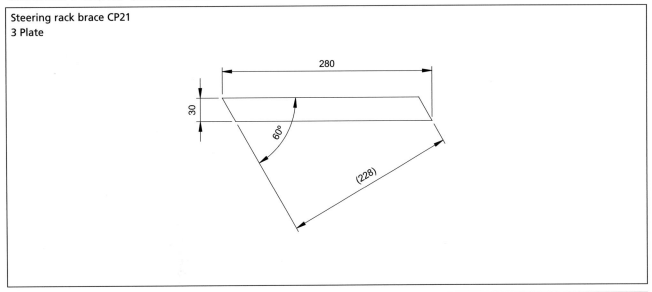

Radiator brackets CP22 x2
3 Plate

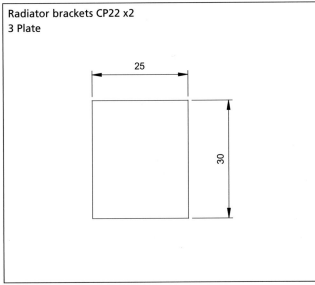

Front and rear flexible brake pipe mounts CP23 x4
3 Plate

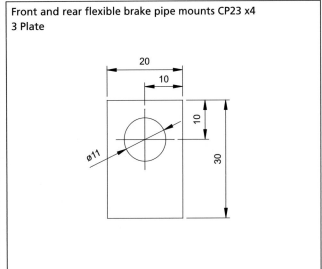

Chassis plate CP24
3 Plate

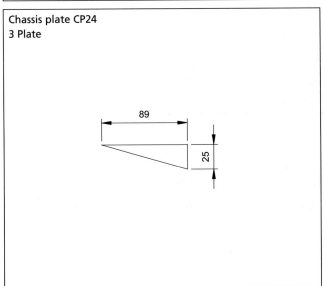

Chassis plate CP25
3 Plate

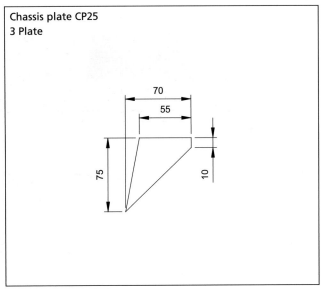

REAR UPRIGHTS

RU1
3 Plate

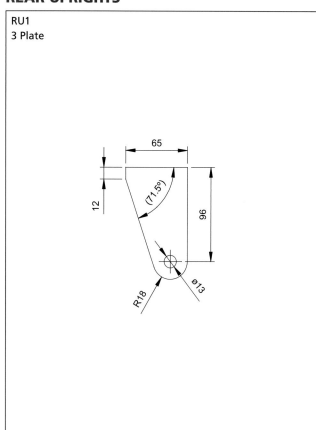

RU2
3 Plate

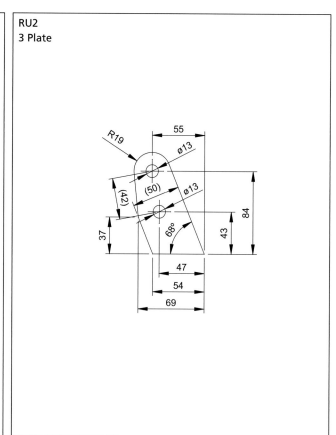

RU3
3 Plate

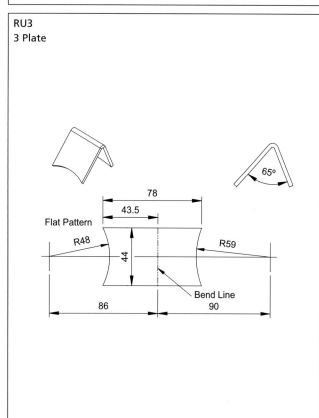

RU4
3 Plate

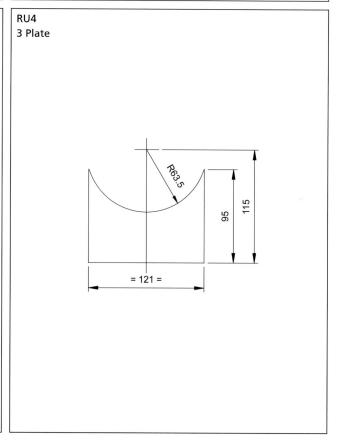

REAR UPRIGHTS CONTINUED

RU5
ø5in Tube

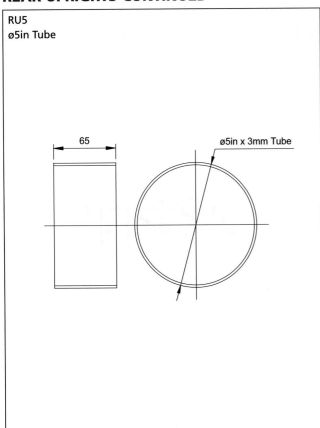

65

ø5in x 3mm Tube

RU6
ø19 Tube

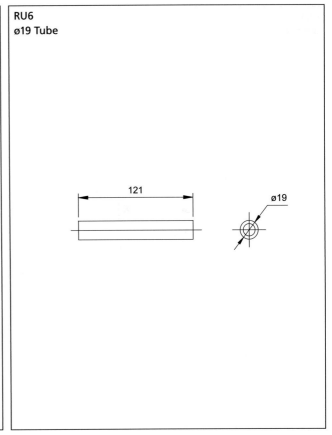

121

ø19

RU7
10 Plate

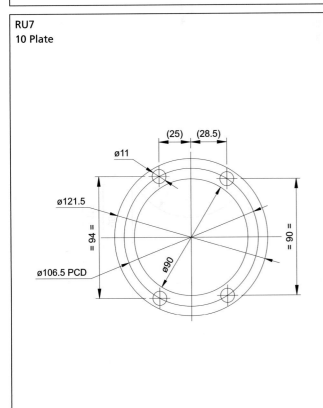

(25) (28.5)

ø11

ø121.5

= 94 =

= 90 =

ø90

ø106.5 PCD

RU8
10 Plate

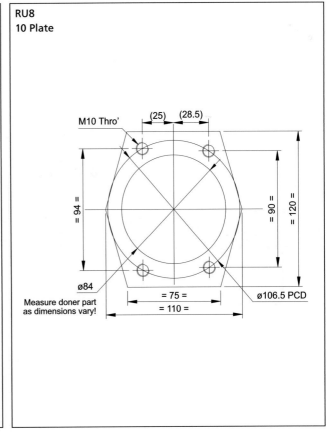

M10 Thro'

(25) (28.5)

= 94 =

= 90 =

= 120 =

ø84

Measure doner part
as dimensions vary!

= 75 =

= 110 =

ø106.5 PCD

ENGINE MOUNTING PLATES

Engine mounting plate EM1
3 Plate

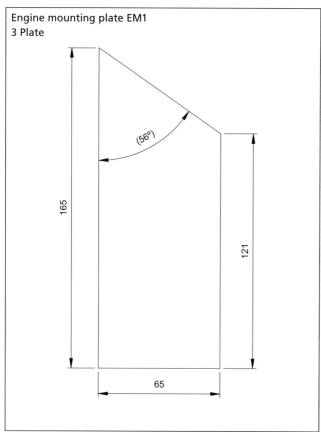

Engine mounting plate EM2
3 Plate

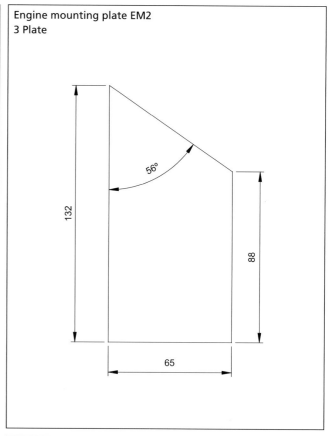

Engine mounting plate EM3
3 Plate

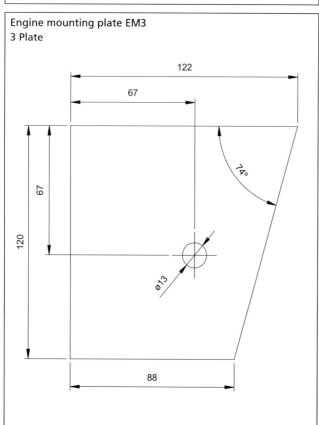

Engine mounting plate EM4
3 Plate

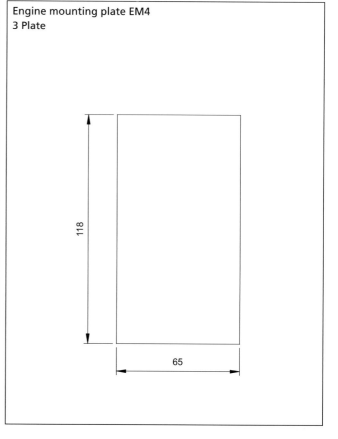

DIFFERENTIAL MOUNTING PLATES

DS1
5 Plate

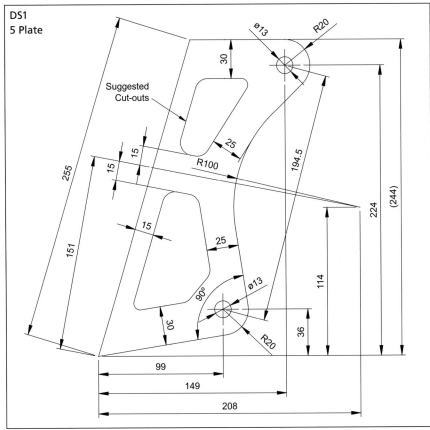

Suggested Cut-outs

DS2
5 Plate

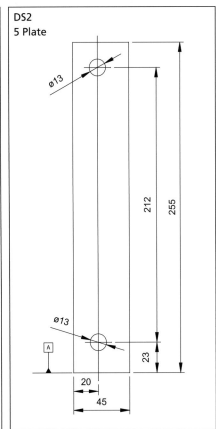

Differential mounting plate DM1 as drawn
Differential mounting plate DM2 opp. hand

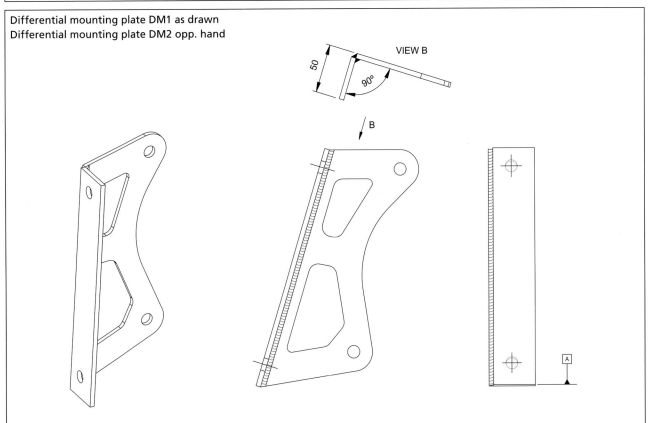

VIEW B

SIDE SUPPORTS

Side support SS1
3 Plate

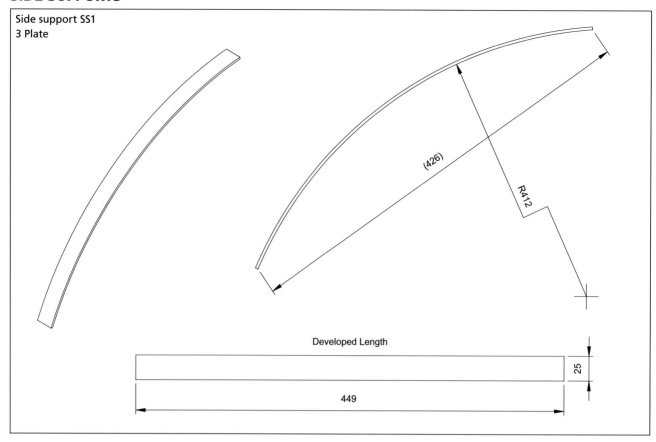

Developed Length

GEARBOX MOUNTING PLATE

Gearbox mounting plate GM1
Gearbox mounting plate GM2
3 Plate

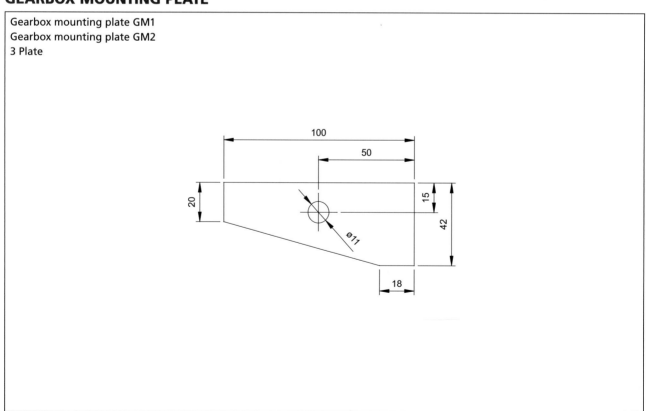

FRONT SUSPENSION BRACKET ALIGNMENT JIGS

Alignment jig for front suspension lower brackets

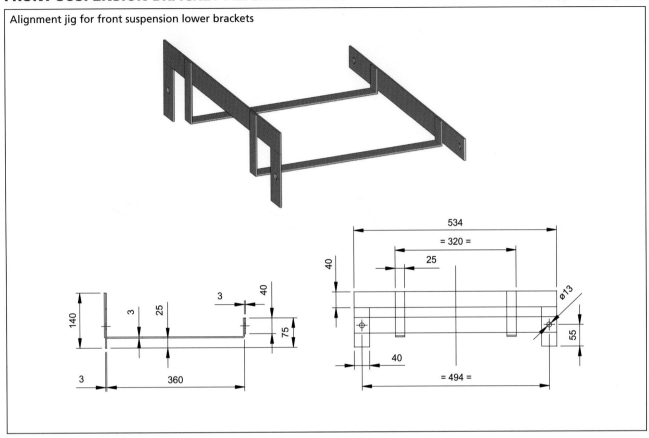

Alignment jig for front suspension upper brackets

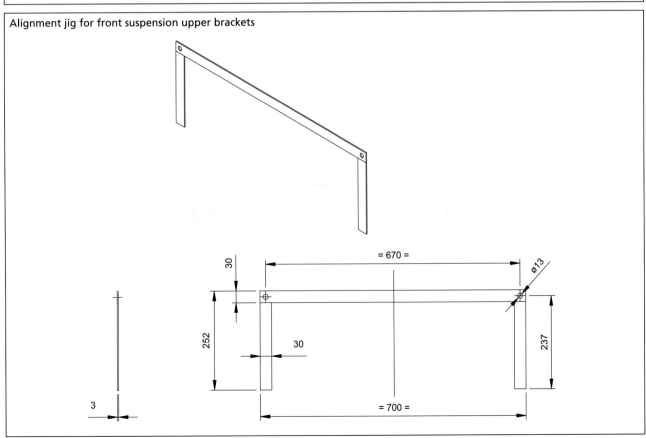

SUSPENSION BRACKETS

Standard suspension bracket x16

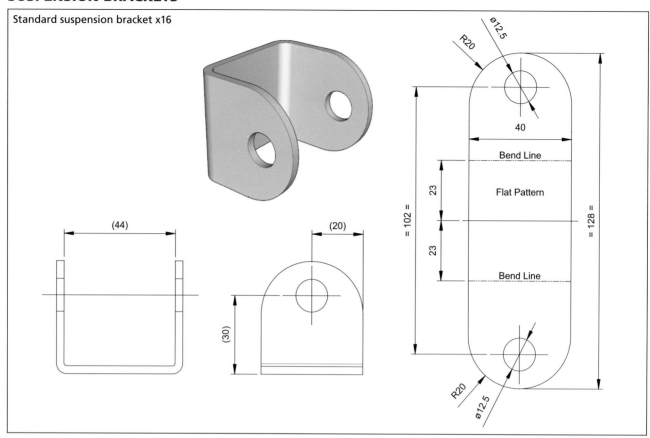

Shock absorber bracket x8

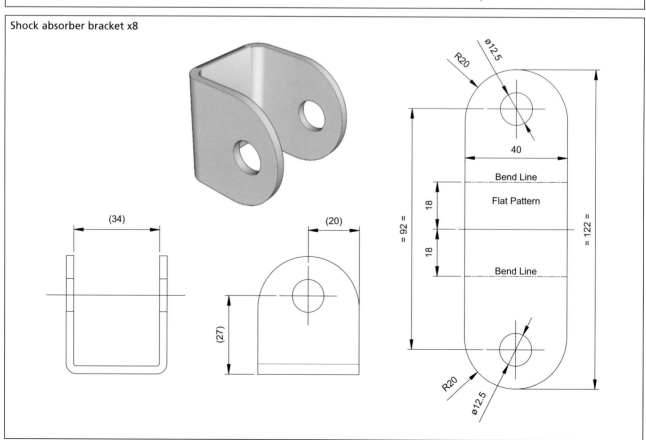

SUSPENSION CRUSH TUBE

Stainless steel inner tube

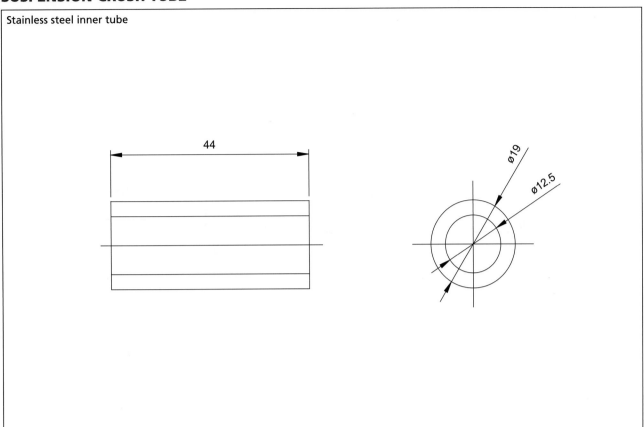

PEDALS

Pedal box plate PB1
3 Plate

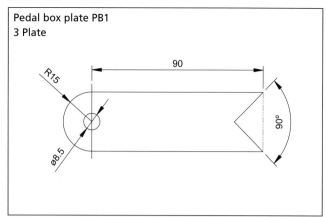

Pedal box plate PB2
3 Plate

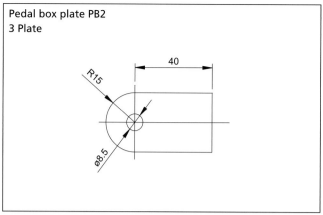

Pedal box plate PB3
3 Plate

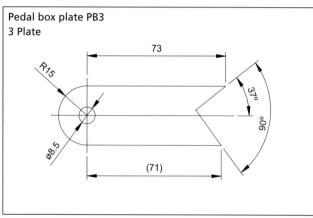

Pedal box plate PB4
3 Plate

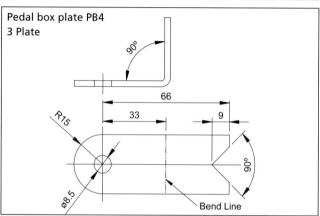

Accelerator pedal

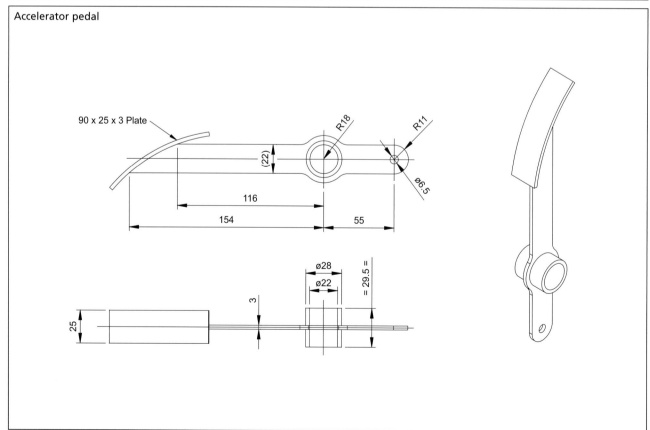

PEDALS

Brake pedal

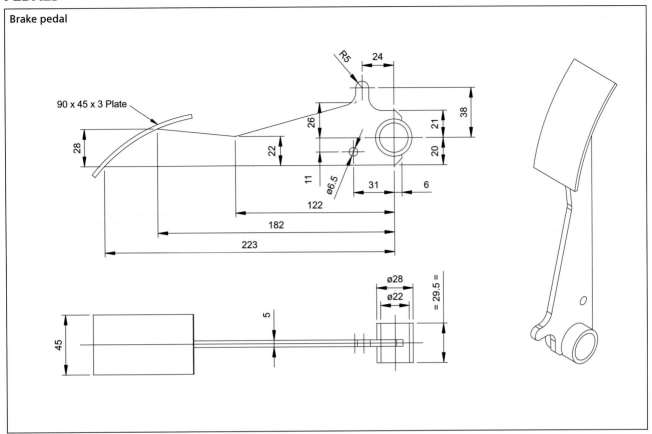

Clutch pedal

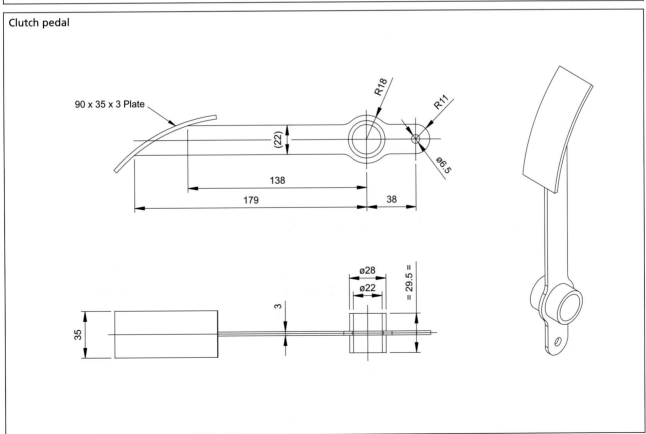

WING STAY

Front wing stay WS1 x2
3 Plate

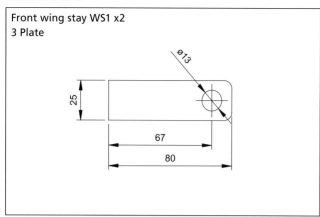

Front wing stay WS2 x2
3 Plate

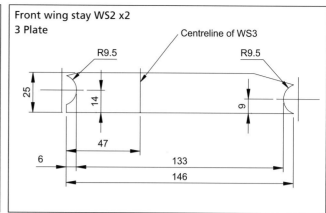

Front wing stay WS3 x2
3 Plate

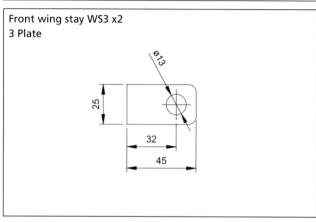

Front wing stay WS5 x2
3 Plate

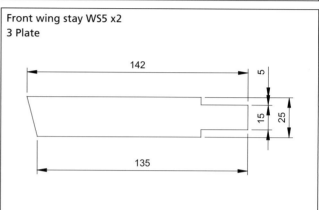

Front wing stay WS6 x2
3 Plate

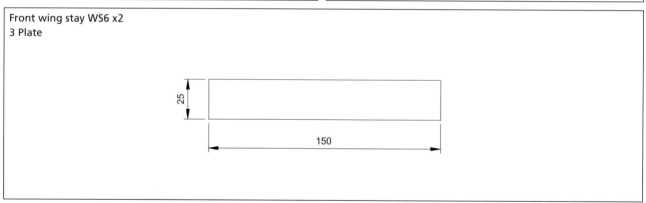

Front wing stay WS4 x2
3 Plate

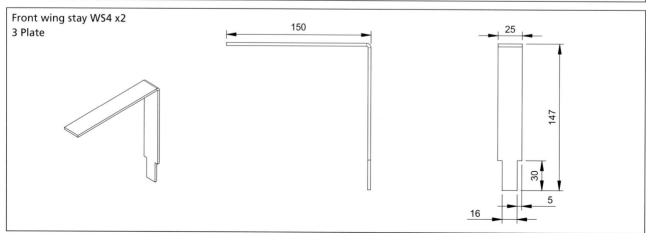

RECOMMENDED READING

The Car Builder's Manual
Lionel Baxter (Haynes)

The Kit Car Manual
Ian Ayre (Haynes)

Workshop Manuals for *Ford Sierra, BMW 3 series (E30 & E36), Mazda MX-5* (all Haynes)

Automotive Welding Manual (Haynes)

Competition Car Suspension 4th Edition
Allan Staniforth (Haynes)

Race and Rally Car Source Book
Allan Staniforth (Haynes)

Kit Cars and the Law
Kitcars Intl. Ltd.

USEFUL ADDRESSES

Locost Car Club
c/o 31 Campion Drive
Swinton
Rotherham
S64 8QZ

The Locost Car Club is ready and willing to welcome builders of the Haynes Roadster. The club is run by builders and is one of the largest car clubs in Britain, with a dedicated website and a 'help a member' scheme whereby names and addresses of club members in your locality can be obtained from the club. Monthly meetings in many parts of the UK are organised, along with a yearly gathering at the Stoneleigh Kit Car Show. Please send an SAE for details to the address above.

750 Motor Club
Rose Farm
Upper Street
Oakley
Diss
Norfolk
IP21 4AX

E-mail 750membership@btconnect.com
Tel: 01379 741641
Fax: 01379 741941

The 750 MC organise the current Locost Championship as well as many other 'grass roots' racing series. There may be a new class for Roadsters.

The Motor Sports Association
Motor Sports House
Riverside Park
Colnbrook
SL3 0HG
Tel: 01753 765 000
Fax: 01753 682 938

The MSA is recognised as the sole governing body of motor sport in Great Britain by the world governing body, the Fédération Internationale de l'Automobile (FIA). The MSA 'Blue Book' is the bible of race regulations.

Hillclimb and Sprint Association
11 Wellington Drive
Bowerhill
Melksham
Wiltshire
SN12 6QW

Tel: 01225 700899
Email: membership@hillclimbandsprint.co.uk

British Motor Sprint Association
Paul Parker
52 Brendon Road
Portishead
Bristol
BS20 6DH

Tel: 01275 843478 or 07710 516758
Email: britishsprint@paulparker.f9.co.uk

British Motor Sport Association for the Disabled
David Butler
BMSAD
Barn Cottage
Commonwood
Nr Chipperfield
Hertfordshire
WD4 9BB

Tel: 01923 265577
Fax: 01923 263872
E-mail: david@justwebs.co.uk.

SUPPLIERS

MK Engineering
2 Addison Road
Maltby
Rotherham
S66 8DG

Tel: 01709 815740
E-mail: martin@mkengineering.co.uk
Website: www.mkdevelopments.co.uk

MIG and TIG welding specialists. MK Engineering can supply everything needed to build a Haynes Roadster, from a nut and bolt to glassfibre sets, and even a complete chassis.

PARTS SUPPLIERS

Europa Specialist Spares
Fauld Industrial Park
Tutbury
Burton-on-Trent
Staffordshire
DE13 9HR

Tel: 01283-815609
Fax: 01283-814976
E-mail: Info@EuropaSpares.com

Demon Tweeks Direct
75 Ash Road South
Wrexham Industrial Estate
Wrexham
LL13 9UG

Tel: 08453306241
Fax: 01978 664467
Email: sales@demon-tweeks.co.uk

Merlin Motor Sport
The Bridgestone Building
Castle Combe Circuit
Chippenham
Wiltshire
SN14 7EY

Tel: 01249-782101
E-mail: info@merlinmotorsport.co.uk

BODYWORK

Tony Skelding
Bodicraft Automotive Renovations
Unit 2, Hinchliffes Yard
Off Church Lane
Maltby
Rotherham
S66 8EJ

USEFUL WEBSITES

■ BUILDING RESOURCES

www.haynes.co.uk/forums/index.php
Haynes Roadster building and news
forum. E-mail: roadster@haynes.co.uk

www.locostcarclub.co.uk
The website of the Locost Car
Club in the UK.

www.locostbuilders.co.uk
Online car building forum.

www.racetech.ee/a/fh12-index.htm
Estonian sports car builders.

www.750mc.co.uk
The 750 Motor Club website.

www.msauk.org
The Motor Sports association.

www.fulframephoto.co.uk
Motorsport photography.

■ SIERRA

www.crustworld.co.uk/sierra/
General Sierra information and
online forum.

www.fordsierraclub.co.uk/
UK-based Ford Sierra club.

**www.madabout-kitcars.com/kitcar/
kb.php?aid=84**
Sierra history and information.

■ MAZDA MX-5

www.mx5-mazda.co.uk
MX-5 information and parts.

www.mx5oc.co.uk
MX-5 Owners' Club site.

■ BMW E30

www.bimmerdiy.com/e30
BMW maintenance.

www.bmwe30.net/
Online discussion forum.

www.unofficialbmw.com/e30.html
Information and sales site.

www.haynes.co.uk/forums/index.php

E-mail: roadster@haynes.co.uk